Postnationalist African cinemas

MANCHESTER
1824

Manchester University Press

Postnationalist African cinemas

Alexie Tcheuyap

Manchester University Press
Manchester and New York

distributed in the United States exclusively
by Palgrave Macmillan

Copyright © Alexie Tcheuyap 2011

The right of Alexie Tcheuyap to be identified as the author of this work has been asserted by him in accordance with the Copyright, Designs and Patents Act 1988.

Published by Manchester University Press
Oxford Road, Manchester M13 9NR, UK
and Room 400, 175 Fifth Avenue, New York, NY 10010, USA
www.manchesteruniversitypress.co.uk

Distributed in the United States exclusively by
Palgrave Macmillan, 175 Fifth Avenue, New York,
NY 10010, USA

Distributed in Canada exclusively by
UBC Press, University of British Columbia, 2029 West Mall,
Vancouver, BC, Canada V6T 1Z2

British Library Cataloguing-in-Publication Data
A catalogue record for this book is available from the British Library

Library of Congress Cataloging-in-Publication Data applied for

ISBN   978 0 7190 8335 8 hardback

ISBN   978 0 7190 8336 5 paperback

First published 2011

The publisher has no responsibility for the persistence or accuracy of URLs for any external or third-party internet websites referred to in this book, and does not guarantee that any content on such websites is, or will remain, accurate or appropriate.

Typeset by 4word Ltd, Bristol
Printed in Great Britain by TJ International Ltd, Padstow

To
Ambroise Kom and André Ntonfo
With gratitude and respect

For my emotional guides
My wife Emily (Meni Nounou)
Elsa-Chloé (Mami Meni Tchoko)
Yves-Michel (Menkam Nzebuki)
Alain-Noé (proud great-grandson of Mami Maria Mamba)

Pour Clémence et Didier Perelly. Love, forever

Contents

List of illustrations

Acknowledgements

When I started this project several years ago, I was far from imagining not only the time it would take, but also the difficulties I would face. I was, however, very fortunate to benefit from the help and experience of friends, colleagues and various institutions throughout.

The Social Sciences and Humanities Research Council of Canada (SSHRC) has been instrumental in the implementation of this project, providing funds for a research programme conducted by Sada Niang, Sheila Petty and myself. Our collaboration over the years has been both intense and exceptionally stimulating, and this work is only one of the outcomes of our intellectual bonds. An SSHRC Institutional Grand Award from the University of Toronto provided additional support.

In completing this book, I was privileged to benefit from useful conversations, exchanges, readings and critiques from colleagues, mentors and friends. I would like to make special mention of Cilas Kemedjio, Célestin Monga and Mireille Calle-Gruber whose support and friendship I value highly. Versions of some chapters have been read at various stages by Akin Adesokan, Kenneth Harrow, Ato Quayson, Etienne-Marie Lassi, Sarah B. Buchanan, Jude Akudinobi, Lindiwe Dovey, Thomas Leitch, Hervé Tchumkam, Kasereka Kavwahirehi and David Murphy, and I am extremely grateful for their very useful comments. I also wish to thank my colleagues and assistants Senai Iman, Irene Krispis, Sébastien Sacré and Claude Zesseu without whom I think this book would still be a work in progress. Myra Bloom stepped into this project at the right time, helping me to better convey my ideas in English. Abdoulaye Gueye, Augustin Simo Bobda, Véronique Bonnet, Boulou E. De B'Beri, Dickson Eyoh, Hélène Tissières, Jean-Philémenon Mégopé, Mathias Rodrigue Tientcheu, Pierre Diderot

Nawe, Aurelien Koloko, Pierre Kemeni, Alain Tchokonte Kamga and George Salla have remained in the background, providing immeasurable encouragement. My 'other' family was uniquely supportive: Sandrine Kamga (with Steve Emmanuel), Marcel Njongwe and Julius Ogunariwo (the unique Dr O.). Needless to say, *Mami Meni*'s spirit is always present, because she was never gone.

Versions of chapters 1 and 7 respectively appear in the *Journal of African Cultural Studies* (Vol. 22: 1, 2010) and the *Canadian Journal of African Studies* (Vol. 43: 2, 2009). I wish to thank the editors and proprietors of these journals for permission to use this material here. In all instances, my work has been substantially revised for the purposes of this publication.

I am extremely grateful to Cornelius More (California Newsreel), Alessandra Speciale (*Ecrans d'Afrique/African Screen*), Rock Demers (*Productions La Fête*), Henriette Duparc (*Les Films Henri Duparc*), Jean Diouf, Mansour Sora Wade, Eileen Julien, Eric Paul Julien and Olivier Barlet for lending me the rare and much needed photographs included in the book. Jeanick Le Naour of the *Cinémathèque Afrique* has remained an exceptionally generous host in Paris over the years.

Introduction

African cinema, nationalism and its discontents

This book revisits the critical paradigms that have prevailed in African film criticism, examines some aesthetic trends in films from the 1990s onwards as well as their attendant discourse and, finally, explores the innovative perspectives that have been opened up by current cinematic productions. Until recently, African film scholarship has been almost systematically dominated by cultural, historical and political considerations that are dated and have become somewhat obsolete. African cinemas now deserve full reconsideration in view of the multiple and transforming facets of a filmmaking landscape where several directors have not only come to see themselves as citizens of a global world, but moreover are experimenting with completely new genres, forms and systems; conceptualizations of nationhood, race, the continent and political contestations appear at times to be almost completely evacuated from these works. This change has remained almost undocumented by scholars, whose projects remain bound to (or by) the nationalist frameworks that have historically over-determined the incipient phase of African cinema.[1] It is within this socio-political and theoretical context that this book positions itself. My study is predicated on the following tenets: a) African cinema has never been as homogeneous as scholars tended to (make us) believe; b) in a new context of transnational circulation, nation building has become a less prominent, if not absent, motivation in filmmaking; c) cultural and nationalist criticism has thus far failed to give voice to the laughter, joy, sexuality and formal experimentation presently being expounded in postcolonial narratives; and d) new analytical categories are needed to theorize a changing corpus that is no longer limited to social contestation, binary oppositions and essentialist cultural considerations. This statement requires elucidation. In this introductory chapter, I will first map out the historical as well as the theoretical foundations of African films. I will then determine their impact on a scholarship that has up to this point consistently reproduced the archetypes inherited from militant filmmaking and cultural institutions. The next section will include an analysis of the benefits and limits of liberationist aesthetics and criticism, which I contend are no longer adequate to the task of analysing innovative productions and narrative experimentation. The final section will lay the foundations of a reinvigorated film scholarship that takes into account emerging genres, representations and functions that are not necessarily tied to specific social, political or historical agendas. Although the genre of committed filmmaking is close to exhausting itself, this has not always been the case because social contestation was almost a sacred norm. As a result, alternative and emerging film praxis was either ignored or dismissed because of the nationalist project which equally dominated cultural criticism. It is within this context that the significance of my scholarship to a renewed investigation of the field needs to be positioned.

1   African cinema and national(ist) constructions

This section aims to show that from the beginning, African filmmakers, like the authors of many postcolonial narratives, were compelled to 'write back' and be militant. This is the case because of specific historical circumstances and what Jean-Pierre Bekolo (2009, 41) calls the 'discovery of cinema medium'. Films were largely concerned with providing a content (i.e. what is shown), and far less so with questions of form (i.e. how it is shown); as such, it is possible to see in what way a diverse corpus generated an impression of uniformity.

As the history of cinema demonstrates (Vieyra, 1975; Ukadike, 1994; FEPACI, 1995), the image industry was born within a socio-historic and economic context where abundance, private property, the industrial revolution and the construction of various hegemonic discourses made it possible for the West to ascend to the status of dominant global power. The encounter of the colonial camera with Blacks perceived as needing 'to be civilized' was thus strongly influenced by this context. Given that the colonized people were regarded as emotionally volatile and easily distracted, it was believed that there could not be a medium more suited to amusing and disarming them than film. Marc Mangin's analysis of colonial films fully explains the link between the construction of primitivism, backwardness, 'civilizing missions' and cinema. He argues that cinema was not a neutral force, but actually functioned

> like an entertainment, attaching [Africans] to the set permissible values, those of the Western civilization. Then came a time when cinema was transformed into tools of effective propaganda in two directions. It 'educated' the natives, while the Europeans, who remained on the old continent, could see for themselves the need for the civilizing mission undertaken by their respective governments. (In Vokouma, 1995, 270)[2]

In *Unthinking Eurocentrism,* Ella Shohat and Robert Stam (1994) show how films were efficiently designed to manufacture otherness, disseminate colonial propaganda, market the 'civilizing mission' and convey ideologies of superiority. A good example they offer is the genre of Westerns, which used point of view conventions to enable the viewer to identify with imperial agents and thus built a sense of dependency 'within the fissured colonial spectator' (103). According to the authors, the subtle link between film techniques and ideology foreclosed the possibility of any sympathetic identification with the colonized, as the viewer was aligned with the colonizer. Robert Stam and Louise Spence argue along the same lines that certain colonial(ist) clichés were successful in taking hold of the public imaginary; they write that 'many of the misconceptions concerning Third World peoples derive from the long [filmic] parades of lazy Mexicans, shifty Arabs, savage Africans and exotic Asiatics' (1983, 6). These personae inevitably fill secondary, negative and degrading roles. In his groundbreaking *Black African Cinema* (1994), Nwachukwu Frank Ukadike methodically and persuasively deconstructs the philosophical, historical, literary and cultural components of a colonial discourse he regards as full of 'vicious misrepresentations aimed at tumbling authentic traditional values' (37). As he puts it, 'Those movies inverted African values by imposing the language and culture of the colonizer on the colonized. They also served to justify "military escapades" and white man's "civilizing mission". [They provided] a false perspective through which the continent was to be viewed' (35). In such a context, the African's reappropriation of the camera necessarily involved a radical reconsideration of the aesthetic as well as the ideological functions of the images being depicted. With the spate of violence and alienation that this takeover generated, colonial expansion compelled the dominated people, as Frantz Fanon (1968) observed, to reconsider the role of culture and its representation. For him, culture ought to become 'national' and contribute to political liberation.

It is within this historical and social context that the *Fédération Panafricaine des Cinéastes* (FEPACI) emerged. This association of filmmakers, which in time became a very powerful lobby group, is central to the inception as well as the ideological and foundational discourse of African films. Even though FEPACI started as an urgent emancipatory body, it was equally dictative in several ways. Central to the arguments developed in this book is a need for a full reconsideration of its shortcomings and dogmatisms that make its principles relatively obsolete in view of today's new standards of production and representation. African cinema is not only known for a number of resolutely revisionist films that have offered alternative images of the continent; it is furthermore associated with a set of assertive manifestos that have shaped the discourse of African films for the past fifty years. These manifestos have made them what they have always appeared to be, and have led younger directors towards an alternative view of the constitution and function of their transnational cinematic landscape. Among these proclamations are the Resolution of the Third World Film-Makers' Meeting in Algiers (1973), the Algiers Charter on African Cinema (1975) and the Niamey Manifesto of African Film-Makers (1982), which are documented in Imruh Bakari and Mbye Cham's (1996) *African Experiences of Cinema*. In order to understand the historical and aesthetic construction of African films and, more importantly, the incredible diversity of recent productions, a brief consideration of FEPACI's plans is helpful. This association in fact had a specific *political* agenda that was developed in response to specific historical, cultural and political circumstances that have since changed. Several of the resolutions of the Algiers Charter clearly espouse the view that cinema can only serve an instrumental function:

> To assume a genuinely active role in the process of development, African culture *must* be popular, democratic and progressive in character, inspired by its own realities and responding to its own needs. It *must* also be in solidarity with cultural struggles all over the world.

The issue is … to allow the masses to take control of means of production of their own developments, *giving them back* the cultural initiative by drawing on the resources of a fully liberated *popular* creativity. Within this perspective the cinema has a vital part to play because it is *a means of education, information and consciousness raising* … The stereotyped image of the solitary and marginal creator which is widespread in Western capitalist society *must* be rejected by African film-makers, who *must*, on the contrary, see themselves as creative artisans at the service of their people. It also *demands* great vigilance on their part with regard to imperialism's attempts at ideological recuperation as it redoubles its efforts to maintain, renew and increase its cultural ascendancy. (In Bakari & Cham, 1996, 25–26, my emphasis)

Such statements by filmmakers are reminiscent of Ato Quayson's (2000, 78) discussion of African writers whose role seems closer to that of journalists than artists because they 'feel themselves part of a larger social struggle in the quest for absent or vanishing agents of democratic social change'.

In his landmark *African Cinema: Politics and Culture* (1992), Manthia Diawara provides very valuable information about the modes of operation as well as the strategies adopted by FEPACI to advance African cinema and discuss issues pertaining to continental liberation. As he puts it,

The commitment to the liberation of Africa meant for the filmmakers the creation of aesthetics of disalienation and colonization.[3] Filmmakers *were told* to use semidocumentary forms to *denounce colonialism* where it existed and to use *didactic fictional forms to denounce* the alienation of countries that were politically independent but culturally and economically dependent on the West. (40, my emphasis)

While it is indisputable that the structural, historical and cultural forces of the 1960s and 1970s construe the liberationist orientations of foundational African films, one also ought to be careful not to ignore that FEPACI's programme comes across as extremely normative, if not authoritarian. The mode invariably used in most documents is that of the imperative: the word 'must' appears no fewer than eight times in a very short document full of other prescriptive wordings like 'demand'. In addition, it is marked by the left wing rhetoric characteristic of the cold war context and the perceived need for liberation. Injunctions concern not only the political content of films. FEPACI moreover encourages specific national(ist) forms to be adopted, such as the 'semi-documentaries' recommended for realist narratives. The language of this document suggests that the association selected, regulated and defined 'African' cinema. In so doing, it also de facto prevented certain genres from fully participating in the nascent landscape of the African imaginary at the time. Although it presents itself as promoting a patriotic duty and ethical imperative for its advocates, this document must also be regarded in its capacity as agent of social and discursive control. A good example of the insidious control of such initiatives can be found in the context of the Algerian film scene, which was for years, along with Ghana and Guinea, the only place for African left wing and revolutionary intellectuals to seek refuge. Talking about the politicization of film, Azzedine Mabrouki writes that

> at the beginning, it was a veritable utopia. The war of liberation had just ended. It was said the cinema was 'the school of the masses'! Nobody thought about producing comedies, or very few. The cinema was in particular not entertainment! It was even the most serious thing in the world. Even the Algerian army owned new cameras and laboratories. Young people were dispatched to Moscow, Prague, Warsaw, Beijing and they returned as film-makers, loaded with skills and knowledge. Scenarios were clear and easy to understand, but above all not contradictory. The message, especially the message of the Revolution. (1993, 40)[4]

Against the horizon of such a dominant (as well as domineering) aesthetic and discursive formation – not any kind of film could be shot, specific contents and features were required – African states and FEPACI's legitimate, timely and useful commitments are paradoxically reminiscent of Michel Foucault's (1972) elaboration on language and discourse control in societies where not every utterance is welcome. Foucault elucidates the forces through which discourse is produced, controlled and selected in order to deal with the chance events of an unexpected, unwanted or even dangerous expression. Looking back at FEPACI, one has to realize that its principles were dominated by exclusion and prohibition, and that filmmakers were prevented from making films that did not correspond to specific aesthetic and political tenets.

One final and most important principle (we might go as far as to say, dogma) put in place by FEPACI, which will be discussed further in this book, was the definition of African cinema as precisely *not* a form of entertainment. Cinema was meant not for pleasure, but for (political) instruction. In keeping with these principles, African cinema, like African literature, could *only* be a cinema of contestation. Not to toe the FEPACI line would represent an aesthetic and cultural anathema. As Kenneth Harrow writes in his remarkable *Postcolonial African Cinema: From Political Engagement to Postmodernism* (2007, 19), 'The terms of resistance were so powerfully set by Sembène [Ousmane] and his generation, it became almost impossible for any filmmaker or novelist not to take a politically engaged position'. African writers and filmmakers in the 1960s echoed in their works the cultural expressions of national liberation struggles being conducted on the political terrain by leaders like Kwame Nkrumah in Ghana, Ruben Um Nyobe in Cameroon, Jomo Kenyata in Kenya and Felix Houphouet Boigny in Côte d'Ivoire. This political urgency also influenced the formation of an 'African' film scholarship, characterized by what David Murphy and Patrick Williams (2007, 19) describe as a form of 'exceptionalism'. This is the term Murphy and Williams use to describe in what way African cinema is generally evaluated within current scholarship, that is, in very different terms from those generally seen in film studies; productions are regarded as significantly separate from other forms of cinematic expression. Most studies were in fact generally concerned with defining African films against a homogeneous 'Western' cinema and hence elaborating what may be called an 'oppositional criticism' which was in fact reminiscent of the dictates of FEPACI. Such intellectual proximity between scholars and filmmakers clearly indicates that critics have almost faithfully espoused the governing ideologies of FEPACI and the reigning political agendas of the time. From nationalist narratives to nationalist criticism, the transition, if not the equation, between fiction and scholarship, looks quite detectable so far. That is precisely what the following section will elucidate and, moreover, interrogate.

2 Wealth and poverty of nationalist scholarship

The thesis of this section is that as a result of political factors, several scholars of African cinema have abdicated their responsibility as intellectuals by uncritically echoing the discourse of FEPACI. It is astonishing how the pronouncements of this association are rehearsed by several critics, who reproduce in scholarship Pierre Bourdieu's (1977) idea of *habitus*. In this case, *habitus*, the indefinitely reproducible practices, dispositions, discourses and languages, can be seen in the praxis of various directors and researchers whose work is permanently marked by pronounced 'Third Worldist terms of cultural nationalism, sometimes inflected by Marxism' (Haynes, 2005, 113) which aggressively promote nation building and liberation. Consequently, Harrow argues for 'a revolution' (xi) in theoretical paradigms so as to 'break with a past that feels like a straitjacket, with its visions of films tied to categories, and categories tied to political agendas' (28), because he believes that scholars 'repeatedly asked the same questions' (xiii). However, if that is the case, it is not simply because African films always said the same things. It is more likely the case that we viewers got used to seeing the same things in early film. We also probably failed to see what else could be learned from most recent films. Clearly, under the sway of FEPACI, pioneer African directors and critics suffocated alternative discourses by committing themselves to speak for the people. As Neil Lazarus (1999, 109) has argued, 'All nationalisms are … appropriative, since they all claim unisonance [sic], and since these claims necessarily involve speaking for – and therefore silencing – others'. Nationalism thus becomes elitist in spite of its claims to represent subaltern classes.

In his influential study *Black African Cinema* (1994), Nwachukwu Frank Ukadike meticulously describes various historical, aesthetic and cultural patterns that characterize films in Black Africa, although his book seems at times to espouse the same dogmatic principles advocated by FEPACI. Ukadike's celebrated work at times comes across as equally nationalistic and at times essentialist as the manifestos that have shaped the foundational films he discusses. Ukadike's project is outlined very early in his book, and shares the same preoccupations as FEPACI, namely nation building and total liberation from colonial oppression. He writes,

> The new black African cinema concerns itself with the role film can play in building African society. Black African filmmakers

contend that traditional ways of filmic representation … *must*
give way to new ones, especially in portraying African culture.
The interest, participation, and collaboration of the people *must*
be secured, stimulated and maintained. (3, my emphasis)

In addition to a questionable, reoccurring concern with 'authenticity,'
Ukadike relates cinema to race and to Fanon's insistence upon Africa's return
'to its true national culture' (96, my emphasis), which he believes will be
achieved by modifying cinematic language 'to suit the culture and situation'
of 'black Africans' (167). Such a nationalist interpretation is further
illustrated in his reading of *Sambizanga* (Maldoror, 1972), one of Africa's first
films about the Angolan liberation. Because this narrative is not exclusively
focussed on the bloodshed and suffering produced by war, Ukadike criticizes
it as 'deficient' in that it 'romanticiz[es] what could have constituted a forceful
delineation of a liberationist uprising' (234). As I will explore in more detail
further on, Ukadike also strongly dismisses any film, for example *Bal Poussière*
(Duparc, 1988) or *Visages de femmes* (Ecaré, 1985) that deviates from the
'established norm' in order to entertain the viewer or cultivate any form of
voyeurism. Other critics share similar intellectual projects.

In addition to Ukadike, the discourse and aesthetics of liberation have
informed the scholarship of Teshome Gabriel and Férid Boughédir in
various ways. Gabriel (1982, 1995) bases his theoretical model on Frantz
Fanon's three-stage linear concept, and situates African cinema within the
general framework of Third World films. Boughédir provides a remarkably
simplistic typology that defines African cinema in opposition to 'Western'
cinema, which is deemed

> the escapist cinema, the evasive cinema that functions outside of
> real life and real life problems. It is the opium cinema; it is the
> cinema that lulls the audience to sleep. 90% of commercial
> cinemas operate in this way, and this explains why cinema is
> universally considered as entertainment. Entertaining also means
> diverting or moving the audience away from reality, granting
> them a momentary escape which delays the conscientization
> process. (1992, 70)

Although not as nationalistic, Joseph Gugler likewise views African
cinema from a strictly socio-political perspective. In his book *African Film:*

Re-Imagining a Continent (2003, 7) Gugler argues that 'Most African films give major play to social, cultural and political issues'. He has emphasized these by organizing this book in terms of five conflicts, and in privileging an analysis focussed on society, culture and politics. Looking at the investigations of these scholars, we can begin to map out the contiguity of the injunctions of FEPACI, the films as well as the academic projects of politically engaged filmmakers. The works of these filmmakers are predicated on an understandable desire to define Africa against a unified 'West', a search for an ontological 'African self', a genuine anxiety over a lost history and a threatened identity. As paradoxical as it may be, from its pioneering phase and for decades thereafter, in a continent desperate for liberation and democracy, African filmmaking and scholarship were reduced to a monolithic trilogy. This trilogy, demonstrated clearly in the above-cited case of Algeria, is comprised of the following tenets: one 'African cinema', one film association (FEPACI) and one dominant (political) discourse. Within such a context, the lack of distance (and of dissidence) between artists, intellectuals and social institutions could be, to borrow from Paul Gilroy (1993, 31) due to an 'ontological essentialist view which has often been characterised by a *brute pan-Africanism*' (my emphasis). According to him, such views are intellectually weak, theoretically unfounded and vague when it comes to coherently documenting the 'essence' of 'black cultures'.

One last critic who must be mentioned within the same nationalist framework is K. Martial Frindéthié, whose *Francophone African Cinema: History, Culture, Politics and Theory* (2009) offers a highly partisan and ideologically simplistic account of African cinema. First, in indicating that 'African filmmakers have generally insisted their work should be both nationally and globally committed to addressing African people's specific ontological, economic, political and social concerns' (4), he shows himself to be a few decades and films behind; most directors, including some of those he discusses, have rejected the ghettoization implied by an 'African ontology'. Second, the triumphant claim, repeated throughout, that 'the book sets a stage for a critical encounter between Francophone African cinema and Continental European critical theory' (3) indicates that this scholar has missed some major recent contributions to the field. Third, and most disputable, is that the narratives considered in his book appear to be simple appendices to or pretexts for weak and controvertible ideological elaborations. A perfect illustration is found in the last two chapters, which do not discuss a single film; rather, they are extensive angry accounts of French and Belgian manoeuvres that have provoked (or accelerated) postcolonial chaos in Côte d'Ivoire and the Congo.[5]

While it is important to note that apart from Frindéthié, the scholars discussed above based their criticism on the films available at the time and that Africa was and continues to be confronted by multiple challenges, one must be mindful of the fact that since the sixties, film production on the African continent has never been as univocal as critics and journalists have generally tended to assert. A good illustration, among the earliest examples, is Senegalese filmmaker Djibril Diop Mambéty, whose oeuvre was formally innovative and diverged from the usually realist films of Sembène Ousmane, to name but one contemporary. Given this heterogeneity, it is important to reassess, as I will endeavour to do, the gains and costs of liberationist praxis in order to address its relevance in a global context of technological, cultural, demographic and structural mutations.

The influence of liberation aesthetics, as well as 'nationalist criticism,' is rooted in a critical stance that has shaped 'African modes of self-writing' (Mbembe, 2002, 239), which, in its various guises, led the 'African collective imaginaire … into a dead end' (239, 240). In spite of clear evidence of formal and discursive innovations beginning in the seventies, African film scholarship seems to have resisted moving beyond the dogmatic viewpoint of the Algiers Charter and its subsequent nationalist/culturalist discourse. Although several critics acknowledge the recent transformations in African cinema, many also strongly contest the implications of this metamorphosis and remain wedded to criticism that maintains an essentialist, if not outright nationalist, framework. A good example is the critical appraisal of Idrissa Ouedraogo's *Yaaba* (1989), which emphasizes tolerance in a rural context of total exclusion, and was widely acclaimed all over the world. *Yaaba* is dismissed as 'elitist and individualistic' by Ukadike (1994, 289), who furthermore wonders whether the director has 'a clear vision of the future of Africa,' and if his approach 'really clarifies social conflicts' (282). According to Manthia Diawara, the film displays nothing but 'a sort of French liberalism' (1992, 164). He equally views the narrative's main philosophy, 'Let's not judge others, they have their own reasons', as decadent and responsible for moral and social turmoil as well as excessive tolerance. Diawara's reading of the film is also problematic as he argues that 'With its bourgeois humanist conception of tolerance, which is imported from the city, the film asks the spectator's sympathy not only for Sana who is an outcast but also for a drunkard and for adulterers within the tight social relations of the village' (162). Such a conservative reading of *Yaaba* recalls Ukadike's authoritarian moralism, which over-dertermines his view of comedy and sexuality in film. Given Diawara's objection and criticism of the narrowness of FEPACI's prescriptions, his interpretation of Ouedraogo's film appears somehow unexpected.

Another critic, Olivier Barlet (2000, 260), writes that 'the successes of African films have left that cinema vulnerable' to the forces of 'Western pressures on the content of films,' thus implying that filmmakers are forced to look towards 'Western' aesthetics to respond to the urgency of raising external funds. Françoise Pfaff (2004, 6) makes a very similar argument in her assertion that 'the serious, didactic, political, social realist' films of the past have been dropped in favour of 'more commercially attractive film products'. Such positions, again, reiterate FEPACI's repudiation of commercial cinema in dominated countries. Ukadike also argues very strongly against formal experimentations and 'proliferations' whereby the 'new breed' filmmakers desperately 'exoticize' their work for foreign markets, a battle which to him is far from won. All noticeable, novel enquiries into alternative film applications remain entirely open to question in that 'some of the conventions used to attain these aspirations have, however, been misappropriated' (Ukadike, 1994, 288).

Yet, for several directors who are at the cutting edge of 'the complex social shifts' that marked the end of the twentieth century, the obvious failure of liberation to achieve 'nation formation and transformation' has generated a series of innovative films that seek to redefine and even challenge existing modes of African representation (Akudinobi, 2001, 125). For example, the 1990s witnessed the emergence of a range of films that deliberately moved away from the ideologically-oriented aesthetics of the pioneer African filmmakers. These filmmakers have in the intervening years been working to create new aesthetic and narrative strategies best suited to communicating increasingly complicated socio-political cultural contexts. Whereas pioneer filmmakers looked within Africa for (post)colonial critique or focussed on rehabilitating a destroyed identity and a falsified history, the new cadre of directors is looking beyond nationalism and situating its discourses in the turbulent cross-flows of globalization. Writing specifically about the case of Burkina Faso, Teresa

Hoefert de Turégano points out that contemporary films are not only technically superior, but 'less moralising, less didactic, less concerned with legitimising the nation' (2004, 195) than their forebears. Such works having '[left] the nation behind' (194), they are now free to participate in a transnational experience and move beyond the realism characteristic of traditional African fiction.

Is it sheer coincidence that *Gito l'ingrat* (Ngabo, 1992), the first film produced in the Republic of Burundi, is a caustic comedy aimed at entertaining its audience? Is it possible to determine inherently common features between *Le Mandat* (Ousmane, 1968), *Afrique, je te plumerai, Yellow Fever Taximan* (Teno, 1993 and 1985) and *Le Ballon d'or* (Doukouré, 1994), *TGV* (Touré, 1999), *Dakan* (Camara, 1997), *Bal Poussière* (Duparc, 1988) or *Les Saignantes* (Bekolo, 2005)? Are the 'African spectators' of *Le Complot d'Aristote* (Bekolo, 1996), *Caramel* (Duparc, 2004), *Bronx-Barbès* (de Latour, 2000) exactly the same? To take the notable case of Sembène Ousmane, is there not a need to rethink the representation of the 'African woman' from *La Noire de...* (1966) to *Guelwaar* (1992) and *Faat Kiné* (2000)? How can one account for the rise of youth and young actors in many narratives? In the case of films like *Totor* (Kamwa, 1994), *Les Saignantes* (Bekolo, 2005) and *Africa Paradis* (Amoussou, 2007), can we locate the rise of sci-fi, dramatic comedies or the fantastic within solely nationalist frameworks? How do (un)masked sexual performances impact individual and national narratives today? What is the place of genre in African films? How do contemporary films represent invisible and other 'limit texts'? How do they entertain without alienating? These important questions have hardly ever been considered by previous scholarship and will be addressed in this book.

As I have argued, it is clear that previous enquiries and narratives were generally motivated by external considerations. These quashed and obliterated the new orientations now being fully explored within heterogeneous postcolonial narratives. In the current global market and in view of recent experimentations, the argument that productions are undergoing rapid transformation appears almost intuitive. Although the films under consideration are exclusively 'African films', there is ample evidence in all these narratives that the 'Africa' being 'imagined' does not correspond to a shared view. By incorporating new visions, genres, representations and aesthetic expressions, today's filmmakers are not only interrogating sub-Saharan African identities, but are furthermore staking out a place for African cultures in global flows where identity oscillates between 'global and local, nation and (non)nation' (Petty, 2008, 1). In a context of transnational, hybrid, shifting and multiple identities, it is difficult to imagine that African productions have remained immune to outside influence. In fact, Jean-Pierre Bekolo almost proudly admits that such influence is central to his own work (Ukadike, 2002, 26). And as Arjun Appadurai (2005, 10) puts it, globalization has

> obscured the lines between temporary locales and imaginary national attachments. Modernity now seems *more practical and less pedagogic, more experiential and less disciplinary* than in the sixties, when it was mostly experienced through the *propaganda apparatuses* of the newly independent nation-states and their leaders … The megarhetoric of developmental modernization … in many countries is still with us. But is often punctuated, interrogated, and domesticated by the micronarratives of film, television, music, and other expressive forms, which allow modernity to be rewritten more as a vernacular globalization and less a concession to large scale national and international policies. (my emphasis)

The current status of African film production, with its multiplicity of issues, discourses and languages, strongly suggests that it is necessary to design a more innovative and inclusive theoretical framework to accommodate a rapidly mutating corpus whose analytical paradigms stretch beyond social challenges, dualities and cultural essentialisms.

This need arises from several factors, the first of which is historical and theoretical. It has to do with the fact that nation building and struggles for political freedom were far from being entirely successful. As Neil Lazarus (1999, 78) asserts, national liberation movements were not what they were expected or claimed to be, namely organizations that aimed at empowering, safeguarding and helping the powerless. Instead, in the words of Franz Fanon (1968, 152), the main project of the local bourgeois nationalists was 'quite simply … [to] transfer into native hands those unfair advantages which are the legacy of the colonial period'. A film like *Xala* (Ousmane, 1974) best illustrates the postcolonial failures that followed the ascension of African elites to political power, namely the much anticipated transformative results of the euphoric nationalism.

The second factor is structural and is related to the natural evolution of FEPACI itself. As an openly political institution that successfully sought affiliation with the Organization of African Unity, it could only end up being an easy site for ideological contestation. As Diawara put it, FEPACI was composed of 'leftists and idealists who were committed to the notion of Pan-Africanism' and who believed in a 'prophetic mission' to liberate and unite Africa (1992, 39). Yet, as we have learned (or failed to learn) from Ali Mazrui (1995, 35), there ought to be a 'distinction between Pan-Africanism of *liberation* and Pan-Africanism of *integration*' (original emphasis). It would not take much to provide evidence that neither form of nationalism has been entirely successful, nor that the latter has enjoyed very little progress, if any, compared to the former. Brutal acts of xenophobia in South Africa, Gabon, Equatorial Guinea, Rwanda, Nigeria or Libya are very common. Considering that not all directors have a first hand experience of colonialism and that not all were trained in Moscow like Sembène Ousmane or Souleymane Cissé, the fact that nationalism and political engagement have lately undergone several attacks becomes less surprising. The decadence of the cinema of endless contestation, represented by Sarah Maldoror (surprisingly), Idrissa Ouedraogo, Jean-Pierre Bekolo and Joseph Gaï Ramaka, epitomizes the opposition to 'traditional' African films.

When she began shooting *Sambizanga,* Sarah Maldoror had a rather modest ambition: 'to make Europeans, who hardly know anything about Africa, conscious of the forgotten war in Angola, Mozambique and Guinea-Bissau' (in Moorman, 2001, 110). Surprisingly, she states that '*I have no time for films with political rhetoric* ... *I am against all forms of nationalisms* ... Besides this, the color of a person's skin is of no interest to me. What is important is what the person is doing' (in Moorman, 2001, 10, my emphasis). As for Idrissa Ouedraogo (1995, 337), his views about nationalism and political engagement are well known:

> African filmmakers reflect on protest discourses rather than on
> cinema in short ... But it is now necessary to stop lamenting,
> and intellectualizing excessively. The African public expects from
> us inspiration, quality and smart getaways. [...] In my next films,
> I will attach more importance to the effectiveness of the story
> and actors than to the beauty of the film set. It will be always the
> same universe, with incredible changes in sound, *mise en scène,*

pictures; the story will be more open, more accessible to other audiences.⁶

Although he is very critical of Ouedraogo's 'bush cinema', Jean-Pierre Bekolo has a similar view regarding boring didacticism. First of all, Bekolo's aesthetic project, as indicated by Akin Adesokan (2008, 1), targets entertainment and constitutes a 'confident mix of aesthetic populism and critical, even *auteurish* staging of conceptual issues in Africa *and* contemporary filmmaking' (original emphasis). Such consideration places him significantly far away from the didactic approach, which he categorically rejects because as he argues it has kept Africans away from movie theatres. In Nwachukwu Frank Ukadike's *Questioning African Cinema* (2002), Bekolo's thoughts about this issue are unequivocal:

> Why do we make films if people would not go to see them?
> Most of [my students feel] that most African films are like tools
> for teaching and that is why I started having problems with that
> definition. Film is a medium of expression and an art form. [...]
> I do not know if African filmmakers can use the film medium to
> teach ... or if they have the right background. I think it is wrong
> for us to teach, even if we feel we have learned something. Film
> could be a good medium for a type of education that is different
> from teaching. I do not pretend to be a teacher. I do not know
> how to do that very well. (2002, 219)

In an interview with Michael T. Martin, the Senegalese director Joseph Gaï Ramaka was equally critical of a cinema mindful only of a politically-motivated agenda and aesthetic. He is very sceptical about nationalist claims, which he characterizes as uncertain in a world of transnational circulations:

> I belong to no cinema organization, or structure, African or non-
> African. I view myself as a global human being and not in
> relation to a nation. I am interested in things that are made by an
> individual. My concerns are not as a filmmaker, but rather as a
> citizen who happens to be a filmmaker ... I do not conceive my
> commitment to social justice as a filmmaker. I am not a
> filmmaker *engagé*. I am an ordinary citizen *engagé*. I want the

rank-and-file, the policeman, the filmmaker, administrator, and judge to be *engagé* as self-conscious citizens. (Martin, 2008, 27–28)

Such stands by Ouedraogo, Maldoror, Bekolo and Ramaka clearly indicate the extent to which Sembène Ousmane's conception of cinema as 'evening school' for consciousness-raising and social transformation has become, in a way, somehow outdated for several directors. This book aims to re-conceptualize contemporary sub-Saharan African cinema by foregrounding the narrative and aesthetic structures of recent films. The failure of liberationist discourses to secure permanent gains has resulted in filmmakers selecting new aesthetic approaches that move beyond anti-imperialist, historical contestations and cultural claims; according to Achille Mbembe (2002a, 272), 'the very project of an essentialist or sacrificial recovery of the [African] self is ... doomed'. Thus, the movement away from liberationist aesthetics may have less to do with the Westernization of sub-Saharan African cinema or a facile 'fashion effect' than it does with the emergence of a hybrid cinematic style intended to interrogate constructs now becoming unsettled in the context of globalization.

The third and perhaps most decisive factor in understanding contemporary African films is the near dissolution of the African nation-state and the resultant need to rethink nationalism. Ato Quayson (2000, 91) links material postcolonial experience with national imagination, stating that

> Africa's literary history is easily transposable onto the evolution of the nation-state and the growing dissatisfaction with its performance. Literary symbols and metaphors are constantly overloaded with meaning precisely because in the real world everything is an aspect of political power and its constant negotiation.

One can argue that cinema is no different. Likewise, Kenneth Harrow's (2001, 33) introduction to the special issue he edited for *Research in African Literatures* on nationalism opens with a truism: 'The nation-state in Africa today is in crisis.' This crisis, in many ways still ongoing, can be read in the multiple conflicts, diseases and disasters that have literally crippled the continent. In a context where, in addition to local 'ethnic' tensions in Darfur or Rwanda, African wars are initiated from the offices of mining or oil companies in Bombay, Beijing or Houston, can nationalism, be it political or cultural, be articulated in the same terms as it was decades ago? What 'nation' exists in countries that rely on American, Swedish or Dutch aid in order to maintain transit, health care or educational systems? What nation is left in war-torn and poverty-stricken countries like Chad or Sudan, where corrupt leaders bask in luxury while children die of malnutrition? And what is the place of imagination in places where the dominant role models are Rambo, Denzel Washington or Lady Diana? How fast has the African imaginary shifted from Hollywood to *Bollywood* (India), and lately, *Nollywood* (Nigeria)? Given the above, can one still proudly believe, alongside Partha Chatterjee (1993, 5), that '[t]he most powerful as well as the most creative results of the nationalist imagination in Asia and Africa are posited not on identity but rather on a *difference* with the modular' forms of the national society propagated by the modern West'?

The decadent nations which have been central in postcolonial imaginations are also, one must not forget, the same nations that have failed to make cinema a priority. With few exceptions like Algeria where culture funded by the newly independent 'socialist' state was assertively nationalist, most postcolonial directors, paradoxically, sought financing from the very colonial France their work criticized. In that sense, FEPACI was not particularly coherent. That is why it was severely criticized by a group of young directors, *Le Collectif L'Oeil Vert* (consisting, among other people, of Cheikh N'Gaido Bâ, Senegal; Sanou Kollo, Burkina Faso; Lancine Kramo Gatiga, Côte d'Ivoire) who insisted that a true liberation of African cinema was impossible without a radical transformation of production strategies (Diawara, 1992, 43). FEPACI's structural weaknesses addressed above are now rerouted by new material conditions of production, distribution and exhibition. It is well known that France has played a central role in the economy of African cinemas. However, in order to fully evaluate current transformations, it is crucial to re-examine its (perverse) nature which makes alternative interventions urgent. Manthia Diawara (1992) analyses the financial as well as political determinants which positioned France as the main 'manager' and 'banker' of African cinema. Funding bodies functioning directly under the authority of the Ministry of Culture or the Ministry of Cooperation, formerly Ministry of Colonies, were created in the 1950s. Among them was the *Centre National du Cinéma* and the *Bureau du cinéma*. These offices decided, through structures like *Le Fond Cinéma du Sud, Ecrans du Sud* or the *Fond d'Intervention pour l'Action Culturelle*, which programmes would be supported. Other bodies like the European Union, the *Fond Francophone* and *L'Agence de la Francophonie* were instrumental in the development of the films that have been available so far.[7] Channel 4 in the UK, ZDF, Arte and WDF in Germany or *Vidéo Tiers-Monde* in Canada have equally been at the forefront of helping African cinemas in post-independence times when emerging autocracies would not fund any entity that threatens their stability. When it existed, the French magazine *Le Film Africain* & *Le Film du Sud* systematically included sections on production, pre-production, distribution or financing, with the list of granting agencies and projects that had been subsidized (see for example issues 33–34, 2000; 35–36, 2001; 37–38, 2001; 39–40, 2002).

However, these crucial transborder financial networks did not come without a price tag which, I wish to suggest, has been high. In fact, *Le Collectif L'Oeil Vert* also strongly – and unsuccessfully – lobbied against French financial grip on productions. As Frantz Fanon indicated with relation to cultural autonomy, 'We have taken everything from the other side. Yet, the other side has given us nothing except to sway us in its direction through a thousand twists, except to seduce us, *and imprison us by ten thousand devices*, by a hundred thousand tricks. *To take also means on several levels being taken*' (1968, 163; my emphasis). Diawara (2005) also shows how, on a perverse ideological level, the French promoted a primitive image of Africa. That is why they would not rush to fund the films of Sembène Ousmane who was known for his critique of (neo)colonialism. Olivier Barlet (2010, 221) rightly argues that subsidy commissions influence the content of films because they base their judgement on perceptions of a continent that are, to say the least, problematic. A good example is the case of Paulin Soumanou Vieyra whose *Afrique sur Seine* (1955), which was made under the auspices of the *Comité du Film Ethnographique*, simply reproduced the colonial idea of the African 'Other'. Funding agencies which emphasized 'Africanness' and primitivism have consequently had a lasting negative effect: the development of difficult to market auteur films without an audience. In a provocative essay 'Cinéma noir, public blanc' (in Elisabeth Lequeret, 2003, 78–79), Congolese director David-Pierre Fila labels African cinema as confidential, made for elite intellectuals. He further adds that Africans do not see films because they are not made for and not funded by them. Differently put, for Fila, the marketability of African cinemas is rendered impossible because funding, therefore content, in a way, is foreign. In *Creative Destruction*, Tyler Cowen actually contends in relation to European cinema that subsidies 'encourage producers to serve domestic demand and the wishes of politicians and cinematic bureaucrats, rather than produce movies for international export. Many films will be made, even when they have little chance of turning a profit in stand-alone terms' (2002, 81). In the specific case of African cinemas, French bureaucracy has subsidized films which alienated indigenous audiences because they targeted a foreign market that directors could not control. Instead of concentrating first on the anxieties, concerns and joys of local spectators, filmmakers generally focussed on an 'African' cinema consisting of nationalist or 'exotic' anthropological genres of 'village films' suited for European 'art' cinema and television. Rod Stoneman (1996) offers a useful typology of these productions and suggests that for each African film the funding source be a balanced combination of different partnerships: indigenous and foreign, television and cinema, commercial and state (177–178).

The danger of foreign aid is therefore evident, and directors have experienced it first hand by systematically generating ethnographic and nationalist 'African' films in spite of transnational circulations that could have accommodated diverse contents and aesthetics. That is why most filmmakers explore alternative sources of funding in Canada, South Africa and Switzerland with limited success. This strategy, it is hoped, can put an end to the old current bi-nationalist model with the European Union or France and its ex-colonies. Most importantly, a few African countries, especially Burkina Faso, have taken decisive steps to fund their national cinema. Although not numerous, some local private companies (telecommunications, breweries, lottery, etc.) now contribute to funding African productions. However, what seems to have saved some directors from exclusively foreign dependency is new technological transformation which allows them to make absurdly low-budget films without subjecting themselves to all kinds of financial acrobatics. Digital video and editing have significantly reduced production costs. For better or worse, the Nigerian *Nollywood* phenomenon is the extreme case of a revolution against the (post)colonial entrapment in foreign charity, high costs and discursive discipline. All these paradigms have reshaped the relation between African filmmakers and the ex-colonial nation – France – which, over time has ceased being the unique funding source or site for post-production. Not only do directors seek support elsewhere, but they are no more compelled to protect French jobs by operating their postproduction in Paris. Morocco, South Africa and even Nigeria are now in that equation, about forty years after such initiatives were recommended by *Le Collectif L'Oeil Vert*. In addition to trying to further develop what Rod Stoneman called the 'South/South Axis' for production options, filmmakers also look for other venues and strategies to publicize and disseminate their work.

Films, like people, can only circulate because specific channels are in place. However, in the case of African cinemas, especially in recent years, these circuits have changed and established new interrelations between the specific local, national and international networks that have enabled productions to remain not only transnational but radically postnationalist in their discursive articulations. In addition to multiple festivals in the West where directors promote their works (see Barlet 2000 for a list of these festivals), Bassek ba Kobhio has also miraculously succeeded in organising another African film festival – *Ecrans Noirs* – every summer in Yaoundé since 1996. By convincing the Cameroonian government and local businesses to fund culture, he has succeeded where most other entrepreneurs have failed. In 2009, in addition to the expensive and glamorous settings, his festival awarded seven prizes ranging from US$2,000 to 10,000.[8] Although this adventure started rather modestly, *Écrans Noirs* has become a major cultural attraction on the continent after the Pan-African Film Festival (FESPACO) held every two years.

Various directors and distributors are equally promoting films by putting some excerpts on YouTube where one can see Jean-Pierre Bekolo, Ousmane Sembène, Ngangura Mweze, Moussa Sene Absa, Djibril Diop Mambety, Idrissa Ouedraogo, Gaston Kaboré, Jean-Marie Teno, Bassek ba Kobhio, Manosur Sora Wade or Joseph Gaï Ramaka. Such exposure places their work in a larger public sphere. If one adds the massive online information about them, it becomes clear that these films are now visible in a global setting. Sylvestre Amoussou has gone a step farther by creating a website (http://www.africaparadis.com) for *Africa Paradis* (2007) which, together with the television series of the group *Les Guignols* from Côte d'Ivoire (and a few other titles), is one of the very few African DVDs sold by the major French bookstore FNAC. More importantly, these works are not ghettoized in an exotic 'World' or 'African' category, but placed under the comedy section. *Ma Famille*, a very popular television series in West

Africa, is now available online at http://www.tou.tv/ma-famille. Several African titles, including those studied in this book, have now become 'classics' and can be purchased through California Newsreel in the USA or *La Médiathèque des Trois Mondes* in France.[9] Another distributor has also started a business in South Africa, The African Film Library (http://www. africanfilmlibrary.com). This new initiative aims at showcasing African films and to make them available to all movie lovers.[10] Jean-Marie Teno has added some commercial sophistication to the concentration of roles in his work. Not only is he the narrator, producer and director of his films, but he also distributes them through two websites, *Les Films du raphia* (http://www. raphia.fr) which has recently had a sister company (http://www.jmteno. us) in the USA where the Cameroonian director now lives.[11]

All the above however does not solve the *invisibility* of these works in Africa where movie houses are close to completely disappearing – a few quartier houses left in Senegal, about two in Cameroon. There is in fact no evidence that the production of African films ever depended on their distribution in African movie theatres. That does not mean Africans do not see films. Rather, those that are available, African or not, are spread through routes that defy all economic rationalities. While one cannot blame Sembène Ousmane, Med Hondo or Kwah Ansah who, for years, did not want their films to be put on VHS format because of concerns over piracy, all empirical research unfortunately indicates that contraband and black-market production are central to the dissemination of culture by business people and consumers to whom the word copyright is non-existent. One can even strongly argue that, unfortunately, African cultures only become popular with viral piracy. Brian Larkin (2004, 307) once rightly suggested that watching Hollywood or Indian films on VCDs in Nigeria means watching the dub of a dub of a dub, and that perfectly applies to African films and television series as well. In order to reduce the rationale for piracy, *Nollywood* has increasingly turned to English, whereas in Senegal Wolof is used and in Ghana Twi or other non-English languages. There is a national and regional market in Africa where almost all productions can be found. However, the rules that govern their accessibility are resolutely unconventional and subvert mainstream economic controls. As Manthia Diawara writes,

> Markets in West Africa clearly undermine official forms of
> globalization according to which a nation-state attracts the

investments of multinational corporations after undergoing a measure of structural adjustment, that is, devaluation. By producing disorder through pricing, pirating, smuggling, and counterfeiting, they participate in the resistance to multinational control of the national economy and culture. (1998, 121)

One cannot therefore discount the fact that the cultural landscape is changing, especially with the advent of satellite television channels like TV5 and CFI which have allowed a number of films to be seen in Francophone Africa. In any case, some directors have stopped trying desperately to conquer only foreign spaces and spectatorships, and have even been successful. The box office triumph of Boubacar Diallo in Burkina Faso and the burgeoning popularity of videos in Cameroon, Senegal and Côte d'Ivoire – all far from the unprecedented levels of *Nollywood* in Nigeria or Ghana – clearly signal that African cinemas have moved in the crucial direction of a popular cinema. This cinema both federates local spectators around ordinary characters they can identify with and appeals to transnational horizons through generic categories which are reworked with sophistication. In other words, contemporary productions have significantly modified their formal and discursive architecture for a public which only wants to see good films, be they 'African' or not. As Olivier Barlet writes, directors now

> envisage the world in its globality. [...] To be able to ask about one's place in the world independently of where one comes from demands a new aesthetics, a new language that reflects this. This is why the films of a new generation of filmmakers are experimenting with new forms better suited to sharpen the awareness they have of the problems facing Africa and the world at large. (2010, 223)

Given the new material conditions just outlined and the formal transformations, one is left to wonder if the failed and oppressive nation can remain a central signifier in postcolonial narratives. If, as Kathleen Newman asserts (2010, 4), filmmakers around the world have always been in conversation with each other, and audiences are generally exposed to more than one cinematic tradition with which they develop an *active*, not passive, engagement, how can African directors or spectators remain un-transformed over time and space? In *Africa for the Future*, Jean-Pierre Bekolo asks an essential question (2009, 49), the implied answer to which is negative: how can one possibly differentiate what is French or American from what belongs to one's African world? In other words, is the African cinema of today ontologically different from dominant cinemas? If not, why? If there has ever been something like an 'African form', has it remained the same after encountering the Other? There may not be clear answers to these questions. What is indisputable, though, is that liberationist aesthetics and paradigms seem to have played themselves out. The following section therefore proposes some alternative representational strategies.

3   Postnational(ist) imaginary and new paradigms

Given the nature of contemporary productions, keeping the same theoretical structure of jingoistic frameworks would consolidate two dominant thrusts of critical thought which, according to Achille Mbembe (2002a, 240–243), have shaped 'African modes of self-writing'. Describing the first as 'Afro-radicalism,' Mbembe argues that 'Marxist and nationalist' mechanisms became imbricated in discourses of 'victimization' as a result of colonial intervention. African identity politics are concerned with repudiating Western imposition, developing instead a language infused with African 'authenticity' (244). The result of such attitude is the invention of a narrative of liberation built around a dual temporality: on the one hand, the mythical, glorious, vanished past tradition or history, and on the other the hope of a better future to be secured through commitment to nationalist ideals (249–250). Typical of this tendency is Manthia Diawara's 'return to the source' films which he uses in his typology (1992, 159–164).

The second thrust, which Mbembe refers to as 'nativism,' foregrounds 'the idea of a unique African identity founded on membership of the black race' (2002a, 240– 241). In this view transnational solidarity is built on a collective narrative that emphasizes a past of slavery, colonization and apartheid. Recovering these past identities involves recouping cultural imperatives, real or imagined, from a vanished pre-colonial past. Africa thus becomes reconstituted 'in the light of myth' (2002a, 255). Ukadike's *Black African Cinema*, Frindéthié's *Francophone African Cinema* and Josef Gugler's *African Film* provide excellent illustrations of this conceptualization. These critics all emphasize membership in a racial or geographic category as a defining feature of African cinema, which does not provide much possibility for 'multiple ancestries' or belongings. Given such circumstances, Mbembe's argument becomes almost hyperbolic when stating that the African social imaginary has been reduced to obsolescence and become trapped in a sort of cul-de-sac (2002a, 239–240). When I argue here for a new episteme in African film scholarship, it is because new narratives demand alternatives to nationalist thought.

If one considers the work of directors such as Mahamed Camara, Mansour Sora Wade, Jean-Pierre Bekolo, Daniel Kamwa, Safi Faye, Henri Duparc, Desiré Ecaré, Henri-Joseph Koubi Bididi, Dani Kouyaté and Mwenze Ngangura, to name just a few, it is obvious that 'the nation' becomes a less important, if not totally absent, signifier. Although it has not been entirely abandoned, the idea of nation building has been somewhat overshadowed by a shift in focus to more quotidian priorities. The oeuvre of these directors puts into praxis Paul Gilroy's arguments about black expression by deconstructing the myth of a unitary or 'pure' culture. Motivated by conscious and unconscious influences, these directors, like several others, illustrate Arjun Appadurai's argument that

> We need to think ourselves beyond the nation. This is not to
> suggest that thought alone will carry us beyond the nation or
> that the nation is largely a thought or an imagined thing. Rather,
> it is to suggest that the role of intellectual practices is to identify
> the current crisis of the nation and in identifying it, to provide
> part of the apparatus of recognition for postnational social
> forms. Although the idea that we are entering a postnational
> world seems to have received its first airing in literary studies, it
> is now a recurrent (if not unconscious) theme in studies of
> postcolonialism, global politics, and international welfare policy.
> But most writers who have asserted or implied that we need to
> think postnationally have not asked exactly what emergent forms
> compel us to do so. (2005, 158)

This book takes up considerations which have largely gone unnoticed in theoretical writings by interrogating the ways in which African narratives position postcolonial identities and forms beyond essentially nationalist frameworks. A comprehensive survey of recent publications related to the focus of *Postnationalist African Cinemas* reveals that there are no studies that deal directly with the issues being addressed here. To date, no critic has consistently explored the transformed (and transforming) territory of African cultural productions. Although quite laudable in several of its investigations, Melissa Thackway's *Africa Shoots Back: Alternative Perspectives in Sub-Saharan Francophone African film* (2003) is also based on the 'nationalist scope' of postcolonial theories used in her excellent analyses. She rightly observes that '[m]any filmmakers have increasingly experimented with styles and forms, making it impossible to class their work in a single category' (12), and that young directors reflect the cultural hybridity of urban settings; she does not however document the breadth of these *new forms*, remaining very much preoccupied with challenging 'existing representations of Africa' (1).[12] Josef Gugler's *African Film* (2003) is likewise substantially influenced by anthropology, which can be attributed to Gugler's background in sociology. His book seems at times erroneously to equate cinema to reality. Unlike Thackway, Gugler is not particularly interested in aesthetic concerns. Both authors are engaged in 'oppositional criticism,' a scholarly disposition concerned with defining African cinema *against* other cinemas. The subtitles of their respective books, 'Re-Imagining' and 'Alternative Perspectives,' speak to this postcolonial, revisionist, project which, paradoxically, 'inevitably posits a reductive binary model whose fixed boundaries automatically situate "counter-cinemas" such as Francophone African film, in a simply oppositional, reactive role' (Thackway, 2003, 18).

Roy Armes' publication *African Filmmaking North and South of the Sahara* (2006) offers a detailed thematic overview of African cinema. A chapter entitled 'Experimental Narratives' briefly examines a few transformations displayed in films; however, Armes does not focus much on formal choices, and is also sceptical of the nature and breadth of identity formation, the main goal of his work because

> there has been a constant, dominant stream, over the past forty years, of socially realist films which accept identity as a given and are based on a sense of common historical experiences and shared cultural codes. *Alternative or experimental films which call into question that approach have been sporadic, though nonetheless valuable for that. Most often these have been isolated, individual works within the overall output of a filmmaker who has earlier worked in, or subsequently reverts to, the realist mainstream.* (111, my emphasis)

One of the main arguments of this book is precisely that fixed identities and social realism are no more a fatality, the *must* feature of African films. In *Postcolonial African Cinema: Ten Directors* (2007), David Murphy and Patrick Williams undertake a thorough analysis of ten African directors from various milieus. This is a theoretically sound work but which, with its biographical and socio-historic structure, does not engage the renewal of African film criticism that is the core objective of this book.

Because 'the nature of African cinema has too often been trapped within a reductive opposition between Western and African culture' (Murphy, 2000, 241), in the context of globalization, *Postnationalist African Cinemas* investigates how the emergence of new genres, discourses and representations, some of which are totally unrelated to the nationalist dictates of FEPACI, influence the formal choices made by the new directors. It explores sub-Saharan cinema in terms of 'the emergence of new thought forms' (Meyer, 1999, 108), forms that have little, if anything, to do with moribund fifty-year-old imperatives. The objectives of this book are as follows: 1) describe the limits of current taxonomies and critical investigations in light of new productions; 2) determine the new genres (crime movies, epics, comedies) that have arisen; 3) explore how new aesthetic innovations, issues and concerns are addressed in these genres and set apart from the foundational oeuvres; 4) examine how films propose new modes of representation, sexuality, gender and/or African identities; 5) investigate what role is played by global cultural forces and forms.

Postnationalist African Cinemas expands on the very few existing critical texts that explore the necessity of challenging the assumptions that have governed most African film criticism. Dayna L. Oscherwitz (2008) has published an essay in which she persuasively analyses the effect of globalization in Djibril Diop Mabety's *Hyenas*. She shows how this narrative formally and thematically takes up cinematic codes particular to the Western genre. In a related essay Sada Niang (2008) also convincingly traces the link between Sembène Ousmane's *Borom Sarret* and Italian neorealism. Taiwo Adetunji Osinubi (2009) persuasively theorizes the use of science-fiction techniques in three films from different eras: two very recent, *Les Saignantes* (2005) and *Africa Paradis* (Amoussou, 2007), and the more dated *La Noire de…* (Ousmane, 1966). Osinubi's essay shows how the advanced degradation of the nation-state as well as the emergence of supra-national entities compels postcolonial subjects to reimagine their future. More radically, Kenneth Harrow emphasizes the need to rethink African film criticism in the light of contemporary praxis. However, although it sets coherent foundations for revisiting African film scholarship, Harrow's *Postcolonial African Cinema: From Political Engagement to Postmodernism* (2007) provides a poststructuralist, de-historicizing analysis that also misses (or ignores) the historical and cultural factors that account for certain textual specificities. Furthermore, although there is evidence that a 'new breed' (Ukadike) of African cinema has been consolidating itself and that even Sembène Ousmane's own work is neither homogenous nor immune to 'western aesthetics' (see Niang, 2008; Tcheuyap, 2008), Harrow opposes him to Bekolo facilely. In addition, by arguing that '[t]here is *no history to represent, to correct*, in film. *There is only authority that represents itself*, and in its power represents its images and narrative as authoritative, as authorized, as official, or worse still, as real' (2007, xi, my emphasis), his critique of historiography simply reinforces postcolonial authority. One other problem with Harrow's critique of the categories tied to political agenda is that it does not distinguish between different types of political projects. Counterintuitively, postcolonial autocrats like Houphouet Boigny, Julius Nyerere and Ahmadou Ahidjo all presented themselves or were presented as 'nationalists'. A final point needs to be noted about the landmark studies of Harrow, Murphy and Williams: they generally examine the same small number of male directors, namely Jean-Pierre Bekolo, Sembène Ousmane, Djibril Diop Mambéty, Idrissa Ouedraogo and Souleymane Cissé.[13]

Postnationalist African Cinemas contributes to this limited re-evaluation of contemporary African cinema by foregrounding the narrative, generic, discursive, representational and aesthetic structures of films produced by filmmakers for whom there is no doubt that 'the thematics of anti-imperialism is exhausted' (Mbembe, 2002a, 263). Thus, the distance from nationalist discourse that the book will illuminate may have less to do with an unhealthy contamination by Western codes than it does with the growth of cinematic modes intended to interrogate unstable new social constructs and shifting identities. It will closely examine a wide range of oeuvres (as well as directors) and move scholarship away from oppositional criticism. The path taken here is to determine the new modalities according to which, to borrow from the South African critic Njabulo Ndebele (1994), African directors have shifted their focus towards experimental projects almost unilaterally overlooked by critics: they are engaged in a 'rediscovery of the ordinary'[14] which admits laughter, dance, crimes, vain heroism, tragic love, sex or witchcraft mythologies.

Before elaborating on the structure of the book, a number of quick theoretical and methodological procedures demand clarification. I do not wish to rehearse the already lengthy debates about the contemporary proliferation of the ubiquitous prefix *post*. There are without a doubt several hazards in using it in this context. In *The Postnational Constellation*, Jurgen Habermas (2001) traces the political, economic and cultural challenges awaiting the newly created European Union where nation-states have become micro-entities. Although he briefly – and rightly – mentions (75) that in reaction to the pressures of material world cultures, fresh constellations emerge with hybridized forms – as is the case with postnationalist African films – his focus on trans-border political and economic networks fits best with issues of transnationalism in cinema studies as proposed by Will Higbee and Song Hwee Lim (2010). This paradigm centres on economic and financial considerations in film production as have been addressed above. In this book, I intend the *post* to signify a *process* rather than serve as a temporal – or spatial in the case of Habermas – designation. This does imply that nationalism, understood as '*a mode of representation*' (Lazarus, 1999, 108, original emphasis) that generally produces oppositional discourses, is far from 'exhausted' as argued by Achille Mbembe. A temporally-inflected reading of the prefix would imply that nation building has been successfully completed. However, historical and sociological documentation unequivocally suggest that, if anything, the reverse is actually the case. That is why although this book mostly focuses on post-1990 films, it also includes several others which date from the 1970s or the 1980s, precisely because the post-resistance aesthetic was already then in place.

I am therefore unwilling to state categorically, as Mbembe does, that nationalism has disappeared. Although his view must not be dismissed out of hand, neither should one lose sight of the historical trajectory that produced anti-colonial rhetoric, and continues to resonate, at times too simplistically, in films like Jean-Marie Teno's *Le Malentendu colonial / Colonial Misunderstanding* (2005) or Abderrahmane Sissako's *Bamako* (2006). Stuart Hall's discussion of cultural identity applies to nationalism. He writes, '[i]t is a matter of "becoming" as well as of "being". It belongs to the future as much as to the past. It is not something which already exists, transcending place, time, history and culture' (1989, 73). In *We Who Are Dark*, Tommie Shelbie (2005) also offers useful foundations for what he calls 'pragmatic black nationalism'. He rejects the crude, ahisotorical and dichotomous oppositions such as black/white and African/Western proposed by cultural nationalists. Shelbie instead inscribes Black cultural forces in transnational formations that cannot be limited to an 'ethnic' milieu. The shaping of new, hybrid cultures does not in any way suggest that Blacks cannot build community spirit, or that brute racial discrimination no longer exists in America. Pragmatic nationalism rejects the obsessive recovery of a glorious fallen past, an imaginary 'original' homeland or a racial purity, positioning itself instead within the cultural turbulence of global interconnection. For Shelbie, 'what holds blacks together as a unified people with a shared political interest is the fact of their racial subordination and their collective resolve to triumph over it' (56). In such a context, the concept of nationalism is far from passé, and can be reconciled with the aggressive forces of globalization. Because nationalism thus becomes less overt, the challenge scholars face is to determine the new modalities of its expressions. Subsequent scholarly projects will undoubtedly deal with other forms of nationalist expression, and I have chosen in this study to limit my examination to narratives in which militancy and protest are *not* essential. My emphasis is on new generic classifications and forms of entertainment that have emerged for the most part since 1990.

In this book, I show that the fragmentation of experience and the appearance of transnational associations have brought about national crisis; the reproduction of alternative cultural forms has become accelerated and accentuated in places where nation building and social outcry are no longer priorities. I call narratives created in this context *postnationalist* because they are thematically beyond the mode of resistance. Far from advocating a strict social determinism, my argument here is that new contexts have generated new forms and representations. That does not mean that cultural or liberationist nationalism has vanished. It has simply become less prominent, although more assertive in some narratives such as *Colonial Misunderstanding* (2005) or *Bamako* (2006). In that sense, African nationalism remains a process that cannot possibly be confined to one particular era. However, today there are far more texts aimed at entertaining a public tired of ultra realist codes intended to remind them of an undeniably unhealthy experience. As Jean-Pierre Bekolo and Mwenze Ngangura have argued, obsessive didacticism has transformed African cinema halls into deserted sites because all African films, as summarized by a character in *Le Complot d'Aristote* (Bekolo, 1996), are 'shit'.

It is important to articulate the theoretical underpinnings of this project. Debates have raged in postcolonial and African scholarship about the possibility of using 'Western imperial' theories in order to understand cultures born out of domination. In the introduction to *Less Than One and Double: a Feminist Reading of African Women's Writing* (2001), Kenneth Harrow wonders why scholars working on African literature are almost compelled to apologize when using psychoanalytic frameworks. In an issue of *Research in African Literatures* (2007), Uzoma Esonwanne and other critics took up this question with generative results. One other 'problem' they identified in postcolonial enquiries is the alleged 'saturation' of the field with French (especially Enlightenment) thinkers who may have contributed to the circulation of dominant discourses in the first place. Although it is true that theories cannot be universally applied to any cultural context, as Nwachukwu Frank Ukadike, Ella Shohat and Robert Stam show, neither can they be instantly debunked on the simple grounds that 'white' is tantamount to 'hegemonic'. Paul Gilroy rightly reminds us of 'the complicity and syncretic interdependency of black and white thinkers' (1993, 31), and we must likewise remember that criticisms are seldom levelled at critics who draw on the discourse of Marxism. While this book makes extensive use of postcolonial/cultural criticism as well as 'Western' tools, it does not lose sight of their limitations whenever they occur. That is why K. Martial Frindéthié's claim to have 'finally' connected African cinema with 'contemporary [Western] literary theory and political imagination' (2009, 3) is not merely misleading. A methodology that uses postcolonial narratives as simple receptacles for the uncritical testing of specific theories is also dubitable.

Although we all know that Western scholarship was born within a specific historical and discursive setting that consolidated its hegemony, the encounter with the African 'other' has been, for better or worse, mutually (trans)formative in that directors, writers and artists now experience hybrid identities. African filmmakers have borrowed and substantially subverted categories or codes indebted to foreign spaces and cultures. This indebtedness is clear in moments of comedy and dance in several films I will consider, some of which fuse local and global codes. Many contemporary directors would agree with Kwame Anthony Appiah that 'in this world of genders, ethnicities and classes, of families, religions, and nations, it is as well to remember that there are times when Africa is not the banner we need' (1992, 180); a purely nationalist or African framework is not, against this horizon, the most desirable. Even Frantz Fanon, whose inheritance several postcolonial critics claim, did not view nationalism in a narrow sense, and was never in favour of 'nativism'. It was doubtless openness to otherness that must be considered an ancestor of the global forces that shape African cinema today.

One final clarification to be made is the importance of the plural in my title, *Postnationalist African Cinemas*. Other than Olivier Barlet (2000), critics have invariably used the singular in defining films from the continent. Paulin Soumanou Vieyra, one of the first historians of African cinemas, specified in the seventies that he used the term 'African cinema' because 'the national cinemas of this continent are not yet so important ... that we are led to divide them up and study them separately as Algerian, Senegalese, Nigerian, Moroccan, Guinean, Ivorian or Nigerien cinema' (1975, 7).[15] However, there is little doubt that today, it is methodologically untenable to continue using the singular. The fact that universities and job postings relegate African films to the category of 'world cinema' or remote 'area studies' is not enough to justify the continued use of the singular in a continent where Nigeria, Burkina Faso, South Africa and Egypt have separate and unique film industries.[16] A good illustration of the need to rethink inclusive territorial classifications is offered by Teresa Hoefert de Turégano whose *African Cinema and Europe* (2004) skilfully illustrates the dynamics of Burkina Faso's vibrant national cinema. As she rightly points out, the generic blanket label 'African cinema' is not totally appropriate because it masks the diversity of genres, film languages and narrative forms of a field that is far from being homogeneous (13). However, as she also points out, theories of national cinema ought to interrogate the conceptual limits of the nation, positioning it within transnational and international settings (206). While waiting for researchers to fully document and theorize this phenomenon, technological advances have transformed Nigeria, Ghana, Côte d'Ivoire and Cameroon into huge image industries. The *Nollywood* phenomenon has radically transformed the landscape of African productions, and scholars will need to conceptualize the terms according to which these films can be included in catalogues of (national) cinema.

4   Structure of the book

The book is divided into seven chapters, which examine a variety of texts in relation to entertainment, genre theory and representation, without viewing them as 'exceptional' in the sense deplored by David Murphy and Patrick Williams. These critical axes are not necessarily meant to hold African films up to mythical global standards, but rather to highlight how the chosen directors address *different* issues or address the same issues *differently*.[17] I argue that 1) African oeuvres are now more than ever geared toward entertainment; 2) they can be usefully fitted into Western generic categories; 3) they are now depicting what has historically been considered 'limit' or 'non-representable' subject matter; 4) in this representational process, nation building and 'confrontational' aesthetics are less significant, and I attribute this fact to a change in cultural attitudes. This is due, at least partially, to a global circulation of cultures that influence one another. Consequently, 'there is a clear sense in some postcolonial writing that the postulation of a unitary Africa over against a monolithic West – the binarism of Self and Other – is the last of the shibboleths of modernizers that we must learn to live without'. (Appiah, 1992, 155)

Chapter one analyses the pleasures of comedy. Its main objective is to examine the structural as well as semantic constructions governing the proliferation of comic forms in African films. In spite of the perceived dualistic opposition of film and entertainment, there is more evidence today than ever before that nation building is not incompatible with laughter, buffoonery and the carnivalesque which, as Bakhtin has argued, can equally liberate the subject without heavy pedagogic pretensions in that '[l]aughter ... overcomes fear, for it knows no inhibitions, no limitations. Its idiom is never used by violence and authority' (Bakhtin, 1984, 90). Films such as *Les Couilles de l'éléphant* (Koumba Bididi, 2002), *Quartier Mozart* (Bekolo, 1992), or *Bal Poussière* (Duparc, 1988) can help articulate the emerging role of comic identities, languages and intertexts in African films.

The second chapter interrogates the opposition to entertainment in a context where the putative efficiency of an obsessively political, activist cinema is progressively diminishing. 'Choreographing Subjects' first looks at the innate contradiction that has always existed between manifestos and actual film practice, for, from its very inception, African film always aimed at entertainment. It then examines the place of ritual, popular and social dance in national and individual experiences and determines the discursive implications of a diverse range of films, including *Xala* (Ousmane, 1973), *La vie est belle* (Ngangura, 1987), *Karmen Geï* (Ramaka, 2001) and *Caramel* (Duparc, 2004). It interrogates the performances of the dancing body as a material entity, a discursive construction and a vessel through which to channel the sacred and the profane. Most importantly, it illustrates how the state has lost its role of organizer of public enjoyment to become an absent agent in primarily non-official territories where subjectivity triumphs.

The third chapter focuses on the development of crime fiction which, in spite of a postcolonial obsession with law and order at the administrative level, has surprisingly not featured prominently in African cinema. It first examines the theoretical and historical factors that, along with ideological pressures, have made it virtually impossible to consider African films according to existing theories of genre. The need to re-conceptualize the advent of murder in cinema is more pressing in view of the positions of Ngandu Nkashama (1989) and Jean-Pierre Bekolo (as demonstrated in *Les Saignantes*, 2005) for whom detective movies are virtually 'un-African' or impossible to create in countries with corrupt police systems. This chapter argues that works like *Madame Brouette* (Sène Absa, 2002), *Les Saignantes* or even *Guelwaar* (Ousmane, 1992) can in fact convincingly be read as crime films by looking at how African directors appropriate a genre generally perceived as popular 'Western entertainment'. It also emphasizes how formal choices subvert the rules of this particular category and help elaborate alternative discourses regarding the nation and the status of postcolonial authority.

Chapter four looks at the relationship between myth, tragedy and African cinema. In spite of the strong similarities between films like *La Genèse* (Sissoko, 1999), *Ndeysaan, The Price of Forgiveness* (Sora Wade, 2001), *Tilaï* or *La Colère des Dieux* (Ouedraogo, 1991 and 2003) and some foundational Western myths, scholarship has failed to go beyond general statements about the 'Oedipus drama' visible in *Tilaï* (Diawara, 1992, 164; Armes, 2006, 126; Murphy & Williams, 2007, 152–3), the only narrative it is believed to inform. This chapter establishes a link between the aforementioned films and the myth of Oedipus, in addition to other myths such as the biblical story of Cain and Abel. It shows how tragic forms and psychoanalytic categories can be successfully related to African texts. The cultural and symbolic orders are shaken, revealing narratives focused on individual, private, matters, rather than national metanarratives.

The fifth chapter builds on the previous one and considers as well the relationship between film and epic. It reconsiders the concept of orality and determines one of its fundamental, yet unexplored, connections to African cinema, namely the *formal* relationship of various narratives to the epic genre. Gugler (2003) and Paré (2000) examine the intertextual and historical references in *Keita* (Kouyaté, 1995). Other texts, among them *Ndeyssan, The Price of Forgiveness* (Sora Wade, 2002), *Yeelen* (Souleymane Cisse, 1987) and *La Colère des Dieux* (Ouedraogo, 2003) display formal devices that can be related to epic and other tales.

Nationalist and culturalist discourses have transformed postcolonial subjects into exceptionally ascetic and abstinent characters in African films. Yet, there is a clear link between sex and the nation that needs to be re-examined, especially in view of Achille Mbembe's work which emphasizes, in an almost essentialist way, that sexuality in the postcolony is hyperbolic and abnormal (2001, 126). Aside from *Faces of Women* (Ecaré, 1985), nudity has consistently been the most noticeably absent signifier in films that nonetheless largely *discuss* sexuality. The sixth chapter explores *how* African films talk about sexuality *without showing it*, and examines the link between sex, the body and its cultural/political restrictions. The strategies of certain directors pertain to a set of cultural codes that will be discussed. In the few cases where there is actual nudity, I will examine the ways in which directors 'rehabilitate' and celebrate the beauty of the obscene. I will equally determine the new discourse on decadent nations in pornographic 'limit texts'.

The final chapter focuses on the scientific interest in occult practices as manifestations of postcolonial modernity as portrayed in film. From the dismissive attitudes depicted in films from Burkina Faso (*Yaaba, Wend Kuuni, Delwende*) to the more nuanced ones in Cameroonian cinema (*Le Cercle des pouvoirs* and *Quartier Mozart*), African cinema has not been particularly coherent in its representations of witchcraft, which is intimately related to the discourse on the nation. Furthermore, in attempting to depict the occult on screen, cinema makes visible what was not meant to be visible. It *interprets* witchcraft, and in so doing perhaps demystifies a phenomenon that is meant to remain sacred. This chapter looks at various representations of the occult, examines the strategies used by directors to reveal the invisible and determine its status in the nation.

Notes

1 Before further analysis, I wish to clarify a potentially contentious issue. Throughout this book, 'African cinema(s)' will refer to Sub-Saharan Francophone film praxis. Although films from Burkina Faso are in several ways different from those from Cameroon for example, one must admit that beyond

the linguistic similarity, both countries share a reasonably common socio-political heritage. Francophone Sub-Saharan African countries experienced French colonization which involved specific cultural policies that significantly shaped the nature, context, history and aesthetics of filmmaking before being completely transformed by current technological innovations and the generalization of video production in several countries. As Melissa Thackway puts it, there are 'real convergences in the region that arise from common linguistic ties, a shared legacy of French colonization, and the inheritance of convergent political and economic structures and continuing (neo-colonial) ties with France' (2003, 2). Manthia Diawara (1992) and Nwachuckwu Frank Ukadike provide the most comprehensive history of cinema in this region. Similarly, in her book which pays special attention to violence, Lindiwe Dovey offers a detailed analysis of '[t]he complex and contradictory ways in which the French attempted to create a regional Francophone family based on culture, and particularly, cinema' (2009, 178). In spite of notable differences, Diawara (2000) equally argues that there are common patterns that can be determined and which have been facilitated by the collapse of the nation-state that is no more a viable entity.

2 French original: '*Le cinéma a été introduit en Afrique à une époque où l'homme noir était dépossédé de sa destinée, où il était considéré comme un homme primitif, sans culture et sans histoire. Le cinéma fonctionnait alors comme un pont, reliant des "missions civilisatrices" reliant des "contrées inhospitalières" à la puissance de leur métropole tutélaire. Pour les « bons blancs » résidant en Afrique, déjà le cinéma intervenait comme un divertissement, les rattachant aux seules valeurs admises, celles de la civilisation occidentale. Puis vint le temps où le cinéma se transforma en un outil de propagande, efficace dans les deux sens. Il « éduquait » les indigènes, tandis que les Européens, restés sur le vieux continent, pouvaient voir de leurs propres yeux, comment l'entreprise civilisatrice des leurs gouvernements respectifs était nécessaire*'. (Quoted in Vokouma, 1995, 270)

3 Although the book says colonization, I wonder if it is not a typo which actually meant the opposite.

4 French original: '*Car il s'agissait au départ d'une véritable utopie. On sortait de la guerre de libération. On disait que le cinéma était "l'école des masses"! Personne ne songeait à tourner les comédies, ou très peu. Le cinéma n'était surtout pas une distraction! C'était même la chose la plus sérieuse au monde. Même l'armée algérienne avait ses caméras et ses labos neufs. On expédiait les jeunes à Moscou, à Prague, à Varsovie, à Pékin et ils revenaient: cinéastes, bardés de connaissances techniques. On écrivait des scénarios limpides, mais surtout pas contradictoires. Le message, surtout le message de la Révolution*' (1993, 40). We should not lose sight of the fact that the word 'revolution' in the Algerian context had a specific connotation. It referred to the independence and nationalist movement which laid the foundations of the modern Algerian postcolonial state.

5 This 2009 publication does not mention important interventions such as Sheila Petty's *Contact Zones* (2008), David Murphy and Patrick William's *Postcolonial African Cinema: Ten Directors* (2007) nor Kenneth Harrow's *Postcolonial African*

Cinema. From Political Engagement to Postmodernism (2007). None of Harrow's previous works, which are generally based on strictly poststructuralist, psychoanalytic or postmodern ('Western') enquiries, is discussed. A certain Ken Arrow (Kenneth Harrow?) is included in the acknowledgements, not in the bibliography. K. Martial Frindéthié's simplistic, unfounded charge against a misread Sembène Ousmane would almost perfectly apply to his own book: 'Why would Sembène, at the dawn of the new millennium, shoot a film [*Faat Kiné*] that says nothing, that introduces nothing new? To his credit, let us assume that he really wanted something novel to come out of his art. Unfortunately, however, Sembène has grown too old in the trenches of antiquarian idealism. He has waded for too long in the waters of fossilized beliefs.' (75)

This publication is equally full of historical and political elaborations, with details as useless as the circumstances in which Allsane Ouattara, a prominent politician and former Prime Minister of Côte d'Ivoire, 'inherited' his wife from the former President with whom she was involved. In the end, one is left with the impression that the book includes everything except rigorous film analysis. Among several debatable pronouncements is the fact that Frindéthié almost praises the notorious Charles Blé Goudé, leader and founder of the *Jeunes Patriotes*, a militia responsible for mass murders in Côte d'Ivoire.

6 French original: '*Les réalisateurs africains pensent au discours revendicateur plutôt qu'au cinéma tout court. [...] Mais il faut maintenant cesser de pleurnicher et d'intellectualiser à tour de bras. Le public africain attend de nous de l'inspiration et de la qualité, de l'évasion intelligente. [...] Dans mes prochains films, j'accorderai plus d'importance à la force de l'histoire et des acteurs qu'à la beauté des décors. Ce sera toujours le même univers, avec un travail très différent dans le son, la mise en scène, l'image, l'histoire sera plus ouverte, plus accessible à d'autres publics*'. (1995, 337)

7 The saturation of African cinematic landscape by French presence is best illustrated by a short attempt to place a precredit sequence and logo 'The Minister of Cooperation presents' on the films that were funded (Stoneman, 1996, 177). That has not entirely disappeared and has taken a different form. The *Agence de la Francophonie* initiated a programme called *Cinéma en milieu rural* consisting in showcasing one African film per month in various rural locations throughout the continent where no one would otherwise see them. However, for all films selected, a precredit sequence explains the rationale, with the logo of the *Agence* appearing first in good position on the screen.

8 Prizes awarded in 2009 were *Ecran d'or* (the highest prize) to *Nothing but the Truth* (John Kani, South Africa, 2008); *Ecran d'honneur* to Joseph Essomba for his work on comedy; *Écran du meilleur comédien* to William Nadylam for his role in *L'Absence* (Mama Keita, Guinea, 2009); *Ecran de la meilleure comedienne* to Norah Kafando for her role in *Le Fauteuil* (Moussa Hébié, Burkina Faso, 2009); *Ecran de la meilleure première oeuvre* to Manouchka Labouba for his film *Le Divorce* (Kelly Labouba, Gabon, 2008); *Ecran du documentaire* to Arnold Antonin for *Jacques Roumain, la passion d'un pays* (Haiti, 2008) and *Ecran du court métrage* to Bernard Kouemo for *Warametsubo* (Cameroon, 2008).

9 It worth noting that New Yorker Films, the other American distributor for African films, has gone out of business.

10 Interestingly, this company has listed the films according to specific generic categories: comedy, drama, musical, political drama, ethnographic feature, sci-fi, historical drama and youth drama. The old 'African cinema' classification seems to have disappeared.

11 It is also worth mentioning that over the years, 'African Cinema' has been strengthened as a cultural institution and academic discipline with some important editorial orientations. It has increasingly become the topic of multiple university courses in America, Canada, Britain and Australia. Surprisingly, very few universities, if any, offer such courses in Africa. Moreover, the creation of specialized journals partly or fully dedicated to African film studies (*Journal of African Cinemas, Transnational Cinemas, New Cinemas*) by the British publisher Intellect Books also comes to better position this cinema in a field where it had remained marginal(ized). The magazine and website www.africultures.com, both run by the indefatigable Olivier Barlet, is probably the most extensive online source for African cinemas and cultures, far better than www.cinemafrancophones.org which limits itself to specific linguistic zones.

12 This framework is developed later in the book in the following way: 'Filmmakers working in the postcolonial context have found themselves confronted with a legacy of distorted, demeaning images created by the European colonizer. Both the liberation discourses and works of contemporary filmmakers frequently accord history and memory a major role in reworking this imagery. Reassessing and interrogating the past are posited as a means of recreating and redefining the present and the future. Telling one's own story, recounting history from one's own point of view to reappropriate collective memory and to challenge the erasures of Eurocentric readings of history have become a vital part of the postcolonial process of self-definition'. (2003, 93)

13 Murphy and Williams discuss one female director, Tunisian Moufida Tlati, who does not belong to the territory this book covers.

14 In *South African Literature and Culture: Rediscovery of the Ordinary* (1994, 49), Ndebele questions the ways in which aspects of South African writings and criticism have remained excessively focussed on what he calls a literature of 'the spectacular,' which consistently misses 'the ordinary' because of exclusively political preoccupations. He is extremely critical of a tradition of social contestation that, because it reproduces the same discourse, is bound to become exhausted: 'The spectacular documents; it indicts implicitly; it is demonstrative, preferring exteriority to interiority; it keeps the larger issues of society in our minds, obliterating the details; it provokes identification through recognition and feeling rather than through observation and analytical thought; it calls for emotion rather than conviction; it establishes a vast sense of presence without offering intimate knowledge; it confirms without necessarily offering a challenge. It is the literature of the powerless identifying the key factor responsible for their powerlessness. Nothing beyond this can be

expected of it. Every convention will outlive its validity. Judging from some aspects of the new writing that has emerged recently from the South African townships, one can come to the conclusion that the convention of the spectacular has run its course. Its tendency either to devalue or to ignore interiority has placed it firmly in that aspect of South African society that constitutes its fundamental weakness'.

15 French original: '*les cinémas nationaux de ce continent ne sont pas encore si importants (...) pour que nous soyons amenés à en séparer l'étude en la fractionnant en cinéma algérien, sénégalais, nigérian, marocain, guinéen, ivoirien ou nigérien*' (1975,7).

16 It is interesting to note that in her latest book *50 ans de cinéma maghrébin* (2009), Denise Brahimi also uses the plural form in characterizing the cinemas of Morocco, Algeria and Tunisia.

17 *Omar Gatlato* by director Merzac Allouache (1977) was a huge success in that respect: this film exposes, without heavy didactic presuppositions and militant discourse, the evils that were repressed in Algeria for years. The *form* is crucial in expressing a nuanced content.

1   Sembène Ousmane

2   Jean-Pierre Bekolo

Chapter 1

Comedy and film

The ideological functions attributed to African cinema at its origin in the 1960s could lead to the belief that thinking about these movies as a form of entertainment is paradoxical. This is due to the fact that, in the wake of Frantz Fanon's cultural theories and their African theoretical counterparts such as those of Sembène Ousmane (to give only one example), African cinema was first and foremost perceived as an instrument of social transformation. Going to the movies, to 'night school,' is supposed to teach people to not follow blindly, but to be citizens who are aware of their society's challenges. This early perception of 'African cinema' surely explains a fairly simplistic and essentialist typology such as that of the Tunisian filmmaker and film critic Férid Boughédir who, following the Algiers Charter of 1975, positioned African cinema in direct opposition to 'Western cinema' and to entertainment (1992, 70). According to Boughédir, going to the movies should not lull one into complacency but rather make one think. The image should not serve as a 'diversion', but as a 'conversion' to socio-political causes to which filmmakers themselves are assumed to subscribe. Engaging in 'entertainment' is perceived as a futile and ethically irresponsible affair, while encouraging reflection on 'the real' is the work of the 'serious' filmmaker – the overtly political and subversive filmmaker. In another essay where he provides a typology of the comic genre, Boughédir criticizes the fact that '[t]he implicit ideology of these comedies ... is primarily a conservative one' (2000, 117) because it is always man rather than the institution which is at fault. In a characteristic objection against non-committed filmmaking, he presents comedy as a category that promotes powerlessness, useless cathartic compassion and avoids explicit condemnation of social evils. Similarly, one of the first critics to write a monograph on African cinema, Nwachukwu Frank Ukadike, ultimately dismisses Ivorian director Henri Duparc's most successful and most popular cinematographic achievement *Bal Poussière*, about which he writes, 'On the surface, *Bal Poussière* is a social comedy focussing on polygamy, making references to corruption, contradictions of tradition and culture, *but cannot be taken seriously as the issues are treated with only one thing in mind — amusement*' (1994, 286, my emphasis). Ukadike's charge is rooted in the idea that African filmmaking has a mission and is not meant to amuse spectators. There is also an assumption here that every film has a 'superficial' and a 'deeper' function that are the result of the intentions of the filmmaker; and if the 'deeper' function is amusement, then any alternative and coexistent functions are to be dismissed.

Although rarely mentioned, the African filmmaker's perceived 'mission' as 'serious' rather than 'superficial' was questioned quite early on by Pierre Haffner (1978, 28 and 61) who warned that only a small minority of spectators could actually identify with Ousmane Sembène's militant narratives. Haffner indicated that most Africans are interested in genres aimed at pure distraction, such as burlesque, melodrama and, interestingly, comedy films. Furthermore, he argued that the future of 'authentic' African film language would be based on Koteba, a popular West African theatre practice. In fact, the obsession with a 'mission' has been challenged by contemporary directors such as Mweze Ngangura, for whom militant films are the principal cause of the doubtful future of African cinema. In his incisive article 'African Cinema: Militancy or Entertainment?' Ngangura questions the pertinence of a cinema with militancy as its only goal, to the exclusion of all forms of entertainment. He maintains that many of the 'night school' films, such as those directed by Sembène Ousmane, are economic failures because African spectators, like filmgoers in other parts of the world, are not able to identify with them. For Ngangura, political films that claim a so-called 'mission' often fail to achieve their goals because, ultimately, it is not predictable whether a film will have the intended effect on its audience. As Olivier Barlet (2000, 130–131) wrote in *African Cinemas: Decolonizing the Gaze,* African audiences are heterogeneous and respond differently to different films. Sembène Ousmane himself once acknowledged that it is impossible for a film to be 'revolutionary'; a film can only be 'political' (quoted in José Paré and Anny Dominique Curtius, 1996, 143), and even then there is no way of ultimately evaluating or quantifying what kind of social or political effect it has had.[1] What is worse, according to Ngangura, is that African *auteur* films have become a 'cinema of the elite' and have contributed to the alienation of a public that goes to the cinema for enjoyment rather than to undergo an ideological subjugation. Ngangura explains why the genre of comedy has rarely figured in African cinema:

> in Africa, for many years now almost all African film-makers
> have regarded themselves as authors, as people with a mission,
> charged with carrying a mission to their people. [...] In fact, the
> infatuation with a 'cinema of authors', because it did not
> emanate from a broad, mainstream cinematographic current
> (which did not exist anyway) addressed to the bulk of audiences,
> has only succeeded in alienating the African audience from its
> own cinema, which even today it tends to regard as too 'cultural'
> in the pejorative sense and too didactic rather than a spectacle. It
> is revealing, for instance, that comedies, a popular genre, if there
> ever was one, in Africa just as much as elsewhere, have only been
> rarely attempted in African cinema. (1996, 61–62)

In *African Filmmaking North and South of the Sahara*, Roy Armes also points out that '[v]ery few African filmmakers have produced out-and-out comedies, and comedy can *in no way* be regarded as one of the "traditions" of African cinema' (2006, 110, my emphasis). Although Ngangura's and Armes' observations are valid up to a point, it should also be mentioned that there has throughout history been one exception: for reasons yet to be seriously investigated, filmmakers from the Ivory Coast have developed comedies in lieu of more militant, political films. In this country, there has been what Michel Koffi calls a 'comic tradition'. In his interrogation of this tradition Koffi quotes a local filmmaker, Kramo Lanciné Fadika, who asks a crucial question: 'Why must we be intellectuals when Louis de Funès gets laughs in African cinemas?' (quoted in Koffi, 2003, 147).[2] Similarly, Armes points out that 'those [African] comedies which have been made have often found huge audiences' (2006, 110). Barlet likewise asserts that while African films of a variety of genres have been popular and supported, social parody is unquestionably the most popular genre (2000, 138). Another proof of the preference for less 'serious' films is offered by Mike Dearham, who argues that in South Africa, 'film content that is slapstick, comedic and trivial [is] the most successful' (Thomas McCluskey, 2009, 34).

Fadika's question highlights a troubling double standard: why is it assumed that the majority of Western (and other) spectators watch films largely for entertainment, while African spectators have been criticized for wanting to experience the same cinematic entertainment? It should equally be remembered that while comedy is a genre that can entertain, it is not the only genre that can do so. Also, what a spectator finds 'entertaining' is not only determined by her or his cultural context, but more importantly, is necessarily personal; as subsequent sections will explore in more detail, the 'African spectator' is not a homogeneous entity. It is possible to deconstruct the oppositions between 'politics' and 'pleasure', 'comedy' and 'tragedy', 'entertainment' and 'education', supposed binaries that are actually part of a continuum rather than sharply opposed.

The absence of comedies signals a clear gap between the films being produced and what may be expected by African spectators who have hardly ever been considered as pleasure seekers. This absence is best illustrated in *Aristotle's Plot* (Jean-Pierre Bekolo, France/Zimbabwe, 1997) where Essomba Tourneur anxiously wonders 'why Chapter Two of the *Poetics* is missing'. The 'lost' chapter from Aristotle's foundational work is, obviously, the chapter on comedy. Essomba Tourneur's question points to a key issue often skipped in contemporary African film (criticism), and allows Bekolo to use fiction as a unique allegoric reflection on how 'to reinsert Africans into their own chapter' (Dovey, 2009, 211). Such reinsertion is crucial because African filmmakers and scholars have been so obsessively focused on education, nation building and consciousness-raising that they failed to realize that comedy could also be used as a tool for self-liberation. Unlike the mediaeval carnival participant or the town buffoon depicted in *Yaaba* (Idrissa Ouedraogo, 1989) or *Finzan* (Cheikh Oumar Sissoko, 1989), today's postcolonial subject has been almost systematically denied what he used to freely control, namely the possibility of experiencing the freedom to laugh. According to Mikhail Bakhtin, distraction, and especially comic laughter, is but the cure for alienation as

> [l]aughter *liberates* not only from external censorship but first of
> all from the great interior censor; it *liberates* from the fear that
> developed in man during thousands of years: fear of the sacred,
> of prohibitions, of the past, of power. It unveils the material
> bodily principle in its true meaning. Laughter opened men's eyes
> on that which is *new, the future.* This is why it not only permitted

the expression of antifeudal, popular truth; it helped to uncover this truth and to give it an internal form … Laughter showed the world anew in its gayest and most sober aspects. Its external privileges are intimately linked with *interior forces*; they are a recognition of the rights of those *forces*. *This is why laughter could never become an instrument to oppress and blind the people. It always remained a free weapon in their hands.* (1984, 94, my emphasis)

Henri Duparc, one of Africa's chief producers of comedy, likewise believed that 'humour is a powerful means of getting ideas over … people laugh, but think later. If I use caricature, it is to give us the courage to look at ourselves as we really are so that we can mend our ways' (quoted in Thackway, 2003, 10).[3]

To study comedy in African film might therefore seem risky against the horizon of the scholarly commitment to expounding ideas regarding the importance of authenticity and the political. Although Sembène Ousmane's oeuvre has been analysed in detail, far too little attention has been devoted to its comedic characteristics. According to David Murphy and Patrick Williams, the Senegalese director 'has *also* shown a distinct talent for comedy, which has been a refreshing influence in the sometimes rather didactic and moralistic world of African cinema' (2007, 50, my emphasis). They add that, '[t]his comic dimension of [Sembène's] work is often neglected in critical appraisals but in fact comedy is deployed in most of his films, and it would play a key role in *Xala,* his biggest commercial success in Africa' (53). Although Armes also refers to the fact that *Xala* 'is full of brilliantly comic touches' (2006, 70), he focuses mostly, alongside the majority of critics, on its 'sharp social observation' and 'pitiless dissection of its (unnamed) African setting' (*Ibid*), thereby setting up 'comedy' and 'social observation' as mutually exclusive categories, when in Sembène's films they often overlap. In analysing the same work, Ukadike does not go any further in specifying which parts of the film display comedic elements, relying instead on generalizations: '*Xala* is a comedy told in the typical African storytelling tradition to illustrate a simple moral tale' (1994, 178–9). Nor does Ukadike provide an analysis of the specific comic features of *Bal Poussière* (Henri Duparc, Côte d'Ivoire, 1988),*Yaaba* (Idrissa Ouedraogo, Burkina Faso, 1989) or *Visages de femmes* (Désiré Ecaré, Côte d'Ivoire, 1985) when he discusses these films. For him, '*Bal Poussière* could be read as a political film, *although its few political jabs get lost in the comedic structure*' (250, emphasis added).

The argument of this chapter, then, is that the apparent absence of the *genre* of comedy did/does not preclude the existence of the 'comedic' within African films. From the very beginning of African filmmaking, comedy was present in the verbal, visual, performative and rhetorical elements of many films. More importantly, I establish the historical evolution of comic representations in African cinema by showing how, from the early 1970s to later periods, the comic which, in 'serious' narratives, appealed to a 'global' spectatorship, has been paradoxically replaced by films targeting an audience which can be positioned as 'local', African. I argue that although preference for comedy as 'genre' becomes commonplace with directors such as Henri Duparc or the Cameroonian director Jean-Pierre Bekolo, the 'will to comedy' started with Sembène himself. I also suggest that African filmmakers, especially those of the 'first hour' such as Sembène, regularly cheated on their publicly proclaimed convictions to the extent that comic strategies are regularly integrated into their texts through modalities to be investigated. One question that needs deliberation, therefore, is why comic features were incorporated into films which were primarily made to educate and to 'raise people's consciousness', rather than to entertain. Why might certain directors have subversively included comic elements while publicly confirming their membership of the movement of 'committed', socio-political African filmmaking? Did they assume African spectators would unmistakably identify what they perceive as a 'superficial' or 'deeper' function? And how do other directors who have been less willing to confirm such membership bring into play alternative forms of comedy? Some directors, such as Duparc and Bekolo, foreground gags, puns and jokes in films that do not necessarily aim to participate in nation building or the 'education' of the masses. These directors would seem to have ushered in a major transformation in that, in their work, postcolonial subjectivities are no longer represented in openly confrontational modes. Rather, similarly to how Achille Mbembe sees it, 'the public affirmation of the "postcolonized subject" is no longer found in the acts of "opposition" or "resistance" to the *commandement*' (2001, 129). For him, the postcolonial subjects who laugh in public or private spheres are not necessarily bringing about the collapse of power or even resisting it. As the films under consideration well illustrate, these citizens undergo a new experience which involves exercising the ability to laugh, play and entertain themselves in a context where the postcolonial authority is virtually absent. They are no longer depicted as bound up in unproductive identity politics but rather are immersed in carnivals where, as Mikhail Bakhtin put it, 'the role of the memory is minimal; in the comic world there is nothing for memory and tradition to do. One ridicules in order to forget' (1981, 23). Before one can further analyse this shift in filmmaking in which the comic is foregrounded, however, it is necessary to define 'comedy' which, by '[insinuating] itself into a form, a posture, a gesture, a situation, an action, a word' (Bergson, 1910, 135)[4], displays syntactic (narrative), linguistic, cultural and discursive components.

In *Le Filmique et le comique* (1979), Jean-Paul Simon suggests that comedy can only be defined as subversive which, of course, has implications for the argument forwarded here that certain African filmmakers have precisely used comic strategies subversively. Simon asserts that when comedy appears in a film – usually via a gag – it erupts and thereby disrupts orders, institutions and codes. Perhaps, then, we can think of comedy not as 'distracting' or 'diverting' – as Boughédir emphatically suggested – but as disruptive. The comic effect is generally one of shock or surprise – in turn engendering transgression. In such contexts, far from engendering apathy, comedy in fact 'shakes', 'jolts' or 'shocks' people into a new way of being.

Comedy is also intimately associated with economic and social connotations/stratifications because it has long been related to subjects who belong to the 'lower' scale of society. As suggested by Aristotle, comedy tends to involve 'inferior' people with some kind of defect or who become implicated in laughable disgrace (*Poetique*, 1449a32f, 1448a2–5, 16–18, 1448b24–6). In his study of the mediaeval carnivalesque, Mikhail Bakhtin (1984) similarly points out that the power to laugh, and the right to be laughed at, is the minimal constituent of 'subaltern' people who never miss any opportunity to entertain themselves. Such socio-economic considerations mean that comedy can be synonymous with portraying human life in its barest, most common or trivial reality. Contrary to tragedy which generally involves kings, princes and other noble subjects engaging in 'superior' official or heroic projects, the comic is notable for representing 'ordinary citizens' whose attitudes and language are not necessarily 'sophisticated'. They may be openly scatological and grotesque. That is why Kathleen Rowe suggests that '[w]here comedy is, so are food, sex, excrement, blasphemy usually presented obliquely enough to be socially acceptable' (Rowe, 1995, 44–45). These definitions have important implications when one considers African movie-goers who are, more often than not, of low income and social status.

A crucial element which makes comedy notoriously difficult to define is its pragmatic articulations which can only be judged based on the (inevitably varied) responses of viewers. This aspect is central to the argument of this chapter, mainly that there are two main 'strands' in African comic filmmaking which can be distinguished by the function they are designated by various directors: they appeal to a 'global', 'universal' audience or, more often as will be illustrated in subsequent sections, to a more 'local' one. In relation to the latter case, Andrew Horton argues that 'like language, and like "texts" in general, the comic is plural, unfinalized, disseminative, dependent on *context* and the intertextuality of creator, text and contemplator. It is not, in other words, just the *content* of comedy that is significant but also its "conspirational" relationship with the viewer (reader)' (1991, 9, original emphasis). This genre is, therefore, a strictly context- and audience-dependent mobile category. Furthermore, because 'comedy' encompasses sub-categories such as laughter, humour, satire, parody, farce, and the burlesque, no totalizing theory of it is possible.

Returning to the undefinable nature of comedy due to its pragmatic and contextual basis, one can argue that the genre not only presupposes cultural orthodoxies within which it needs to be understood, but also, to some extent, an in-built, 'target' audience. The desire to establish this connection does not necessarily prevent the films from also being found comic by other audiences. However, while comedy is not always universal, it does tend to largely be based in a shared culture. In this sense, the particular kind of comic strategies employed in films made in Africa might be analysed as 'cultural' elements just as the incorporation of local music, dance or oral narratives might be identified within African films. Given the local nature of comedy, a certain 'cultural competence'[5] often allows for a more accurate or relevant interpretation of it since – while the effects on the local audience, as emphasized above, cannot be quantified – the culturally competent spectator is more likely to be able to infer some of these effects. In his essay 'Mock Realism. The Comedy of Futility in Eastern Europe', Charles Eidsvik points out that 'Eastern European audiences laugh at things that mean little to Westerners' (1991, 91). The same could be said in the case of all localized cinematic traditions, as humour is not necessarily universal. Pierre Yameogo likewise argues that comedy is culturally specific: 'Things which make an African laugh don't necessarily amuse a

European or a Chinese. When a film shows a well-off family grown fat from eating well, Africans laugh, whereas Westerners tend to be more saddened than anything!' (quoted in Barlet, 2000, 130). Attuned to their own linguistic, historical and cultural specificities, African directors use formulas and patterns that may not be fully accessible to a spectator who is not a member of the target audience. However, as Andrew Horton has cautioned, '[f]ilm comedy is deeply rooted in the comic traditions of the cultures in which it is produced as well as in the tradition of film comedy itself' (1991, 18). In other words, comedy is produced at both local and global levels. Although being familiar with the particular culture inevitably enhances the experience of comedy, African directors have been producing works that are inclusive and more universally accessible. In the mostly mundane, vulgar, everyday experiences that shape the comic repertoire, these filmmakers have developed narrative, character-based, performative, aesthetic and linguistic strategies to construct spaces for laughter. I want to examine how these spaces are made, first through an analysis of the use of comic figures in certain African films (in other words, through narrative, character-based and performative strategies), and second through an analysis of the types of visual (aesthetic) and verbal (linguistic) strategies employed by African filmmakers.

1   Comedic archetypes

To address how comedy is articulated through comic figures in African film, I want to consider two recurrent male character types: the mentally colonized (the '*débarqué*') who is obsessed with emulating Western standards, and the puppets whose sexual desire exposes them to various manipulations. Notably, African filmmakers almost always represent these figures, although they often wield power, as victims, allowing spectators to laugh at them and thereby reclaim some of their power. More importantly, these protagonists, in spite of their claims to 'Africanness', are social archetypes that can be identified in transnational settings.

The *débarqué*, the 'been to,' originally referred to characters who had studied abroad and returned to build the nation. The term has now been appropriated to signify something different, and negative. According to Jude Akudinobi, the 'been to'

was a product of a specific historical relation that essentially
valorized the West; not surprisingly, 'refined sensibilities'
however inferred, became a fetishized civilizational accreditation
for some. Thus, their subsequent affected fabrications of self,
identity, and expectations made the term quite pejorative and
positioned them paradoxically in the discourse of 'nation
building' as reactionary' (2001, 130)

My first example of a mentally colonized character is the school principal,
M. Nyemb, in *Sango Malo: The Village Teacher* (Bassek Ba Kobhio, Cameroon,
1991), a film about the difficulties of a young educator who tries to adjust
his foreign-learned pedagogical practices to local realities. M. Nyemb is the
central focus of the film's comic gaze; he is marked out as a comic figure by
his choice of language and his gestures. Any audience in any part of the
world would be likely to laugh at M. Nyemb due to the ridiculous insults
he hurls at his students (he accuses them of having peanut paste for brains)
and the way in which he interrupts a new teacher by speaking *over* him just
after allowing him to speak. However, the film's most humorous scenes are
those that use performative and aesthetic comic strategies. In these scenes,
M. Nyemb is shown spying on his schoolteachers' classes in which the latter
dare to subvert the conventional syllabus by talking to the students about
politics and sexuality. M. Nyemb's gestures and facial expressions –
heightened by his performance – provoke laughter not only for viewers
with 'cultural competence', but universally. Furthermore, Bassek Ba
Kobhio magnifies this humour through his choice of framing and editing.
After revealing first the scenes upon which M. Nyemb gazes (thereby
positioning the viewer *with* M. Nyemb), Ba Kobhio then cuts back to
expose, as it were, M. Nyemb himself, a ridiculous figure, attempting to
exercise his power through surveillance and voyeurism. Through this
framing and editing, M. Nyemb is converted from vigilant persecutor into
laughable victim of his own megalomania and of the spectator's amused
gaze.

Many of the protagonists in Ousmane Sembène's films also become
comic figures because, it is suggested, they have been mentally colonized.
Xala (Sembène Ousmane, Senegal, 1974) is well known as one of the
harshest critiques of vanity, negligence and the perversion of the newly
crowned postcolonial elite. Critics have not however sufficiently studied
the comic aspects of this film. For example, there is a striking artifice in the

actions of the Chamber of Commerce members when they appear to have taken control of the country. Their rapid wardrobe change from African boubous to European suits, the pretext of a selective cultural identity that allows them to only retain the aspects that guarantee their sexual pleasures, the panegyric of the president who glorifies the 'father of the nation' and the peroration about 'Africanness' all contain comedic overtones. These examples, depicted as the fallout of the fight for independence, are also filmic elements that allow Sembène to construct comedy and, in so doing, provoke the spectator's antipathy.

In *Xala,* El Hadji could be seen as a forerunner figure of the principal in *Sango Malo* in that both see France as their defining reference point. El Hadji only drinks Evian water, which he uses, moreover, to fill his car's radiator; he speaks exclusively French, whereas his family, most notably his daughter, speak only Wolof. Apart from the conflicted identities and ideologies at work here, there is something unusual and comic about two people who seem to communicate well but fail to understand what is at stake in choosing one language over another. El Hadji does not understand that his daughter is teaching him a lesson, and is making fun of him. She in turn does not realize that her father belongs to another world, that of totally alienated postcolonial subjects who believe in French cultural superiority. It appears as if both characters are talking without communicating. The exchange between them can be characterized by what Noel Carroll (1991) calls 'incongruity', that is, an association of comic duos that provoke amusement and, depending on context, a sense of superiority on the part of spectators.

In *Guelwaar* (1992), a film by Ousmane that challenges the political and moral perils of receiving aid or engaging in 'international cooperation,' the character of Barthélémy becomes initiated into the realities of his country of origin, Senegal. In the beginning he is a big-talker who behaves arrogantly at the news of his father's death, adopting an artificially bombastic tone and an affected walk. He answers people exclusively in French at first, even when they address him in Wolof. His numerous exclamations of 'what an Africa!' and 'you're making me cry' speak to a pretention acquired in France more than to a concern with the transformation of his native society. The funniest moment occurs when he ostentatiously waves his French passport, which has become a symbol of his cultural superiority. By the end of the film, he has to realize that he has become the subject of mockery among his fellow Senegalese, as expressed in Gora's suggestion that he go back to 'his' country, France. Father Leon also wonders, to Barthélémy's embarrassment, why he keeps speaking French, even with his own relatives. From beginning to end, Barthélémy suffers systematic humiliation at the hands of the villagers.

We can thus see that early African cinema displays a form of comedy that focuses on parodying mentally-colonized characters (inspired, no doubt, by Fanon's observations in *Black Skin, White Masks*). Fanon describes the mentally colonized person as one who is trapped in a double bind. A product of empire, he feels superior to other colonized subjects, although he is in fact never fully accepted into the culture of the dominant power. He therefore belongs to neither world, and his fellow people laugh at his efforts to mimic the colonial power. Fanon describes the colonized subject's daily routines, style of dress and even his walk in an extremely humorous and cynical tone. In *Sango Malo*, Erna only has one desire, namely to 'travel,' to 'get on a plane'. Her dream destination, significantly, is international: she wants to go to Europe or America. This young girl is the antithesis of Rama who, in *Xala*, categorically refuses to drink Evian water, even though her father glorifies its consumption. Her father, who has seemingly 'made it' and become powerful, is, in fact, a victim, insofar as comedy reduces him to a defeated and weak man whose daughter teaches him a lesson in humility. The victim who is mocked, a comic subject, is the person in the social superstructure with the most power. He is the one who maintains the illusion of different kinds of power. The white man, the Other, and Europe are signifiers of the castrating, pathological and psychologically devastating seduction of Western culture, as identified by Franz Fanon. Fanon writes,

> Every colonized people – in other words, every people in whose soul an inferiority complex has been created by the death and burial of its cultural originality – finds itself face to face with the language of the civilizing nation; that is, with culture of the mother country. The colonized is elevated above his jungle status in proportion to his adoption of the mother country's cultural standards. He becomes whiter as he renounces blackness, his jungle. (1967, 18)

It is clear, when one considers in the colonized subject described by Fanon, that a given character's reverence of European culture actually ends up in his or her being mocked by the community. The cultural superiority they thought they were assuming is rather deconstructed by local subjects who do not in the same way equate Western customs with cultural supremacy. The viewer is both embarrassed and amused by the outlandish character of their behaviour.

The second type of comic figure regularly used in African cinema is the puppet, another comic archetype that may be found in non-African contexts. The figure of '*débarqué*' is inevitably also a puppet since they have a servile quality in their relationship with France and its symbolic representations. However, whereas the mentally colonized is *often* a man, the puppet figure seems to *necessarily* be a man in African cinema, for the type of servility that is parodied, at least in the examples given here, relates to men's sexual desires and the subjection these desires spawn. The relationship between comedy and sexuality is by no means solely an African one; as Andrew Stott states, 'Comedy treats matters of sex more often and more openly than any other form' (2005, 62). However, in many African films it is a practice that is widespread in many communities – polygamy – that initiates the comedy. Instead of creating additional sexual pleasure for men, polygamous marriages are shown to turn men into puppets manipulated by their very own desires. In films such as *Xala*, *Bal Poussière* (Henri Duparc, Côte d'Ivoire, 1988) and *Quartier Mozart* (Jean-Pierre Bekolo, Cameroon, 1992), polygamous marriages are presented as completely chaotic, and as ultimately detrimental to the men rather than their wives. While polygamy may be perceived as an 'African' phenomenon, the comedy invested in these male marionettes does appeal to a universal audience, especially in the way the directors use this device to 'deflate' and 'disrupt' typical versions of masculinity. To confirm this universal form of comedy, one might turn to Kathleen Rowe, who writes,

> Comedy often mocks the masculinity that tragedy enobles. The very centrality of sex to comedy and the comedic agenda of renewing life open up space for the presence of women that does not exist in the more masculine world of tragedy. [...] In comedy, sex is not a means toward knowledge or transcendence of the self, as in tragedy, but social. Sex is part of comedy's overall attack on repression and celebration of bodily pleasure, a means of connection within the space of family and the time of generation. (1995, 45)

My first example of a comic figure represented as a puppet comes from Sembène's *Xala*. El Hadji is a kind of marionette that his wives and colleagues gleefully manipulate. When he is supposed to celebrate his third marriage, Oumy, his volatile and demanding second wife treats him as though he were a doll. He is unable to defend himself and is ridiculed by Oumy, who pushes him toward the door and the car. Once inside the car, he is squeezed between his first and second wives, as between the hammer and the anvil – a symbolic directorial decision on the part of Sembène. In this way, Sembène – like Bassek Ba Kobhio in *Sango Malo* – uses the aesthetic possibilities of the film camera to *fabricate* the comedy, emphasizing the narrative, character-based and performative comedy also through stark visual choices. This scene is captured in a close-up of the man, silent and visibly beleaguered by the events. His power as head of the household, and his social standing in general, is in decline, as emphasized by the comical absurdity of his squished position between the two wives. The subject who used to be all powerful is offered up to the viewer's antipathy.

In *Bal Poussière*, Demi-Dieu (Half-God) is, like El Hadji in *Xala*, manipulated by his wives' ruses. After fighting to win the privilege of spending the night with him, the wives end up forming two sides that Binta calls 'les robeuses' (the women in dresses), still young and pretty, and 'les pagneuses' (the skirted women), whose natural beauty has eroded with age and who are therefore less desirable to Demi-Dieu. When he calls them all together in the beginning of the film to announce his decision to take a sixth wife, he explains that each of them will have their own day with him, and that the seventh day will be reserved as a kind of bonus for the wife whose 'performance' has been 'remarkable'. Demi-Dieu is caught in a web of his own contradictions: his oldest wives all remind him of the promises he made them exclusively and then broke by taking on other wives. Even if the man seems to be in control and blithely moves about in a space where his seated wives desperately watch him, the spectator perceives from this moment that he suffers from some confusion. The 'power of the phallus' begins to crumble, and it is not surprising that his wives later begin to wage battles in which he ultimately becomes the comic victim.

The expressions that Binta insists Demi-Dieu use when he wants to make love come from a French card game: 'bid' (*belote*) for the request, 'raise' (*re-belote*) if she agrees, or 'pass' if she doesn't want to, which she rarely does. Unhappy, and even furious, the frustrated protagonist is seen jumping on his wife, who is at first amused by then becomes horrified as the camera cuts from what appears will be a rape scene. As viewers, we witness the feebleness of a man who is incapable of containing desires in the face of his wife's provocation. The latter flirts with him, arouses him, and then refuses his advances just at the moment when he desires her the most, without even censoring her mocking laugh. Demi-Dieu's desires reduce him to his most base attributes, taking away all the power (except the power to rape) conferred upon him by money and social status. When, at the end of the film, he surprises Binta kissing her lover, she responds 'raise' in their ritual verbal play, in other words propositioning him, to which he responds 'pass' in a state of breathless despair. The all-powerful husband, always conquering and victorious, discovers that he is a cuckold and that his wife is ready to give a musician the favours he has desperately sought for long.

Demi-Dieu's vulnerability is revealed in the antics of his wives, whether they are plotting against him or each other. Several times as he sits down to eat, he realizes with the first bite that his meal is overspiced with strong chilli peppers. He spits it out immediately, disgusted, while the hidden wives laugh behind his back. Binta, the paragon *par excellence* of feminine manipulation, decides to take the 'place' of one of her co-wives although she has exhausted Demi-Dieu the night before. When she enters the bedroom, the camera frames her from above, in a relatively high-angled shot. Next we see the husband in bed, surprised to see Binta coming in when he is not expecting her. He is obviously not happy about this and dreads what is going to happen. However the young woman, still visibly resourceful, shows with her gaze that she is perfectly in control of the situation. She arouses her husband's desire, which she had so recently sated, although the viewer sees how tired he is. Unusually, for she almost always refuses to make love with him, Binta here offers herself to Demi-Dieu, the sexual champion, clearly to punish him. She gives him what he desires in order to kill him, an act that places the vain male in the fragile position of puppet, compelled by his powerful desires and open to all kinds of torture. Because these intimate scenes between Demi-Dieu and Binta are imbued with humour, sarcasm and manipulation, they remind the viewer of the desperate scenes in which El Hadji tries to deflower his youngest wife though he is stricken with impotence. In such a context, romance is absent; sexuality becomes correlated to bestial behaviour and a lack of control. The privileges and sexual predation of the male characters are turned into objects of derision, and the desiring male subject becomes the object of the viewer's scorn. Demi-Dieu and, to a certain degree, El Hadji belong to the category of 'odd beings who are out of step with the people around them, with the spectator who laughs at what they, with their slow reflexes, don't even suspect' (Meyer, 2003, 10)[6]. Furthermore, their addiction to sex makes them even more vulnerable and exposes a severely ridiculous/ ridiculed masculinity. Such buffoonery built around bedroom performance is not, I must stress, specifically African. What equally needs to be noted is the way in which several 'early' comedies address issues such as sexual predation/impotence that may appeal to a non-African audience. This suggests a careful global positioning rather than simply taking on the role of 'educating' local postcolonial subjects. There is no question, then, about whether the first African filmmakers drew on comedy or not. Rather, the issue seems to turn back to whether scholars want to acknowledge the comedy or not, for in such a way they would seem to signal their membership (or not) of the group of committed, socio-political African filmmakers.

2   Verbal and visual comedy

The following section illustrates the transition from global to local comic experiences as theorized by Horton (1991) and Jean-Marc Defays (1996). Given the pragmatic and cultural components of comedy, I look at the ways in which narratives establish 'context-specific' verbal and visual strategies to generate a comic effect.

Ludwig Wittgenstein (1968) was the first to characterize comedy as a set of practical 'games,' wherein language holds an important place. To play is, first and foremost, to play with language, to challenge conventional meanings. Comedy is also, essentially, a journey to undermine denotative finality. Derrida developed the idea of language games even further. Particularly pertinent to the present discussion is his comment that '[t]o risk meaning *nothing* is to start to play ... and first to enter into the play of *différance,* which prevents any word, any concept, any major enunciation from coming to summarize and to govern from the theological presence of a *center* movement and textual spacing of differences' (1981, 14, my emphasis). Geoffrey H. Hartman further stresses the importance of the 'attacks' that form part of the playful agreement between writer and reader by generating 'a sense of a serious, unending game, both in the writer who plays language against itself and in the reader who must uncover without losing track, the gamut of language' (1981, 1). One other theorization that would perfectly fit this analysis is T. G. A. Nelson's work on 'The Language of Comedy' (1990). He pays special attention to jokes and puns – comic strategies which are frequently used in *Bal Poussière, Quartier Mozart* and *Sango Malo.* Duparc, Bekolo, and Ba Kobhio systematically use language and numerous enunciative postures to prop up their comedy – these are props which require, however, a certain level of cultural competence without which Wittgenstein's 'game' would be inconclusive. This type of comedy can be identified in the choices for the names of places, objects and characters, on the one hand, and in the linguistic register used in the films, on the other.

The filmmakers named above enhance characterization by playing with names in a symbolic, evocative, connotative or denotative manner. The names chosen draw on the local lexicon and are therefore humorous for spectators who are able to understand them. That is best illustrated in the choices regarding the names of places, objects and characters, on the one hand, and in the linguistic register used in the films, on the other. Bassek Ba Kobhio's choice of names of characters is deliberate: the hairstylist who abandons his client while raging against 'communism' is named 'Sans Rival' (Without Rival); the tailor is 'Chaud Gars' (Hot Guy); and Honba's labourer is called 'Commando'.[7] The importance of naming is even more pronounced in the films of Jean-Pierre Bekolo in which names equally point out things about characters.

In *Les Saignantes*, the two girls who create chaos in the unnamed republic are called Majolie and Chouchou, two popular nicknames for hot young girls in Cameroon. In *Quartier Mozart*, Atango[8] calls himself 'bonbon des jeunes filles' (candy for young girls), and says he is a graduate of the Sorbonne. Samedi's (Saturday's) little brother is well named, since his name, 'Envoyé Spécial' (Special Correspondent/Envoy) matches perfectly with his function in the film, which consists essentially of playing the go-between for Saturday and her admirers. Acting like a diplomat, he accomplishes difficult missions, since he has to get past his aggressive father who, for his part, is called 'Chien Méchant' (Mean/Mad Dog), an animal metaphor given to Cameroonian fathers who insist on controlling the lives and sexuality of their children, and especially of their daughters. Mad Dog's second wife is Kongossa, meaning gossip. The shopkeeper is called 'Bon Pour Est Mort' (Credit Dead For Good or H.P Is Dead)[9] because he categorically refuses to sell his goods on credit. 'Mon Type' (My Guy), like 'Samedi' (Saturday), is also a name that reveals Bekolo's desire to remain in a register that is both comic and colloquial. 'Chef du Quartier' (Queen of the Hood) is a name given to any person who knows almost everything about the life and activities in his or her neighbourhood. This name is therefore attached to knowledge, to power over one's entourage. In this film, the names are working-class nicknames that would be likely to amuse any Cameroonian, while they are more likely to baffle non-Cameroonian spectators. Although *Quartier Mozart* is characteristically global and postmodern in terms of composition, narrative and visual effects, the choice of comic names is deeply rooted in local practices.

In addition to the choice and meaning of names, Bekolo's films also build their comic atmosphere through casting from the local star system. Many of the actors in *Quartier Mozart* and in *Les Saignantes* are popular Cameroonian comedians, such as: Essindi Mindja (Atango and Essomba), Atebass (one of Panka's friends and a right-hand man for Atango), and Jimmy Biyong (Mad Dog and taxi driver for Bekolo; shop owner and pimp for Ba Kobhio). The same applies for *Sango Malo* where M. Nyemb, the village teacher, Big Eyes and the drunkards who mislead the storekeeper, are well-known comedians who have entertained the Cameroonian public in some of the most popular TV series and films (*L'Orphelin, L'Etoile de Noudi, Japhet et Jinette*, for example) which the national television corporation (run then by Marcel Mvondo, Jean Endene, E. Keki Manyo, Salomon Tatmfo and others) used to produce. Their appearance in these films constitutes a promise of, and often generates, comedy and laughter for informed spectators. In these films, name typing and the 'comedy of names', as well as the names and presence of well-known stars, play an essential function: this allows the filmmaker to seal a pact, and to dialogue, with a targeted local public. Thus, even if the comedy may at times appear universal, the gap fostered by comedy is eminently cultural, contextual and specific, as Jean-Marc Defays has said:

> the comic author and his audience, while delighting in their complicity, congratulate themselves for **mastering** language (logic, culture) to such a degree that they can play with it and display it. Conversely, their laughter punishes the fictional person (in the story) or real person (in the audience) who doesn't have the same level of mastery. (1996, 37, original emphasis)[10]

Playing with language and names is also well at work in *Bal Poussière*. The name Demi-Dieu (Half-God) is in itself rather unusual, especially since he claims to be second in the village only to God. But the explanation that Porte-Clés (Key Carrier) gives for his name – that he is dangerously driving a car without breaks and that only God is great and will save him if he has an accident – offers an explanation. He calls himself Porte-Clés because he opens doors, hearts and even the legs of women. This name is synecdochic: the subject is designated in terms of the role that he plays, namely that of a tool (in this case, the key). On the basis of the functions performed and their association, an analogy is created between the character and the tool. As for Beau Gosse (Beautiful Kid), his character is a striking illustration of a biting irony, dissimulation and oxymoron. The subject is a dwarf, afflicted with a large hump on his back; his face is not likely to grace the cover of a beauty magazine. With such inconsistency between the name and the character, the name Beau Gosse registers, perhaps, the conflicts over naming and meaning in the local postcolonial context.

Beyond the comedy associated with naming, there is the comedy generated through the wit and repartee of the dialogue. Porte Clés's sense of humour is to the point, and he never misses an occasion to show it. When a shopkeeper says that God is great (a refrain that is repeated often in the film), he responds that God would do better to become small because by staying great he ends up only seeing the great people of the world. Binta's mother's bawdy language is equally comical, but moreover contains many games with words. She insults her daughter's 'cheeks' and says that she has legs like matchsticks, which she claims allows her daughter to light men's fires. Demi-Dieu, the conquering male, makes an association between virginity and fidelity when addressing his wives. As previously mentioned, Binta divides the wives of Demi-Dieu into the *robeuses* (dress wearers) and the *pagneuses* (skirt wearers). Infuriated after Binta makes an accusation against the old *pagneuses*, he responds with a rhyme: 'il n'y a que des emmerdeuses!' (you are all pains in the ass!)[11]. This rhyme manipulation expresses the despair of the character.

On the other hand, an anonymous alcoholic character called 'l'ancien/the elder', who typically plays the role of a comedian in the film, comes up with an original interpretation of the French language. For him, French can't be 'une langue de cons' (an idiot's language) because it perfectly captures things. He explains that *les citrons* (lemons) contain vitamin C, that *la farine* (flour) gives fortitude with vitamin F, and that he always eats bananas because they contain vitamin B which makes a man *bander* (get an erection). Along the same lines, *Les Couilles de l'éléphant* (Henry-Joseph Koumba Bididi, 2002) opens with a show where actors put on a play with very eloquent costumes, postures, diction and make-up. During their spectacle, they make ironic comments on national politics, suggesting that the official state verbs are to lie, to steal and to embezzle[12]. In all of these films, a radical subversion of language, which other characters and spectators enjoy, allows comedy to articulate a fundamental critique of the negligence of the postcolonial elites in a roundabout way. African directors also draw on non-verbal comic strategies, however.

If Mweze Ngangura and Roy Armes are able to claim that comedies are not a common genre in African cinema, one can nonetheless remark that *Quartier Mozart, Les Couilles de l'éléphant* and, in particular, *Bal Poussière*, are interesting examples of comedies of manners that focus specifically on word-play, some of which appeals only to local audiences, and some of which can be read by a global audience. *Bal Poussière* can be read both ways. For example, Demi-Dieu's attempt to write poetry would be amusing to any audience. He enthusiastically declares to Binta that she is as beautiful as a grasshopper upon which she grows irritated because she thinks the insect is hideous. There is also a blind man in the film who is an incorrigible alcoholic. When Demi-Dieu feels sorry for his lot in life and suggests that he drink water because he is poor, the man responds that he will never again drink a drop of water because it gave him an onchocerciasis that made him go blind. Another instance of universal comedy occurs at the end of the film: at a restaurant, Demi-Dieu orders a good wine. But when the waiter presents a bottle of wine more than ten years old, he gets upset. He demands a 'younger' wine.

Some filmmakers also include spectacular comic shows within the narratives themselves, dealing with comedy in a meta-fictional way. My first example that showcases a comic performance is that of the man in *Bal Poussière* who makes the spectators laugh uncontrollably during the marriage of Demi-Dieu and Binta. He is given the honour of making the first toast, but he arrives drunk, salutes, and looks in vain for the speech he prepared. He mumbles and stumbles, causing the audience to burst out laughing. He rummages through his pockets without finding anything, ultimately taking instead the bottle of whiskey next to him. Another example of the spectacle comes from *Sango Malo*, where the same process is repeated several times: at regular intervals, Sans Rival (Without Rival) and Chaud Gars (Hot Guy), both well-known Cameroonian comedians, get together at Honba's bar and use a battery of different ruses to convince the employee, Commando, to give them beer on credit. Each time, after they have got their beer, they burst out laughing, as if making fun of the gullibility of a manipulated employee. Their tactics, as well as those of Big Eyes, are skillfully inserted into the narrative for a *comic pause* because, like gags, they are not 'an elementary building of narrative', although they are dependent upon it (Gunning, 1995, 95). More specifically, they are not essential to the main plot, but rather disruptive of it. That is precisely one of the narrative functions of comedy. For Kristine Brunovska Karnick and Henry Jenkins, 'if a narrative is understood as the process a spectator undergoes in constructing a continuum … comedy arises as a momentary break in some aspect of this continuum' (1995, 80).

Notably and somewhat contradictorily, the most interesting example of a combination of narrative and performative entertainment spectacle is to be found in a 'militant' film by the Cameroonian documentary filmmaker Jean-Marie Teno. In his documentary, *Afrique, je te plumerai* (Cameroon, 1992), Teno makes wide use of comic spectacle via two popular local actors, Kouokam Narcisse and Essindi Mindja. The former acts out a meeting between the film director and the director of the national television station with whom Teno meets in order to try to involve the station in the production of his film. The *mise-en-scène* is comical, insofar as the actor imitates, in the local accent, the words and gestures of a television director who categorically refuses to show Teno's film. He asks to be paid, arguing that it is easier for him to broadcast American sitcoms or other low class films that are given to him free of charge. Essindi Mindja's comedy act, to be discussed below, is rooted in parody, just as is Kouokam's dramatization. These cases are apt examples of how, even in more contemporary African films, comedy and politics are entwined. Comedy here is used to make a political point, but it is not necessarily oppositional in the Marxist sense of the word.

In *Afrique, je te plumerai*, Essindi Mindja plays the role of an African Head of State who grants an interview to the local and international press. When he entertains the questions asked by the journalists, he imitates several accents: French, Italian, Arabic and Cameroonian. But in his responses, he especially stresses a Cameroonian accent to draw attention to the comedy not only in what he says, but also in how he says it. His responses are often unexpected: he 'secures' the State's capital in Switzerland because 'les petits nègres' embezzle it whenever they get the chance; he decides to deport citizens of a neighbouring country because he can't believe that after giving them a warm welcome and letting them marry Cameroonian daughters they would ungratefully beat his country in a soccer match. Teno's film, which involves characters and jokes familiar to Cameroonian spectators, are illustrations of the ways in which Ukadike's implied two 'levels' – the superficial and the deep – are not mutually exclusive, but work together. They can be reconciled and in fact complement each other.

After painting a tragic and dark atmosphere in *Afrique, je te plumerai*, Teno decides to conclude his film with a show put on by Essindi Mindja. As Teno says in the narrative voice-over in the film, it is better to laugh than cry. In his show, Essindi Mindja carries out a radical subversion of a French song. He takes up the refrain of 'Quand le film est triste' by Sylvie Vartan, while giving it a twist that is dialectically opposed to the original. He transforms the meaning and, instead of singing the original lyrics – 'Quand le film est triste, ça me fait pleurer' (When the film is sad, it makes me cry) – Mindja transforms the lyrics to 'Quand le film est triste, ça me fait rigoler' (When the film is sad, it makes me laugh). When he sings this refrain for the final time, he emphasizes the last verb, ri-go-ler, dividing the word into three separate syllables whose pronunciation ends the film. In other words, the film concludes with laughter to ward off everyday tragedy. This radical semantic subversion comes from what Gérard Genette called transtextuality in *Palimpsestes* (1982), which proceeds here not only by a kind of parody, but also by a complete semantic transformation. All this requires not only linguistic competence, but also a cultural understanding of French-Cameroonian speech and events. These strategies and metatextual elements confirm Andrew Horton's point that 'like language, and like "texts" in general, the comic is plural, unfinalized, disseminative, dependent on *context* and the intertextuality of creator, text and contemplator. It is not, in other words, just the *content* of comedy that is significant but also its 'conspirational' relationship with the viewer (reader)' (9, original emphasis).

Teno's combination of the genres of fiction, documentary and performative comic entertainment is important to his subversive humour. Contrary to the majority of the films analysed in this chapter, *Afrique, je te plumerai* ends not only with a comic scene, but, furthermore, with a *mise-en-scène*, as well as a *mise-en-abyme*, a show within the show of the film itself. In *Bal Poussière, Quartier Mozart* and *Sango Malo*, for example, comedy penetrates into the narrative, as suggested by Gunning; laughter that is provoked in the characters, and, perhaps, in the competent spectator, allows the narration as a whole to be more embellished. Sembène Ousmane's *Guelwaar* is an excellent illustration of a 'comic pause' performed through what Christian Metz calls a 'transvisualisation', that is, in the framework of a memory, the character becomes the site of the primary enunciation.[13] In the cemetery, while attending Guelwaar's burial, Alfred tells the story of one of the deceased's many sexual misadventures. He is caught in the act after arriving at the home of one of his lovers (the village chief's wife) disguised as an old woman. He runs off completely naked. Despite the context of mourning, everyone laughs at this escapade. What is important to notice here is especially the release of tension and the laughter, brought about in the context of sorrow.

However, in *Afrique, je te plumerai* and in *Xala*, the most overtly comical or tragic scenes occur at the film's conclusion, serving to emphasize the satirical content. The appalling spitting scene at the end of *Xala* is accompanied by the crying of El Hadji's family as they witness their father's humiliation, and even more notably by the laughter of the 'human waste' as they spit on El Hadji, who hopes to be cured of his sexual impotence through this act. This laughter is vengeful, biting, and is a 'revenge from below'. The juxtaposition of laughter and tears renders the scene particularly painful, but dramatizes the shift in social power. Likewise, Teno's decision to end his film in a comedy show makes an oblique statement regarding the political tragedy in Africa. These decisions on the part of filmmakers substantiate the idea that humour is the only weapon available in a dictatorship, and laughter the only form of resistance. Unlike the films of Jean-Pierre Bekolo, Henri Duparc or Bassek Ba Kobhio, laughter and humour become, in a tradition inherited from the ancient Athenian dramatists, necessarily political. In the case of Teno and Sembène, eruptions of comedy constitute a strategy of resistance against tyranny because, as Francis Bebey put it in one of his songs, it is better to laugh about tragedies that arises than to cry about them. Another very interesting example is furnished by Pius Ngandu Nkashama in his play, *La Délivrance d'Ilunga* (1977) in which the humour of a storyteller, The Old Kafeuta – the only survivor of a world of death – allows him to give courage to the fighters tempted to give up, and to cast doubt upon the all-powerful nature of the oppressor. Using humour as a means of resistance is a thoughtful praxis that must be given due consideration. For the philosopher John Morreall,

> The person with a sense of humor can never be fully dominated,
> even by a government which imprisons him, for his ability to
> laugh at what is incongruous in the political situation will put
> him above it to some extent, and will preserve a measure of his
> freedom – if not of movement, at least of thought. (1983, 28)

The first body of African films may not seem to be constituted of many comedies. However, comedy has, from the earliest days of African cinema, been used as an important element in films. As I have argued, in these early narratives, comedy may not be a genre, but rather a subversive strategy which seems important to its specific function as a political weapon of resistance. The imbrication of comedy and the political in early African cinema, and in much contemporary African filmmaking, thus makes it impossible to create a distinction between the political and the pleasurable, entertainment cinema and 'evening school' cinema. What is most interesting about the comic strategies in many of these 'serious' African films is that they appeal to universal spectators rather than only to 'culturally competent' spectators. In the later postcolonial period, as I have shown, comedy becomes a *bona fide* genre in African cinema. Far from this genre simply 'selling out' to the principles of commercial entertainment, however, in many ways it at times reinforces what is specifically 'African' in filmmaking as a form of cultural production. For these comedies seem to appeal more to 'culturally competent' spectators, particularly through forms of verbal comedy – their playful use of naming, or wordplay – and also through their appeal to audiences' knowledge of local stars. These films, while seemingly offering more pleasure than politics, could be seen as political in their insistence on local rather than universal forms of comedy and humour. Furthermore, although many African nations are in crisis and authoritarianism remains, perhaps the shift from subversive forms of political comedy in early African films to a more open focus on the need for, and success of, comedy as genre signals that there is, in fact, more freedom of expression allowed today than there was in the immediate post-independence period.

Notes

1 Stuart Hall's influential essay 'Encoding/Decoding' (1973) argues that it is
  nearly impossible to fully reconcile the 'intentionality' of the filmmaker with

the 'effect' of a film on the audience because the process of signification requires 'at the production end, its material instruments – its "means" – as well as its own sets of social (production) relations – the organization and combination of practices within media apparatuses' (107). For him, the circulation of information, as well as its distribution to various audiences, takes place in a discursive form, which may make an essentially unstable category. See Stuart Hall et al (eds.), *Culture, Media, Language*, London, Routledge, 1980.

2 *'Pourquoi ne ferions-nous que de la haute réflexion alors que Louis de Funès fait rire des salles africaines?'*

3 *'l'humour est une arme puissante pour faire passer les idées ... on rit, mais après, on réfléchit ... Si je caricature, c'est pour avoir le courage de nous regarder tels que nous sommes pour nous corriger'.*

4 *'s'infiltre dans une forme, une attitude, une geste, une situation, une action, un mot'.*

5 By this, I mean that certain features may only be best understood by those viewers who are familiar with the cultural, historical and social heritage at play in specific comic strategies. That is why, for example, it is very likely that a Cameroonian spectator understands the language used in Jean-Pierre Bekolo's *Quartier Mozart* much more easily that a non-Cameroonian.

6 *'êtres singuliers qui sont en décalage avec leur entourage, avec le spectateur qui rit de ce que ces êtres en retard d'une réponse ne soupçonnent même pas'.*

7 The car that transports Sango Malo in the novel which inspired the film is called 'S'En Fout La Mort', that is, 'Gives a damn about death'.

8 In southern Cameroon, this is also a popular diminutive, the short form of the last name Atangana. All these names are mostly used by youths.

9 In Cameroon, when you go to a store and are unable to pay for what you need, the owner may make you sign a document, a sort of 'account', called 'Bon Pour' in which you acknowledge that you owe the shopkeeper money for merchandise. So those shopkeepers who do not wish to sell on credit any more simply post a note which says 'Bon Pour Est Mort', which means no loan is granted and every one must pay cash. The reason is that 'Bon Pour', the 'loan provider', now personified as in the film, is dead! The alternative expression, which is the name of the official blog of the Congolese writer Alain Mabankou, is 'Le Crédit A Voyagé', meaning 'Credit is Long Gone'.

10 *' l'auteur comique et son public, tout en se réjouissant de leur connivence, se félicitent de maîtriser à ce point le langage (la logique, la culture), qu'ils peuvent jouer avec lui et se jouer. Inversement, leurs rires sanctionnent la personne fictive (dans l'histoire) ou réelle (dans l'assistance) qui ne partagent pas la même maîtrise'. '*

11 Translated into English, Demi-Dieu's reaction loses its phonetic connotation because the translation does not have the French sound in the ending 'euses'.

12 State verbs in French (to be, to become, etc.) are different from action verbs.

13 Christian Metz describes 'transvisualisation' as a *'récit second [qui] commence en voix-off par le personnage, puis la voix se tait; on considère que ce qu'il dit est "remplacé", mis en actes, par les images et les sons; mais en vérité, on ne peut pas savoir ce qu'elle dit, puisqu'elle n'en dit plus rien. C'est donc ce qu'elle aurait pu dire qui*

est "tranvisualisé". Le spectateur en oublie d'autant mieux qu'elle a parlé, qu'elle a désigné le récit comme emboîté, et c'est maintenant "le film", tout court, qu'il regarde: la source a aboli le personnage' ['a second story that begins in voice-over by a character, and then the voice is silenced; it is as though what is said is "replaced," put into acts, by the images and the sounds. But, in truth, we cannot know what the voice says since it doesn't say anything more. It is therefore *what it could have said* that is "transvisualized". The spectator forgets about it, especially since the voice did speak, since it designated the narration as fitted together, and now it is "the film" – period – that he watches: the source abolished the character' (*L'Énonciation impersonnelle ou le site du film,* Paris, Méridiens Klincksieck, 1990, 120, original emphasis).

3 Henri Duparc

4 Bassek Ba Kobhio, *Sango Malo*

5 Henri Duparc, *Bal Poussière*

6 Sembène Ousmane, *Guelwaar*

Figure 7   Jean-Marie Teno

Chapter 2

Choreographing subjects

As I argue in the introduction and first chapter, the perceived political mission of African cinema has been increasingly questioned by several filmmakers, critical of an institution that embraces militancy over entertainment. Scholars have likewise almost entirely overlooked the fact that in all films, entertainment and dance in particular is present and central to various ceremonies. The striking proliferation of social entertainment on screen speaks to preoccupations beyond those outlined in ideological manifestos. If cinema is an 'evening school' intended to stimulate the intellectual faculties alone, why have dance scenes abounded in African films since the seventies? Does this fact not contradict the self-proclaimed political agendas of filmmakers? Postcolonial scholarship has pointed out the negative view of cultural practices such as dance by the Western philosophical and ethnographic tradition; against this theoretical landscape, how do we interpret the prominence of dance in films?

These questions are all the more essential given that very few fictional films, if any, overtly correlate artistic choreography to national identity. Apart from *Xala*, all the films included in the following analysis involve dance either as a ritual or as social entertainment. Nevertheless, almost every newly independent postcolonial nation had a national ballet, which was considered nothing less than 'machinery for uplifting culture' (Apter, 2005, 109). Senegal's National Ballet, for example, is regarded by Francesca Castaldi as 'the official embodiment of Senegalese dance, invested by the state to construct, represent, and preserve the cultural patrimony of the nation' (2006, 2). In addition to its National Ballet, a country like Cameroon also had a National Orchestra (*Orchestre National*) and a National Theatre Group (*Théâtre National*). In the national culture deliberately manufactured within postcolonial states, annual festivals served an important function; dance, now reduced to a social commodity for disenchanted citizens, was essential to all extravagant and grotesque state rituals. Even African political parties made great use of these artistic manifestations in order to rally people behind obscure ideologies and empty slogans very few could actually understand. Any official ceremony, from the most important to the most trivial, became a pretext for dancing. That is why performance in Sembène Ousmane's *Xala* (1974), where it occurs as a celebration of independence, is in no way similar to the pre-electoral hysterical agitation in Henri-Joseph Koumba Bididi's *Les Couilles de l'éléphant* (2002). The song '*Independance Tchatcha*' by the Congolese band OK Jazz, featured in Bassek Ba Kobhio's *Le Grand Blanc de Lambaréné* (Cameroon, 1995) is well known among Africans and speaks to the social and political role of dance.

Forms of entertainment and dance in particular are historically and philosophically important for several reasons. Léopold Sédar Senghor, we recall, suggested that emotion and rhythm, not reason, were the defining traits of the Negro. His notorious and essentialist contention '*Emotion is Black as reason is Helenic*' (1964, 24)[1] has established a lasting stereotype regarding the representation of black African people. He went further in emphasizing that it is in the area of rhythm that the Black man's contribution to world civilizations has been the most important and the most undeniable. For Senghor, the Black man is rhythm incarnate (1964, 37). Although his simplistic views did not withstand close examination, they have contributed to a stereotypical portrayal of postcolonial subjects by presenting them as easily distracted and pathologically emotional. Films like *La Vie est belle/Life is Rosy* (Ngangura, 1987) that are openly organized around rhythm and performance may indeed serve to shore up his claims. In my view, dance in films are illustrations of a clear opposition between political manifestos such as the Algiers Charter of African cinema and works designed to entertain.

In addition to Senghor's pronouncement, we can also recall Aimé Césaire's *The Tragedy of King Christophe*. In response to his wife, who complains that he asks too much from his citizens, King Christophe states that Blacks have more existential challenges because of their unique history. He castigates the overly frequent tendency of his people to play, and especially to dance:

Listen. Somewhere in the night the tom-tom's beating ...
Somewhere in the night my people are dancing ... Everyday
they dance ... and every night ... the ocelot's in the bush, the
prowler is at our doors, the manhunter is lurking in wait with
his gun, his net, his muzzle; the trap is ready to be sprung, our
persecutors are dogging our heels, and my people dance! (1969,
Act I, Scene 8, 42–42)

This clearly shows that when it is used for entertainment, dance is
considered to be alienating. Alongside Christophe's castigation is the
colonial project of systematically denigrating African dance as devilish,
backward and savage, and the attendant construction of a discourse of guilt
regarding any celebration of the body. In *Théâtres et scènes de spectacle,* Pius
Ngandu Nkashama (1993) describes this colonial strategy:

the castigation of dance by the colonial system was not
prompted solely by its suspicion of the body, a tradition handed
down from ancient theological movements and which holds a
negative view of physical materiality. The first missionaries on
the continent blindly and violently clamped down on all forms
of dance, because they considered the latter to be the *work of the
devil*, the concupiscence of the flesh. In fact, they held the view
that any actions that sought the 'glory of the body' revealed the
fallen nature of the individuals who carried them out for
themselves. [...] The incoming 'civilization' was driven by a
purpose: the complete negation of the body and the absolute
exaltation of the spirit. (1993, 67, original emphasis)[2]

Given this colonial and postcolonial objection, one is left to wonder why
directors have kept including dance scenes in films where old and young,
villager and city dweller alike, give their bodies over to motion. Why do
people dance in Africa? Why do directors make dance a signifying art form
and create alternative heroes who are not militants, but *social performers*? If
dance has remained an essential feature in postcolonial societies, what is its
meaning in fictional films? How can traditional celebrations of the body be
interpreted in postcolonial and global settings that are now reclaiming what
was banned or dismissed under colonial regimes? The difficulty with King
Christophe's position, which is equally dismissive as colonial discourse, is

that, according to this reasoning, dance is reduced to a suspicious bodily bacchanalia. Alternatively, Senghor equates blacks with emotions, but this characterization does not fully explain the social function of dance either. The subsequent sections will be given over to a discussion of exactly this point.

In *Anthropology and the Dance: Ten Lectures*, Drid Williams suggests (1991, 21) that when people dance they reinforce social relations, and also enact historical, mythological, religious, or political roles. This assessment holds true in Africa where, according to Pearl Primus, dancing is involved in almost any activity:

> People use their bodies as instruments through which every conceivable emotion or event is projected. The result is a hypnotic marriage between life and dance. The two are inseparable. When a child is born, when a person is buried, there is the dance. People dance the sowing of the seed and the harvest, puberty rites, hunting, warfare. They dance for rain, sun, strong and numerous children, marriage and play. Love, hatred, fear, joy, sorrow, disgust, amazement, all these and all other emotions are expressed through rhythmic movement. (1996, 6)

Alphonse Tiérou (1983, 1989, 2001), an African choreographer, has written on the subject of dance and his views are different from both Senghor's and Césaire's. Although his analysis seems to reflect the expectations of an exotic Western public, he believes Africans were not born with an extra dancing chromosome, and that dance can become a tool for development. This view is shared by Ngandu Nkashama, whose book is probably the most influential semiotic study of performance in contemporary Africa. Achille Mbembe's *On the Postcolony* describes dance as a cultural and, essentially, political phenomenon; he points out the fact that during the parades and public ceremonies of postcolonial authorities (*commandement*), dance served to promote its propaganda stick goals and enhance its visibility. For him,

> In the world of self-adoration that is the postcolony, the troupes summoned to dance bear witness to the central place accorded the body in the process of *commandement* and submission. [...] In

the postcolony, bodies have been used to entertain the powerful
in ceremonies and official parades. On such occasions some of
the bodies have borne the marks of famine [...] Others have
attracted small crowds of flies. (2001, 122–123)

According to Mbembe, it is easy for the postcolonial subject to be
manipulated because he displays a 'deployment of a talent for play, of a
sense of fun that makes him *homo ludens par excellence*' (2001, 104). This
disposition reinforces the *commandement*'s aspiration to regulate and
organize everything, including public happiness. The latest theorization of
entertainment is offered in *Nihilisme et négritude: Les arts de vivre en Afrique*
(2009), in which Célestin Monga describes dance as everything but ascetic.
Although he concedes that performance and thought are intimately
associated in Africa, he also links it to a kind of sophisticated nihilism that
involves a dose of paganism and Epicureanism.

Dance accordingly plays an important part in the cultural, aesthetic and
political postcolonial experience, and the anthropological discourse of guilt
about the body is lessening. Yet dance has been systematically ignored
by film scholars perhaps themselves under the sway of the directors
who contested the relevance of entertainment in spite of its inclusion in
their own films. The lone work that discusses dance in an African film is a
brief section of Nwachukwu Frank Ukadike's *Black African Cinema,* where
the author convincingly examines the significance of dance as a socio-
cultural practice in Désiré Ecaré's *Visages de femmes.* Following Ukadike's
study, this chapter explores the complexities of dancing as postcolonial
dramaturgy. It positions dance as a central form of entertainment that
involves many generations, spaces, languages and signifying modes.
Dancing is so important that it constitutes the inaugural or terminal
sequence of several films. It also establishes a bond between the
postcolonial subject and his environment, as between the sacred and
the profane. Dance does not disrupt the narrative; significantly, filmmakers
have systematically made dance an essential part of it, in both official
and non-official circles. Most importantly, dance ceremonies, as will be
seen, play an essential role in what Mikhail Bakhtin calls 'non-official
cultures' in that most often, 'they [are] sharply distinct from the serious
official ... political forms and ceremonials. They [offer] a completely
different, nonofficial ... extrapolitical aspect of the world, of man, and
of human relations; they build a second world and second life outside

officialdom' (1984, 5–6). Dance is described in African films as an activity of ordinary, even lower class, people, (*la plèbe*) who seek nothing more than to have fun, in spaces where political or national(ist) concerns are literally absent. It is significant that music and dance are the main subject matter of Mwenze Ngangura's *Life is Rosy*, where dance appears in social and religious contexts alike. This film, like several others, defies the classificatory systems of classical dramaturgy because the stage, central to conventional theorization of performance, is in this context multiple: people dance everywhere, at different times and for different reasons.

1   Dance on stage

Dance as social practice appears in many African films, early and recent, of which the following constitute the basis of this chapter: *Xala* and *Faat Kiné* (Sembène Ousmane, Senegal, 1974 and 2000), *Bal Poussière* (Henri Duparc, Ivory Coast, 1988), *Delwende* (Pierre Yameogo, Burkina Faso, 2005), *Quartier Mozart* (Jean-Pierre Bekolo, Cameroon, 1992), *The African Child* (Laurent Chevalier, Guinea–France, 1995), *Karmen Geï* (Joseph Gaï Ramaka, Senegal, 2001), *Madame Brouette* (Moussa Sène Absa, Senegal, 2002), *Pièces d'identité* and *La Vie est belle* (both by Ngangura Mweze, Democratic Republic of Congo, 1987), and *Sango Malo: The Village Teacher* (Bassek Ba Kobhio, Cameroon, 1991). In *Choreographies of African Identities*, Francesca Castaldi carries out a study of the national ballet of Senegal and shows how a connection is frequently made between dance, primitivism, the transitory, and the nonverbal. Dance, especially when it is popular or profane, as in comedies, tends to have an atemporal quality. The subject is often not bound to a historical context, but is rather immersed in his/her present life, worrying only about the immediate. Castaldi's analysis however focuses primarily on an institution (the National Ballet) and, to a lesser extent, on dance as a sacred form that enables subjects to fit within a past-present-future time continuum. Kariamu Welsh Asante's *African Dance: An Artistic, Historical, and Philosophical Inquiry* provides a more comprehensive study of various aspects of African dance. His analysis is useful in understanding the complexities of the performances displayed in the films studied in this section, especially when it comes to their relationship to the sacred.

Although the majority of films deal with ordinary popular dance, there are a few that depict dance's significant relationship to the sacred, spiritual world. The opening scene of Pierre Yameogo's *Delwende*, which precedes the credits, involves a sacred dance in which the whole community thanks the gods for their bounty and requests their protection against a curse that is being inflicted upon them. An overseer supervises the ritual, which ends in a long joyous dance by the female youth of the village. Dance as a sacred cultural practice is best illustrated in *Pièces d'identité* because it is clearly related to the main character's concept of belonging. At the very beginning, we are introduced to Mani Kongo, the king of a small community. He visits Brussels in order to find his daughter Mwana, who left Africa more than twenty years earlier. Although Mani Kongo eventually does find his daughter, along the way he comes into contact with a foreign culture and consequently comes close to losing his identity.

In one of the opening scenes, as Mani Kongo gets ready to leave his home and board a plane, his community helps him to prepare for this voyage by dancing. Their dance does not include Mani Kongo but, rather, serves to determine whether the spirits will approve of the king's long journey. The dancers perform to the beat of a traditional drum. As a panoramic shot pans the village and its enormous vegetation, thunder can be heard in the distance. The thunder does not signify the onset of rain, but more importantly acts as an omen that the king's visit will be successful. Nature agrees with the king's project, as we can intuit because the heavy drumbeats coincide with the sounds of distant thunder. A wide-angle shot encompasses everyone. When the king is ready to leave his home, the entire group of performers sends him off, dancing behind him.

One important feature of sacred dance as depicted in many of the films under consideration is costume. Apart from *Delwende,* where all the young female dancers have different outfits, symbolic clothing in sacred performances is special either because of the nature of the fabric or the richness of the colour or design. In any case, costumes in ritual performances generally differ from the quotidian variety found in popular dance. Ngangura's film shows the relationship between costumes and the invisible world, as well as the diversity and banality of those worn in popular performances. This is even more so the case in *Caramel,* where the religious choir members all wear a shiny white uniform during the performance that follows the death of the beautiful ghost woman.[3] The aforementioned scenes help illustrate Pearl Primus's point that

Costumes for dance vary from the most elaborate and exotic to the smooth bare body. Some costumes cover every inch of the dancer. Even the eyes are hidden by nets of straw or fiber. Some conceal their dancers, manipulators for the Spirit World, with elaborately carved ceremonial masks. Some extend the dancer into space by the use of stilts and layer upon layer of raffia. (1996, 8)

One of the most interesting scenes in *Pièces d'identité* that illustrates the relationship between dance and the spiritual world comes when Mani Kongo drifts off to sleep outside during the day after having taken a walk on the streets of Brussels. He hears a woman's voice, followed by the camera's close-up shot of her face. At first we only see a ghost-like image of her before she comes into better focus. Mani Kongo dreams of his 1958 visit to Belgium. At that moment, he awakens and sees directly in front of him the face of the woman who calls herself Noubia, the Republic of Black Africa. She wears a drum and moves her body to its rhythm before stopping to speak. The interaction that follows between these two characters is very interesting, but it is unclear whether a real interaction has taken place, or whether Noubia's presence was part of Mani Kongo's supernatural experience. Either way, Noubia has served a purpose, for it is she who takes Mani Kongo to the graves of Africans who were brought to Belgium at the end of the nineteenth century to entertain the country's king. They died unclothed in the cold while on their tour and were not shown respect; instead, they were treated like circus performers for the pleasure of the colonizers. Clearly, her dramaturgical function is linked to history and memory.

Ngangura has dedicated two main scenes to dance in *La Vie est belle*. In order to deal with his concern that he may no longer be virile, the nightclub owner consults a medicine man who suggests that he marry a virgin. He is advised to perform a ritualistic 'dance' that will consist of dancing first on his right foot, then with his left, while reciting the words 'push-push piston'. The camera takes several full-length shots of him performing this dance in private, and once even with his new wife Kabibi watching him. But one of the most significant performances in *La Vie est belle* is linked to the invisible, and occurs when Kabibi falls down and cannot be revived by her relatives. Immediately, she is taken to see the medicine man who instructs the men to dance around her body. They take their positions to dance around her. To add to the aura of mystery, the entire scene takes place at night. The eeriness of the scene is intensified because each time the camera focuses on a particular dancer, the viewer sees his serious facial expression staring down at Kabibi; the effect of this camera work is the appearance that the dancer is staring at the viewer of the film. This exercise is meant to frighten whatever has caused Kabibi to fall down, thus treating her ailment and perhaps driving out negative spirits from her body. At some point, the camera focuses on Kabibi, who has got up and now begun walking off in a trance-like state with her eyes closed. The camera follows her to the club, where Kuru, who has always been infatuated with her, is singing on stage in a concert. One gets the impression that it was the voice of Kuru that brought Kabibi out of her trance and not the efforts made by the medicine man and his dancers. In any case, what seems to be at work is the power of music. These examples indicate that Ngangura views a power in entertainment, and blends sacred and profane dance in his film. Characters are joyously involved in earthly matters, but are also intimately linked to the supernatural by dances that fortify their sense of belonging. According to Tracy D. Snipe,

> Dancing is an expression of a physical, psychological and spiritual state of being that enables people to give meaning and context to their greatest joys, hopes, frustrations, fears or sorrows. This expression contributes to a sense of wholeness. … [T]here is a sense of beauty and life in the dance. To dance is to live. In Africa, dance forms a vital bridge between the dead, the living and the unborn. (1996, 63)

The films studied above show that with sacred dance comes a cultural involvement in a generally crucial timeline. Sacred dances are generally collective in their expected impact and they can have a significant influence over a character's destiny.

However, the context and the significance are completely reshaped when it comes to popular dance. This point recalls Michel Meyer's and Mikhail Bakhtin's observations about comedy. For the former, one of the characteristics of comedy is that in this genre, history is 'offside' or absent because historical events have already been accomplished and are thus taken for granted. As for Bakhtin (1981, 23), the role of memory is minimal, and there is no place for ritual in comic settings. What is more, against a widely cited (and rightly questioned) Cartesian dichotomy, popular dance in African films exposes the artificial split not only between body and spirit, but also between body movement and speech. In these films, the protagonists and the community dance mainly at marriages and popular parties, which are not only venues for socialization, but also for collective practices; in certain cultural celebrations, these dances facilitate a declenching of the ego, body and libido of subjects who sometimes face serious existential crises. Moreover, beyond the ritualized and mechanical movements, a radical subversion of discourses and collective institutions is often at work.

Marriage is the subject matter of five films: *Xala, La Vie est belle, Bal Poussière, The African Child* and *Karmen Geï*, in which the discursive and aesthetic modalities of its representation as well as the function of dance vary remarkably. *Xala* opens with folkdances performed by populations bewildered by the supposed onset of national independence. It should however be noted that the second scene of the film, and one of the longest at over twenty minutes, is almost exclusively devoted to a performance of dance. For the celebration of his third marriage, El Hadji hires an orchestra to entertain his guests. For several minutes, the film is almost silent because no character speaks, with music being the only auditory detail accompanying the procession of guests. The camera gently sweeps from one side to the other of the home of the newlywed, dwelling on several objects. Amidst a thunder of applause, El Hadji inaugurates the dance. As he approaches the newlyweds, the camera shows the contrast between the woman's shockingly miniscule stature, as contrasted with the man's literally towering figure. However, this physical disproportion is less remarkable than the presence of a strange couple, which turns out to be the president of the Chamber of Commerce and the second wife of El Hadji. The rather tiny man is stuck to his partner like a mosquito would stick to an elephant. The difference between the two couples is rendered more noticeable by the position of the camera, which very often takes closer shots, making it possible for the audience to better appreciate the syntax of the image.

In *La Vie est belle,* there is also a lot of dancing when the bar manager and Kabibi get married. The couple is filmed first face-to-face and then from the waist up. Her hands are on his shoulders, and his hands are around her waist. Once the first wife (Mamu) comes in to dance, we see a change in body positions. The two wives of the club owner dance with their hands together and on each other's shoulders. As the evening draws to an end, the viewer notices that all the invited guests are dancing in traditional dress under the patio lights. This scene is in sharp contrast with a previous scene in which young, urban couples are dancing in non-traditional African clothes in the club under the lights of the disco ball, rather than beneath simple patio lights outside in the open air.

The film *Karmen Geï* uses well-deployed choreography to emphasize the rivalry between co-wives. As in the fourth sequence, Karmen, released from prison after performing sexual favours for a lesbian warden lured by her dancing, is shown attending the wedding of Corporal Lamine Diop. Karmen, a veritable femme fatale, lures the corporal thanks to the great feats of dexterity she accomplishes with ease. The camera tracks Karmen's highly suggestive and very erotic gestures, concentrating primarily on the most erotic parts of her athletic body, which the corporal watches covetously, to the absolute despair of his wife. Exasperated by Karmen's ability to flaunt her sensual body in a rhythmic and athletic fashion, the bride finds herself obliged to rise and compete with Karmen. The relationship thus becomes evident between dance, eroticism and power, as these forces cause the rival women to clash. Athletic movements, body twisting, lighting and camera angles emphasize the women's ability to function as active autonomous subjects who are conscious of their influence. Francesca Castaldi makes a similar remark about choreographies deployed by the *babar* dancers at the *tànnebèer* ceremonies in Senegal:

> The relationship between eroticism and dancing performed at *tànnebèers* stresses the agency of women as independent erotic subjects. Unlike western models of femininity promoted in the printed media and on the screen, where women pose seminaked as passive objects of an active (male) gaze, in the circle of *tànnebèers* women engage in spectacular kinetic stunts that both tease and resist visual objectification. The best dancers control the gaze of spectators, dramatically shifting between carefully choreographed stillness that allows the viewers to apprehend with leisure the dancer's body and extraordinary kinetic engagement that resist visual objectification by its active intensity. (2006, 82)

In *Karmen Geï*, dance is not only for pleasure or innocent enjoyment: it is also symptomatic of conflict and major social disorder. It is a sign of competition between rivals that allows Karmen to act as an agent of social and marital disturbance. When the camera approaches the braless female torso and shows close-ups of waists twisting suggestively, it functions to eroticize the dancing body. Dance thus assumes a primarily negative political and social role, since all misfortunes that ensue in the film are more or less related to dance: Karmen 'buys' her freedom after having enticed the warden with daring gesticulations; the marriage of the unfortunate corporal Lamine Diop begins and ends in the time it takes her to make a round of the floor.

In *Pièces d'identité*, there are several dancing scenes. Mwana is both an exotic bar dancer and a practitioner of African dance in the bar Le Katanga. The dancing here is not like the sacred dancing we saw during the early scenes of the movie. There is not any symbolic or mystical significance to this bar dance; rather, as the close-up shots of couples attest, the clientele is in a romantic mood and interested in having a good time. Drumbeats are replaced by modern music pleasing to the young people. The drumbeats return later, however, in the studio of an African dance class. Participants dressed in leotards and casual clothing dance to a rhythm played by three different drummers. Blacks and Whites are present in the studio. It is here that we see Mwana take part in the traditional dance class and are thus reminded of her roots in spite of her having lived in Brussels for over twenty years.

The audience eventually comes to see Mwana dance in another context. She works as an exotic dancer at a bar and by way of the camera's many close-up and full-length shots of her body, we see her African dance attire of casual clothing and a bandana replaced by a more risqué outfit in the nightclub. As the male patrons look at Mwana, the camera also follows their eyes. Mwana dances in full make-up, wearing high heels, a bikini top, a headdress and many bracelets. While dancing, she winks at one of the patrons and casually looks around her audience while performing in a sensual fashion. Compared to her African dance classes, where she is moving freely and energetically about alongside her classmates, this sequence shows her dancing alone and pleasing only the male onlookers. The camera's passage from the soles of her shoes, up her legs and then to the bodice of her outfit reiterates the gaze of the male patrons. In this case, dance functions less as a pleasure for the performer and more a pleasure for the onlookers, whose entertainment occurs at the expense of Mwana's dignity.

On the whole, dance, performed in well-measured choreographic styles, appears to be a strategic interlude in many films. The way in which the camera approaches the body (mainly in close-ups, big close-ups then high-angle shots), the carefully targeted body parts, and the omnipresent dim lighting in general, make dance, even in ceremonies like marriage, a primarily subversive and even perverse practice as it sows the seed of discord and disunion or causes melancholy where one would expect a happy celebration. With the many popular balls staged in other films, dancing makes it possible to fulfil other functions.

Henri Duparc's film *Bal Poussière* implies, from its title, the centrality of dance. As in Jean-Pierre Bekolo's *Quartier Mozart* and Moussa Sène Absa's *Madame Brouette*, the actors in Duparc's film dance on an important day, in this case 31 December. *Bal Poussière* starts and ends in dance, which makes sense given that the protagonist of the film, Binta, is in love with a musician. The first two minutes of the film feature music and dance. The film opens with a night-time shot of streets crammed with people, accompanied by background music: it is, without any doubt, another festive night. We can assume that such nights, of the sort despised by King Christophe in Césaire's play, occur frequently. The camera sweeps the street, moving towards the room playing the music with which the film opened. We see people dancing cheerfully, among them Binta, who is in high spirits. The camera then moves towards the podium where her male lover is performing. Close-ups and extreme close-ups show her insistently kissing him; the focus on this couple suggests the central role it will play in the narrative's plot.

The final sequence takes place one 31 December, a date on which Demi-Dieu, Binta's husband, must go downtown with his four wives. As this day is, in many African countries, traditionally accompanied by dancing, it is fitting that a ball entitled '*Bal Poussière*/Dancing in the Dust' should be taking place that evening. The lighting is poor in this part of film, and not only because it is night-time, but also because the floor is so dusty that the many steps of the dancers raise clouds of dust. Dance is important in this film primarily because it enables dancers to indulge libidos far too often repressed, and helps the characters to fulfil their desires. It is through dance that Binta, who is married, nevertheless reconnects with her true love who has, after the first sequence, disappeared from the film and only reappeared on 31 December. It is night-time, she goes towards him, kisses and caresses him, then acquiesces to his invitation to make love.

In *Quartier Mozart*, the evening of 31 December is a decisive one for Saturday, in terms of her libidinal and corporeal freedom. It is especially on the level of form that Bekolo's film stands out from the others. Amidst American and African music, one sees black and white still images on screen, as if the director has taken photographs of the character and displayed them for the audience. These images recall the trajectory of the relationship between My Guy and Saturday. As in animated cartoons, viewers can read the words and the thoughts of the characters. The most interesting shots are the vertical pans that explore the athletic body of Saturday, the big close-ups on her lips in which we see her putting on her make-up, and the many other big close-ups of her and My Guy dancing. The evening provides the characters, who are all smiling broadly, with a chance to relax.

Another essential function of this fateful evening is to allow Saturday and My Guy to meet each other. Saturday states on several occasions that it is on this date that she will claim her full independence. Her decision to emancipate herself from her parents is inaugurated by her erotic experiment with My Guy. The dance enables her to get closer to this character with whom she regularly flirts. It is while dancing that they embrace each other for the first time. In *Bal Poussière*, dance is depicted as a form of entertainment that allows various subjects to achieve precise goals. In this context dance encourages socializing and promotes interpersonal relationships. Saturday's burning desire occasions the (perhaps premature) emancipation of a young person indulging in forbidden pleasures of which the girl's parents do not approve. Dance, one observes, does not only entertain, but also liberates. This is however not always true, as we will observe in the case of *Karmen Geï*.

Although it functions as a prelude to seduction and gives insight into lesbian relations, dance in *Karmen Geï* has the additional function of representing one of the only authorized amusements in prison. It is primarily dance, involving daring shots of Karmen's body, which sustains her seductive power, establishing her as a torturer of hearts and a homewrecker. Music makes it possible for the female prisoners to relax in their confined circumstances (although admittedly the time they spend telling erotic jokes and laughing among themselves gives the impression that the women's prison is not especially hard to bear). The entertaining dimension of dance is thus emphasized. In *Sango Malo*, one of the first sequences takes place in a bar: shortly after having arrived in the village to

which he has been transferred, the young teacher Malo Malo Bernard goes
to a dancehall bar. Beer is plentiful, people are drunk, and sex is negotiated
without much discretion.

It is clear, from the above examples, that dancing functions to magnify
banal practices where history and nations are absent. Simply put, dance is
intimately essential to postcolonial experience. As Ukadike put it,

> music and dance serve as bridges to the animating forces of
> nature, which is why in traditional cultures they are inextricably
> linked with aspects of everyday life. In this function, every
> rhythm generated is associated with particular activities, where
> rhythmic complexities serve to differentiate one particular song
> and dance from another and one function from another. [The
> rhythm of African music] evokes and manifests the cadence of
> creation, life and death struggles, and generally accompanies
> ordinary ceremonies usually requiring a group of musicians and
> dancers who perform communally. (1994, 215–216)

But beyond the analysis of dance as a social practice, one can also look at the
ways directors use syntax and camera movements to elaborate a specific
discourse.

2   Dance, syntax and discourse

It is not simply coincidence that music or dance is present in the opening
sequences of *Xala*, *Delwende*, *Life is Rosy*, *Karmen Geï*, *Bal Poussière*, and *Sango
Malo*. Dance also concludes Duparc's film as well as Sembène's *Faat Kiné*. It
is as if music constituted the minimal unit for the construction of a
narrative. It is important to pay attention to sequential organization, for,
according to Michel Foucault,

> it is in vain that we say what we see; what we see never resides
> in what we say. And it is in vain that we attempt to show, by the
> use of images, metaphors, or similes, what we are saying; the
> space where they achieve their splendour is not that deployed by
> our eyes but that defined by the sequential elements of syntax.
> (1970, 9)

How does one, in this context, interpret the inclusion of dance in film and, in particular, its privileged position in the narrative sequence? Wouldn't such frequent inclusions reduce the films to mere entertainment, diluting their intended political or moral content? How does one explain the fact that entertaining scenes are equally frequent in films whose directors disavow comedy and entertainment? What is the role of dance in postcolonial experience? Closer observations show that representations differ when one moves from Ngangura or Henri Duparc to other directors. For instance, Ngangura's *La Vie est belle* is, to date, probably the only African film whose narrative structure and theme is completely centred on music and dance.

La Vie est belle opens with a full-length shot of Kuru (as performed by Papa Wemba, a popular Congolese musician) as he is walking alone on a village road clad only in shorts and a tank top. The camera does a close-up shot of his bare feet. He is preparing to entertain the villagers with his musical skills, though his percussion instrument is primitive. Once the villagers join in with him to sing, the viewer sees many close-up shots of them, in particular shots of their feet. Many of them dance barefoot, while others wear simple sandals. The villagers are clearly enjoying being entertained by Kuru, who, although he is poor, enjoys playing for his audience and singing a favourite song, whose lyrics feature the line 'La vie est belle/Life is rosy'. The film begins and ends with his song, which speaks to his love for music and dance.

The next time we see Kuru, he is trying to run after a truck so that he can get a ride to Kinshasa. Kuru takes his gift of music to the big city. As soon as he arrives there, he comes across a club playing lively music. Kuru walks right into the club, gets up onstage and starts singing. The club owner will not give him a job at his bar, but nevertheless brings him home to his wife so that he can help her with the cleaning. The only entertainments that Kuru has during the hard times he spends cleaning are whistling and singing. While he washes his boss's clothes, he comes across a large sum of money and, by stealing it along with the boss's clothes, he is able to sneak his way into the bar. Once there, the camera focuses on the different couples and small groups dancing. The dancers appear to be carefree, waving their hands in the air to the music. The moving figures blend together as the camera does a wide shot of all the dancers together on the floor.

With *La Vie est belle,* Ngangura has chosen to illustrate the easy life, characterized by stress-free entertainment. There are two important moments in the film where a link is made between work and music. The first occurs as Kuru and his friends are shining shoes in the streets. To lighten their workload and make it more bearable in the midday sun, they all sing in unison, 'La vie est belle'. Some bystanders begin swaying gently to the music; others clap their hands to the beat in lieu of the workers themselves, whose hands are busy polishing their patrons' shoes. There is a contrast between the workers crouched down doing their job, unable to dance to their singing, and the others around them free to enjoy the singing as they stand idly by. In this scene, workers and bystanders alike appear happy, dancing and singing; the point is that the entertainment is free and allows everyone to enjoy the moment.

Another scene where music and dance become intertwined with daily work occurs in the outdoor market where the women sell fabric. Mamu is shot from the waist up dancing gently behind her table and clapping her hands. Whether she dances to encourage buyers to come to her table or simply to entertain herself is not entirely clear. However, it is evident that both these elements are important aspects of marketplace life. Another of the bar scenes shows women entering the local club, singing in unison. They also dance while descending the stairs to the club, and they are filmed walking down the steps singing 'Time lost is forever'. Although there is much dancing in the club, the dancing and singing do not serve the same function of uniting the community as in the shot with the men working outside. Rather, in the bar scene, people dance simply because they are in a club and it is expected of them. The jovial community spirit is much more pronounced in the shoe-shining scene where enjoying being in the group takes precedence over enjoying oneself. Here, it is obvious that questions of social and national historicity are bracketed, as the dancing postcolonial subjects are totally immersed in ephemeral, self-indulgent pastimes. They are wholly present in the moment, not worried about the past or future of the nation. The recurrent choruses 'Life is rosy' and 'Time lost is forever' are obviously, as illustrated by Monga, crucial battles to control or halt the inevitable passage of time. The secular, spontaneous movements of the dancers in the club are necessarily nihilistic:

> [the] random gesture is actually a nihilist plea: while refusing to subject themselves to the linearity of the movement, dancers call upon pagan gods who could offer them a world stripped of the dictatorship of the inevitable, and a life where individual and

collective destinies would not be the subject of any
predetermination. The race towards nonbeing is expressed here
in the form of a voluptuous celebration of a life outside life, of
an imaginary location that enables one to steer clear of this
imperfect and unbearable reality. (2009, 116)[4]

In *Sango Malo*, it is not a coincidence that the people dancing in Honba's bar
are all filmed from a high angle, as this technique serves to diminish the
subject. The scenes that take place in the bar are meant to criticize the
patrons, who are occupied with getting drunk and destroying their meagre
fortunes. The bar owner does something even more reprehensible when, to
avoid going bankrupt, he imports prostitutes from the city and precipitates
an outbreak of venereal diseases in the village. Culture and entertainment
are replaced by dance, fornication and alcoholism. The light and camera
movements are similar to those in *Bal Poussière,* where actors dance in a
rather dimly lit environment. Too often, the camera, placed at a very high
vantage point, makes sweeps of the subjects more or less involved in a
rhythmic step dance.

In *Xala* and *Madame Brouette*, dance helps bring to light the most overt
evidence of postcolonial negligence and corruption. In *Xala,* it is while
people are dancing at a ball that a parliamentarian, who doubles as a
member of the Chamber of Commerce, makes an illegal deal with an
entrepreneur. The 'contract' is sealed after a promise to provide fifteen
percent 'commission' in cash to the parliamentarian, who insists that there
must be no traces of the transaction. It is also during this ball that one hears
the members of the Chamber of Commerce in conversation, using many
metaphors with lecherous undertones. In *Madame Brouette*, it is also in the
character London's bar/brothel that strategies for the smuggling and
trafficking of prostitutes are elaborated. London controls a social network
and a fortune that make him an intimidating power to reckon with. London
primarily owes his status, in decline by the end of the film, to the power he
wields over the public authorities, to whom he lends money and women.
Considering the diversity of the preceding cases, is it possible to establish a
coherent theory of entertainment and dance?

It is noticeable that in several films examined, dance and music, while
entertaining, equally facilitate the emergence of a subversive discourse.
Dancers like Karmen can be catalysts for socio-cultural disorder, or they
can serve to corrupt or induce desire, as London, El Hadji and Naago do.

The dancers in most films are not even named. Even in *Bal Poussière*, where dance enables Binta to attain self-fulfilment, the same dance can alternatively be perceived as a deleterious activity that subjugates its participants to their base bodily needs. Dancing can as such reflect a collective cultural and political degeneration.

Another important aspect of dance is its association with eroticism and sexuality. Besides the numerous abilities of Karmen or instances of pleasure implied in *Xala* or *Madame Brouette,* one should not forget what an unnamed actor in *Bal Poussière* describes as his 'war strategy': before inviting a partner, he intentionally puts a piece of bread in the right side of his pants. During the dance, he presses the partner to his right side. As she moves toward the left side, 'Toto [i.e. his erect penis] awaits her'.[5] In *Quartier Mozart*, dance also catalyses the first encounters between Saturday and My Guy. All these examples, together with Karmen's erotic movements, illustrate Simon Ottenberg's observation that

> Sexual matters sometimes play a role in African dancing. Males who are superb dancers ... [attract] females and, equally, the other way round. Dance may involve sexual-like movements and gestures which are acceptable in performance but not otherwise in public non-secular dances which serve ritual purposes. Dance situations may create an air of sexual freedom that encourages liaisons and matings. (1997, 13–14)

In such a context, where senses and pleasure prevail, one could genuinely share the concerns of the protagonist of Aimé Césaire's play, as the pleasures and recklessness of characters constitute a kind of time-bomb waiting to explode social structures.

As mentioned, dance opens and closes Duparc's *Bal Poussière*. This film is considered a comedy, which explains its ending in this way. However, it is equally clear that this film displays some questionable social practices, and that the joyous ending might actually function as subtle social satire. Not surprisingly, popular dance also appears at the end of Ngangura's *La Vie est belle*. This final sequence, which takes place in the nightclub, functions, crucially, as a celebration of Kuru's triumph over his humble beginnings. Overhead shots of the club give the viewer a sense of how much power Kuru has accrued, a fact which is especially on display when he succeeds in getting everyone up and dancing. This final shot also unites him with

Kabibi, his sweetheart. In the last scenes, the camera is overhead and the dance floor is depicted as almost completely empty in the darkness of the club. Within seconds, however, singles and couples fill the dance floor and acclaim Kuru, their new singer, with their raised hands and voices. The close-up shots become less frequent as the camera moves higher to show the viewer what is happening outside the club, where the appreciative audience has spilled out into the street.

Another interesting example of dance featured at the end of a film occurs in Sembène Ousmane's *Faat Kiné,* where a celebration for recent graduates is taking place. We get a glimpse of the festivities taking place in Kiné's home. We get an overhead shot of crowds of young people dancing in the daylight. Both the grandmother and Adèle are watching from a nearby balcony to see who is entering. The camera pays particular attention to the grandmother, who is seated in a chair, clearly enjoying the view from above. Although she is too frail to dance, she claps her hands to the loud music coming from downstairs. The camera's wide-angle shots from above follow her gaze, allowing us to see from her viewpoint what is going on down below; when the camera shows that the grandmother is smiling, we realize that she approves. As the film nears its end, the dancing continues into the night, conveying the sense of freedom from the everyday challenges of life shared by the younger and older generations. The evening belongs to everyone, and coincides with the freedom of choosing a new path. The party and dancing celebrate the completion of an old era and the beginning of a new one. Referring to Monga (2009, 114), one would state that in all these cases of secular movements in quotidian contexts, postcolonial subjects experience a full expression of their primitive needs. Dance hence becomes a unique opportunity to release unconfessed violent desires and other brutal cravings; dancers are released from the underhand resentment buried deep in their bodies, and they appear like quiet outlaws or unrestrained delinquents because of hidden urges and guilty desires.

Although the original intentions of colonial cinema were to distract, alienate and dominate people through the perpetuation of colonial discourses disguised as entertainment, African directors have in recent history significantly reconsidered the social and aesthetic function of cinema. Most importantly, their ideological manifestos purporting to 'fight' entertainment have not prevented them from exploring the art form. That is particularly true in their incorporation of dance and music, which take on different meanings in different circumstances. Dance, whether popular or, more importantly, sacred, is crucial in promoting a sense of belonging. It helps to connect with the spiritual world and brings together subjects in their shared hopes and desire for happiness. In this context, postcolonial entertainment differs radically from colonial entertainment, reorienting African cinema. The films of Mweze Ngangura and Henri Duparc suggest the development of a new pride in reclaiming what were formerly dismissed as 'distractions', 'emotion' and 'backwardness'. By replacing resolutely nationalist films with comedies and more popular genres, Mweze Ngangura, Jean-Pierre Bekolo, Henri Duparc and many other post-1980 directors have paved the way for a redefinition of African cinemas. The inclusion of dance is just one aspect of this metamorphosis. A question remains: can the staging of popular entertainment forms, even for the purpose of social criticism, continue to serve a didactic function? Should it? Is entertainment (in films) compatible with development or social transformation?

Nationalist and committed film directors like Sembène Ousmane are quite hopeful in this regard. To subvert what he perceives to be an alienating social order, he builds a cinematographic discourse that blends entertainment and social satire. However, to engage in action or, at least, in reflection, it is important that the audience avoid the same slavish adulation of the image they have become accustomed to bestowing upon political powers. Furthermore, that would require a real pact, an active complicity between the film director and his audience, which is far from the case in African cinema. It is not the case that simply because they entertain, dance and music do not have a role to play in political discourse. On the contrary, forms of entertainment remain at the heart of a political economy of desire, leisure, pleasure and anxiety. Although dance is not regarded in the same way by Joseph Gaï Ramaka, Henri Duparc, Mweze Ngangura, Moussa Sène Absa or Sembène Ousmane, it inevitably reveals an alternative political discourse to that of nation building and the development of engaged realist narratives. Some directors believe in celebrating the things that make postcolonial subjects happy, whether for the right or wrong reason, and have decided to represent these rather than the images of humanitarian disaster and despair associated with Africa. The nationalist 'crusade against entertainment', which is in reality a myth, is based on problematic assumptions. A question remains: what is the real impact of African films on African moviegoers? Christian Zimmer once noted that it is an illusion that art will actually change the world:

The audience believes going to the cinema helps them forget, escape from their thoughts. In reality, they go there to ascertain that their world is still the same, that it has not changed, that the values underpinning its existence are still in place, they go there to *recognize*, not to discover. Every system provides a sense of safety and assurance. (1970, 20–21, original emphasis)[6]

This quest for pleasure and its representation is without a doubt fundamental in the staging of dance which, thanks to its attendant syntactic and visual languages, enables the construction of a new social discourse where pleasure and entertainment may not always be viewed as antithetical to the construction of social or political identities. Although one could also detect a rapidly changing society in the bodily contortions featured in *Karmen Geï, La Vie est belle, Sango Malo, Xala* or *Madame Brouette*, it is important to point out that a lack of entertainment is still a problem. The explosion of the video industry in various African countries is a clear indication that spectators need and are desperate for entertainment. The inclusion of dance and the multiplication of comedies are important steps towards the complete redefinition of cinema in Africa, as old rigid parameters are called into question or, more radically, become obsolete.

Notes

1 '*L'émotion est nègre, comme la raison est hellène*'.
2 French original: '*la condamnation de la danse par le système colonial ne procède pas seulement de la suspicion du corps, laquelle dérive des mouvements théologiques antiques et tourne à la négation de la matérialité physique. Les premiers missionnaires venus sur le continent avaient pu s'insurger avec une violence aveugle contre toutes les formes de danses, parce que celles-ci étaient perçues comme des œuvres du diable: la concupiscence de la chair. En fait, ils considéraient tout ce qui pouvait rendre la « gloire du corps », la déchéance des peuples qui les exécutaient pour eux-mêmes. […] La « civilisation » qu'ils apportaient avait pour but de nier le corporel, afin de pouvoir exalter exclusivement le spirituel.*' (67, original emphasis)
3 Although not directly related to dance, Daniel Kamwa's film *Totor* (Cameroon, 1994) also links costumes and the spiritual world. In the final scene, in which the two young protagonists Mentse and Ngantse meet with the 'gods' in the fairy world, their costumes are completely different. They are now wearing bright new shiny attire which, in the traditional Bamileke tradition, is very formal and is only used for special circumstances.

4 French original: '*[La] gestuelle aléatoire est donc en réalité une prière nihiliste: en refusant de se soumettre à la linéarité du mouvement, [les danseurs] invoquent des dieux païens qui pourraient leur offrir un monde dépouillé de la dictature de l'inévitable, et une vie où les destins individuels et collectifs ne feraient l'objet d'aucune prédétermination. La course vers le néant s'exprime ici sous la forme d'une célébration voluptueuse d'une vie en-dehors de la vie, d'un lieu imaginaire où l'on se situe pour ignorer ce réel imparfait et insupportable*' (116).

5 In many regions of French-speaking Africa, 'Toto' refers to the idiot or the least intelligent member of the classroom. In colonial schools, the expression '*Toto ne comprend rien*/Toto just does not get anything' was very popular.

6 '*Le public croit aller au cinéma pour oublier, pour s'évader, il y va en réalité pour s'assurer que son monde est toujours le même, qu'il n'a plus bougé, que les valeurs qui soutiennent son existence sont toujours en place, il y va pour* reconnaître, *et non pour découvrir. Tout système sécurise, rassure.*'

8   Bassek Ba Kobhio

9   Ngangura Mweze, *La Vie est belle*

10　Joseph Gaï Ramaka

11   Ngangura Mweze, *Pièces d'identité*

12　Henri Duparc, *Caramel*

13　Moussa Sène Absa, *Madame Brouette*

Chapter 3

Crimes, society and the 'commandement'

Previous chapters examined a central contradiction between African film practice and the political manifestos that shaped its development, emphasizing the ways narratives strategically entertain specific audiences. I discussed films such as *Karmen Geï, Xala* and *Delwende,* each of which is equally organized around the search for truth and the solving of a mystery: why has El Hadji suddenly lost his virility? What is the cause of Caramel's death? Karmen is not only an insubordinate woman, she is also a smuggler and a criminal. Not only does she use her body to buy her freedom, she and her accomplices moreover launch an assault on the police station. Although structured around choreographic scenes and the oral performance of singers, Moussa Sène Absa's *Madame Brouette* is first and foremost the story of a murder committed by a rebellious woman. The carnage perpetrated by Mati constitutes a turning point in the determination of female subjectivity. The almost heroic murderer represents new female agents whose rise, according to Kenneth Harrow, makes us 'lose most if not all our sympathies for fathers as they are increasingly portrayed as licentious, greedy' figures (2010, 191). In such a context, the assassination of abusive or authoritarian males is not only the sign(al) of a disintegration characteristic of the postmodern 'age of man's decline' (Harrow, 2010, 194). Homicides and manslaughters, especially when they target lecherous postcolonial authorities, speak to a new social, aesthetic and political *order* in which legal and social concepts of crime take completely new rationalities.

Yet, the issue of crime in African films, specifically the ways it fosters new subject positions and challenges dualistic thinking, has not yet been given adequate attention. In films like *Xala* or *Karmen Geï* the identification of postcolonial authorities with syndicates of criminals appears all too clear. Considering recent productions, it has been difficult to estimate the imaginative potential of creators. Previous critics seem to have caught a rather narrow perception of, or missed, the new aesthetic dynamics now at work on the continent. With the current cultural, technological, economic and demographic changes, Africa is diversifying its modes of expression. Filmmakers are becoming more interested in detective fiction, a genre popular not only in the huge Nigerian video film industry, but also in Francophone Africa, where crime is becoming a major plot driver. Mamady Sidibé's *Inspecteur Sory, le Mamba* (2005) is organized around the investigations and heroism of a detective, while Mahamat Saleh-Haroun's *Daratt* (2006) relates the psychological itinerary of a boy who is unable to fire his gun at the murderer of his father. The man, who has been transformed, adopts the protagonist as a son, making the avenger and prospective criminal renounce his quest for revenge. Even Idrissa Ouedraogo's *Samba Traoré* (1992), with its robbery and killings, is a classic thriller set in an African village whose story ends in a satisfying conclusion. The most noticeable developer of crime plots is Boubakar Diallo, from Burkina Faso, whose films attract large crowds. Apart from the sentimental comedy *Sofia* (2004), his oeuvre is comprised entirely of detective and Western genres: *Open Water* (2005), *Traque à Ouaga* (2004), *Dossier brulant* (2005), *Code Phoenix* (2005), *L'Or des Younga* (2006), *Série noire à Koumbi* (2006), *La Belle, la brute et le berger* (2006) and *Sam le Caid* (2008). Yet, if one looks at the structures, theorizations and various conceptions of crime genres, and if one agrees with Kirsten Moana Thompson that 'every national cinema has created crime films' (2007, 1), it is possible to see how they relate to African productions that display or challenge their patterns. When one considers the syntactic and discursive structures of recent productions like *Les Saignantes* (Jean-Pierre Bekolo, Cameroon, 2005), *Madame Brouette* (Moussa Sène Absa, Senegal, 2002), or *Guelwaar* (Sembène Ousmane, Senegal, 1992), it becomes clear it is possible to examine African productions in relation to the canons of crime fiction.

Accordingly, I want to examine how the detective genre reflects and shapes subjectivity, governing norms, and systems of policing and law. In this chapter, I interrogate an evolving trend not yet addressed by African film criticism: the transformation of crime fiction by postcolonial directors. More specifically, I deconstruct the myth of 'impossible' African crime fiction, determine the strategies used to subvert crime film conventions and ensure the triumph of postcolonial authorities, and, finally, examine the weaknesses of the few existing burlesque enquiries leading to the irreversible decline of such authority.

1   Africa and theories of (impossible) crime fiction

It may seem problematic to examine African cinema using theories of crime in fiction. Few scholars have ventured into this terrain, 'mainstream' critics having reserved theories of genre for Hollywood and other dominant cinematic traditions. Examples include Jon Thompson's *Fiction, Crime and Empire: Clues to Modernity and Postmodernism* (1993), Thomas Leitch's *Crime Films* (2002), Nicole Rafter's *Shots in the Mirror: Crime Films and Society* (2006), and Kirsten Moana Thompson's *Crime Films: Investigating the Scene* (2007), which all develop interesting analyses of the rise and development of crime fiction in Western and, most specifically, in American culture.

Yet it is clear that detective fiction originating from 'subaltern' or 'peripheral' traditions has not been sufficiently studied. What is more, the ways in which such productions shape 'traditional' crime fiction, subverting its paradigms and epistemic standards as well as its canons of rationality, are yet to be adequately considered. Such enquiries, especially within the African context, may from the outset necessitate a study of the inception of detective narratives. Founded in Europe, the detective narrative very quickly became a victim of its own success. This situation, some critics suspect, may explain the genre's 'obsolescence' and lapse into outmoded conventions, features that may have led to its 'disappearance'. Analysing remarks made by Alain Demouzon, for whom 'the detective novel is dead,' André Vanoncini argues that

> the production of the last twenty years does not at any time
> point to an emerging new form of composition. The great
> majority of the somewhat original creations of this period
> embrace the narrative model of the Gothic novel: a private or
> public detective elucidates a crime at the same time as he/she
> unravels the aspects of specific settings and/or socio-historic
> problems. (2002, 102)[1]

Besides the alleged 'exhaustion' that typifies the genre, one can also point out the scepticism generated by several critics about the possibility of an

African crime fiction. Such scepticism is due both to the genre's datedness and its supposed inapplicability to specific African socio-political and cultural contexts.

In *The Post-Colonial Detective,* Ed Christian (2000) maintains that the structures of the detective novel are static and have not been able to transform themselves with the passage of time. He contends that crime fiction can hardly become a non-Western genre because, his facile argument goes, there is virtually no 'good' detective fiction in most 'post-colonial' countries. Those who have tried to write any have ended up with 'ugly' or 'failed' narratives. Without providing any evidence, he gives as a reason for the limited inclusion of non-Western narratives in his volume a lack of translations for Americans who 'seem uninterested in books set in (much less written by authors from) lands other than England and the United States' (5). He further writes:

> It would be nice to see a volume entirely on post-colonial
> detectives by post-colonial authors ... Are there indigenous
> schools of detective fiction in, say, Pakistan, or the Philippines,
> or Iraq or Turkey, or Angola, Venezuela, Jamaica or the Ukraine?
> The difficulty is unless the books show up in English in our own
> countries, we do not know about them. It may be that there are
> some fascinating mystery writers undiscovered by us because of
> the marginalisation caused by language and culture. (6)

In spite of the reductive character of Christian's assertions, one realizes that it is in fact true that the issue of genres has generally been avoided when one scrutinizes African criticism. In *La Philosophie africaine* (1995), Jean-Godefroy Bidima outlines a set of theoretical considerations that were systematically ignored by African philosophers obsessed with issues bearing on development or politics. Because of what Bidima terms 'phallophilosophy', most African thinkers considered philosophical thinking as a serious exercise that could not accommodate 'flimsy' topics like genre, gender, sexuality, the body or childhood, as if addressing them could result in a guilt backlash. Bidima's reproval of a lack of seriousness points to a fundamental presupposition in many African writings. Although it is outdated and contested today, many theorists, filmmakers and writers regarded their work as a tool vested with the mission to articulate social concerns and incite transformation. This argument implies that philosophy, like literature or film, should not aspire to be popular, as the detective genre necessarily does, but rather should set out primarily to convey 'African' values and to foster nation building. Given such considerations, African crime fiction theories might be regarded as impossible. Detective fiction as perceived in Western societies would thus constitute a utopian form in Africa.

The first example illustrating this 'impossibility' comes from Pius Ngandu Nkashama, who admits in *Ecritures et discours littéraires* (1989) that 'the detective novel is, judging from all assessments and all investigations, the book most read or most consumed in Africa. Most available also ...' (209).[2] At the same time, however, he maintains that it is impossible for the genre to emerge in Africa, a place where the pursuit of truth, a crucial concern in this type of fiction, is not a value shared by criminal (post)colonial State administrations:

> Detective fiction can by no means develop on two incongruous
> planes; namely the search for truth and the denunciation of the
> system in which this search is carried out, or which underpins
> the principle of truth. A sense of constant frustration looms as
> the relationship between the subject and plot development
> witnesses a shift in terms of enunciation. (1989, 209)[3]

This institutional hypothesis is all the more significant because the detective story often maps out and celebrates the trajectory of a subject whose intelligence makes it possible to dissipate a crisis. Famous detectives, among them Hercule Poirot, Maigret and Columbo, are upstanding and respectable heroes.

Foucault (1997) regards political life not only in terms of surveillance but also as involving 'biopower', the ability to decide who is entitled to life or death. It is common knowledge that the police force in Africa is, on the contrary, a force of repression, quite similar to the one which Napoleon Bonaparte reformed in the nineteenth century with an intention not to protect citizens, but to repress various factions that sought freedom from a nascent despot. In *Nihilisme et négritude,* Célestin Monga (2009, 13, 21) confirms this characterization is a description of the Cameroonian police force, which no citizen trusts because the policemen are all perceived as criminals. Postcolonial Africa has revealed itself to be susceptible to regimes whose authorities have 'a carnivorous aspect' (Mbembe, 2001, 200) and do not differentiate between human and animal life. For Mbembe,

any practical distinction between the task of conducting what
would properly be called public affairs (government) and the
institutional and unbridled use of violence and coercion [is]
virtually non-existent. The organs for carrying out violence, and
the means of punishment, [are] systematically brought into
service to put down dissidence, crush rebellions, stifle
challenges, or simply seize power. (2001, 43)

In such a context, genuine crime, according to Ngandu Nkashama, is
the attack on illegitimate institutions and their attendant floating legal
arsenals fashioned according to the whims and caprices of 'untouchable
castes' (read, postcolonial authorities) for whom 'the law is not a
prescription, but a circumscription' (1989, 200). Accordingly, readers or
citizens ought not to sympathize with the 'law and order' which structures
the genre. They instead sympathize with the dissident 'criminal' who
ensures collective salvation. How would a detective narrative celebrate
agents of torture or genocide? Such a juridical-cum-social construction
would preclude any heroic or even sympathetic portrait of an African
detective.

Another factor that renders the development of the investigative genre
almost impossible is that in traditional African societies, Ngandu Nkashama
argues, it is regarded as the responsibility of the group, and even the dead,
to deliver justice. In conventional thrillers, such responsibility is entrusted
to the detective:

> The belief that the revenge of the dead would haunt its murderer
> beyond the grave … would be sufficient to generate, in
> investigative ways, non-novelistic behaviours. If the spirit of the
> dead can take revenge, 'seize the soul of its murderer', pursue
> dreams and experience hallucinations as a ghost, stretch out its
> mental faculties, it becomes superfluous to begin a search for
> clues. The fate of the murderer is already sealed by its very status
> and it would no longer be necessary to seek redress from other
> jurisdictions. (200)[4]

In traditional societies, a criminal's weapon, the 'exhibit A', is shrouded in
magic and traditional religion in a manner unfathomable to the Western
subject (Nkashama, 1989, 206); one can thus understand the institutional,

cultural, aesthetic and anthropological difficulties that would inhibit the emergence of an African detective fiction.

The analysis of crime in fiction must be complemented by another notion, that of 'the theoretical imaginary', a recent idea espoused by Cilas Kemedjio to describe the ability of fiction to anticipate or state theoretical problems. This idea is demonstrated in Jean-Pierre Bekolo's film, *Les Saignantes* which contains motifs pertaining to detective films, science fiction, action and horror. Nonetheless, in various segments of the narrative, the film uses subtitling and captions to state the impracticality of making genre-specific movies, including detective movies, in Africa. 'How can you make an action film in a country where acting is subversive?' 'How can you make a love story where love is impossible?' 'How can you make a horror film in a place where death is a party?' 'How can you make a crime film in a country where investigation is forbidden?' In an interview with Olivier Barlet, Bekolo also reveals that for the granting agencies in which he participated, 'Anything genre-specific is systematically shunned, under the pretext that it would constitute a misrepresentation and stereotype' (www. africultures.com).

The 'mode of impossibility' could therefore partly explain the limited number of detective narratives released so far and the few analyses devoted to them in literary studies, not to mention cinema studies. However, Pim Higginson (2005, 2007) claims to be witnessing a 'proliferation' and a 'boom' of a genre which hitherto did not warrant any attention. With the exception of Christine Matzke and Susanne Mühleisen's *Postcolonial Postmortems* (2006), which explores only a limited number of southwestern African novels, very few publications address the principles that might possibly characterize an African detective fiction. The only other examples are two studies by Ambroise Kom (1999, 2002) and one by Emmanuel Yewah (1990), all published in the aftermath of Ngandu Nkashama's foundational work. As far as film productions are concerned, no single study has ever addressed this issue in African cinema, where genre theories are likewise almost nonexistent. That absence may be due, at least in part, to what David Murphy calls 'a reductive opposition between Western and African culture' (Murphy, 2000, 241), a nationalist opposition which views 'culture specific' African productions against others – read Western – generally considered commercial and alienating. In *50 ans de cinéma maghrébin*, for example, Denise Brahimi (2009) briefly mentions the Western in order to argue that this genre has never taken root in the

Maghreb in spite of a desert landscape which was previously used for such films by foreign filmmakers (13). For her, geography is not enough: a specific cultural and historical orthodoxy is necessary for specific forms. While her view is defensible to a certain extent, one must equally not lose sight of the fact that genres as theoretical categories cannot be identical across space and time. Because differentiating between what is 'African' and what is 'American' or 'French' is no longer possible, as Jean-Pierre Bekolo (2009, 49) argues, it is crucial to generate novel narratives from which new ideas will grow (25). Although *Les Saignantes* is rather ambiguous (if not dismissive) about its existence, as mentioned above, Bekolo is equally very specific about the relevance of genre in Africa:

> genre films are part of our culture, as Africans. There's no doubt about that. But the thing is always not just to use them, but to question them in relation to the choices we have to make in the context of African cultures. It's a question of how to appropriate the cinema that's out there … It's not just about following what's being done like sheep … So we have to raise these questions: why am I using the horror film style? Why am I using the sci-fi style? … The typical thing is to say if you use any of the genres, then you have moved African cinema to the next level. (Adesokan, 2008, 3)

Probably without having read Bekolo's recently published writing (2009), some academics are moving African film scholarship beyond the liberationist criticism that previously dominated it. Dayna L. Ocherwitz (2008) has analysed the effects of globalization in Djibril Diop Mabety's *Hyenas,* demonstrating how this film imports and 'tames' some codes of the Western. Sada Niang (2008) also established the link between Sembène Ousmane's *Borom Sarret* and Italian neorealism. Taiwo Adetunji Osinubi (2009) theorizes the use of science-fiction techniques in *Les Saignantes, Africa Paradis* (Sylvestre Amoussou, Benin/France, 2007) and Ousmane Sembène's *La Noire de...* (Senegal, 1966). Mindful that postcolonial entities are obsessed with order, that 'the state [considers] itself indistinguishable from society and as the upholder of the law and keeper of the truth' (Mbembe, 2001, 105), one wonders why crime fictions, a complex category to define, did not emerge earlier.

Most theorists agree that 'crime fiction' is a broad term that includes categories or sub-genres as varied as film noirs, cop films, police procedurals, gangster films, etc. The most difficult task in defining the genre is to articulate a definition of crime films that encompasses several historical, theoretical, and even cultural periods. According to Jon Thompson, the term crime fiction 'is used to denote all the genres and subgenres that concern themselves with violation of the law, whether or not this violation actually took place, and whether or not this violation is sanctioned by the novelist' (1993, 3). For Kirsten Moana Thompson, 'the crime film foregrounds the commission of a crime, and/or emphasises its investigation, prosecution, prevention and/or punishment' (2007, 2). For Thomas Leitch, the 'trouble' with crime films first lies in the difficulty of offering a coherent understanding of the generic 'crime fiction,' as well as the many sub-genres that it involves. Furthermore, Leitch (2002, 11) raises the question whether the subject, the effects, or the visual style are most useful in defining crime films. He argues that although '[a]ny film in which crime occurs can fairly be considered a crime film; the test of the classification, as of the resulting definition of the genre, depends on its usefulness in illuminating individual examples and the relations among them' (302). Most importantly, Leitch's examination of the crime film's various sub-genres focuses not on their blurred borders but on their common structural patterns: 'Every crime story predicates three leading roles: the criminal who commits the crime, the victim who suffers it, and the avenger or detective who investigates it in the hope of bringing the criminal to justice and establishing the social order the crime had disrupted' (13).

This narrative organization, involving a set of stock characters and formulaic conventions, is typical of most 'mainstream' cinemas. Although hard-boiled detective stories are almost always critical of the system they represent, they also presuppose a specific social order where all institutions generally function as they should: the state is responsible for and guarantees the welfare of the citizens; the police and lawyers enforce legal rules and protect the vulnerable. Structurally, most crime films end by reinstituting the disrupted order, a narrative construction that makes the genre ultimately conservative. Yet, as Barry Keith Grant (2007) puts it, filmmakers have adopted Hollywood genres with more or less success. According to Tom O'Regan (1996), national cinemas have managed to 'carve a space locally and internationally for themselves in the face of dominant international cinema, Hollywood', hence succeeding in 'indigenising' genres and 'reworking them according to their own cultural sensibility' (1996, 5). O'Regan's point is particularly relevant to this study because contrary to the films of Ouedraogo, Diallo or Sidibé, which all have titles, narrative structures and aesthetic features that recapitulate American or French traditions, *Guelwaar, Madame Brouette* and *Les Saignantes* substantially subvert the conventional patterns of the genre.

The following sections examine the aesthetic and discursive modalities of crime in African films which illustrate the rationalities used by political power to shape postcolonial settings and rule. Dramatizing or examining crime in (postcolonial) Africa becomes synonymous with determining a political economy of *death* and its new redistribution between the upper and the lower echelons of the social ladder: the state has lost its entitlement to kill and deliver justice. Furthermore, the absence of investigation is no longer a means of covering up the criminal state's own illegal actions, for the state's top officials become vulnerable to being murdered by ordinary people, who subsequently get away with their crimes. Such an extreme case occurs when the *commandement,* the ruling system which 'embraces the images and structures of power and coercion, the instruments and agents of their enactment, and a degree of rapport between those who give orders and those who are supposed to obey (without, of course, discussing) them' (Mbembe, 2001, 134) becomes fractured. When one examines the foundational oeuvre of Sembène Ousmane, for example, one realizes that some of his works structurally display the dynamics of 'biopower' in effect (Tcheuyap, 2008); moreover, the *commandement* is 'reduced to the right to demand, to force, to ban, to compel, to authorize, to punish, to reward, to be obeyed − in short, to enjoin and direct' (Mbembe, 2001, 32). The consequence is a death provoked by political assassination, which in *Guelwaar* is never investigated by the authorities.

2 Absent investigation and the triumph of the *commandement*

Although specific historical and ideological challenges resulted in the proliferation of discussions about the politics of film, it is, alternatively, possible to re-examine some foundational films, as well as others released since 1990, in relation to aesthetic patterns of crime films. In fact, a film like *Guelwaar* by Sembène Ousmane presents what Elana Gomel calls a setting of 'ontological crime', that is, a 'world where the action takes place [which] becomes an object of investigation, a mystery to be solved, a secret to be uncovered' (1995, 345). But beyond this generic similarity, what is essential is the set of narrative and discursive modalities governing the investigations that lead to the revelation of the truth. More importantly, it would be useful to examine not only the benefits of using generic categories to explore African cinemas, but also to look at the risks, theoretical challenges, pitfalls, and limits of a set of conventions that, according to Barry Keith Grant, 'threatens to overwhelm any distinctive national features that may be expressed in cinema' (2007, 105). In the specific case of Sembène Ousmane, for example, one can see that although no charges are laid against criminals, which means there is no formal investigation, the narrative itinerary of some characters helps to uncover the truth about specific crimes that have been committed in contexts where the police are either absent, corrupt, or in some cases, deliberately undermined by the criminal state. Most African films in which crime occurs usually involve not only criminal, but also social investigations, where Western rationality and 'the burden of proof' are most seriously challenged. This is the case in Sembène Ousmane's work, in which absent investigations speak to the lack of significance placed on criminal activity and the triumph of the *commandement*.

Guelwaar begins as a conventional crime movie. It opens with the death of Guelwaar, an elder who has openly criticized foreign aid. The film's central issue is the disappearance of his body, which has mistakenly been buried in a Muslim cemetery. The main role of Gora, the *gendarme* who appears early on, is not only to find Guelwaar's body but also to make sure the man is buried in accordance with Christian rites. However, the Muslims will not allow Christians in their cemetery. After the officer discovers that an administrative error has sent the body of a Christian to a Muslim grave, generating serious social unrest, several parts of the narrative movement become largely associated with the officer's trips to the village, where he has to negotiate in order to 'rescue' that body.

However, the enquiry into the location of Guelwaar's body takes precedence over the one that should have actually taken place, namely the circumstances surrounding his death. It ultimately comes to light that, in fact, the dissident was assassinated; like most crime films, *Guelwaar* opens with a murder; however, the viewer will only discover that this is the case very late in the narrative. Like all victims, Guelwaar is a character *in absentia*. The narrative structure provides several flashbacks that explain what happened. Before his assassination, which is not shown on screen, one flashback shows evidence that Guelwaar is wanted, or is at least under serious scrutiny, by the police. This flashback appears when Guelwaar's son Barthélémy goes to the police station to report the disappearance of his father's body, prodding Gora to begin investigating. Barthélémy's complaint sparks off the memory of the officer's meeting with the deceased person. During a conversation, after Gora says he remembers Guelwaar, there is a dissolve followed by a flashback. The past scene, as mentally relived by the officer and reproduced on the screen, takes place in the police station, where Guelwaar had come to complain about a group of vandals. As soon as the rebel comes in and presents his case, Gora and his colleague look at each other in a way that implies that they are aware that the complainant has a reputation for being a social dissenter and will thus be difficult. In the next shot, a close-up shows Gora opening a file in which one can read, 'Pierre Henri Thioune alias Guelwaar. Dissident.'[5] The final word is written in French and underlined several times. In this sequence, Guelwaar is obviously presented as a potential target, though he is not an outright criminal.

The exchange between Guelwaar and the officer clearly illustrates the rebellious attitude of the deceased. It is in fact an overstatement to say that he files a complaint, for Guelwaar actually comes to warn the police that he will take steps to protect women against vandals. His body language and his tone are not those of a citizen intimidated by authority; on the contrary, he points his finger threateningly at Gora when addressing him. He also puts his hat on the desk, maintains a firm voice, leans towards the officer when he speaks, and laughs at Gora. Finally, when the officer requests that his colleague write down a report of Guelwaar's complaint, the rebel takes out a signed petition and yells at the policeman before leaving. Guelwaar literally controls the official space where Gora is supposed to be the boss. As the police are generally notorious for their inclination to repression, Guelwaar's defiance and initiative are radical.

Other than to show Guelwaar's defiant attitude, this flashback sequence also functions, as in much crime fiction, to convey the distribution and status of knowledge. Here, it is clear that Guelwaar is less privileged than the viewer, who knows that his impertinence will undoubtedly be punished, and that there in fact exists a plot against him. This discrepancy corresponds to what François Jost (1987) calls a 'focalisation spectatorielle', the dramatic irony whereby the viewer has an epistemic advantage over the character. Guelwaar's predicament indicates the trajectory of victims in detective fiction. It also shows how criminal behaviour appears where it is least expected (in the state apparatus), as well as the corruption of the very authorities that are supposed to guarantee peace and order. His subsequent assassination, as announced in another flashback, is a motif in many crime films that depict political struggles; in every case, murder is used to end political disagreements and eradicate political dissidents.

After Gora goes back to the village, there is almost an open conflict between the Muslims and the Catholics. When the *Préfet* remembers the food aid rally, subjective camera and point-of-view shots replay in flashback the powerful speech Guelwaar gave which resulted in his murder. His (body) language, as well as camera movements, show the man in all his tragic majesty. There are several close-ups. His voice, absolutely firm, is the only audible sound. His threatening finger points at the corrupt elite and the passive populace. He is also often filmed from below, making most characters look tiny next to him. For an actor who is already tall, the fact of standing on a podium, with a voice that has silenced even the wind, there could not be a more efficient positioning. This very long speech could not be delivered at a better time, or, as it soon becomes clear, at a worse one, because the ceremony is in celebration of food aid. While he speaks, the local MP requests from Samba that Guelwaar be interrupted; Samba's reply is unambiguous: 'Don't worry. He has spoken for the last time in public.' After the flashback, Gora asks whether Guelwaar died at the hospital after the attack. The *Préfet* says Guelwaar's statements caused trouble 'en haut lieu'.[6] For viewers who recall that Barthélémy told Gora right from the beginning that Guelwaar died of internal bleeding after an attack, several questions arise: Who attacked and killed him? Who had an interest in having him killed? Who gained from his death?

Although the spectator can guess, the film does not provide any answers. Most troubling is the fact that no member of the victim's family knows what really happened, ignorance being a central motif of the diegesis. In spite of his endeavours and his rare professionalism, Gora, like the *Préfet*, limits himself to uncovering that a rebellious citizen was attacked and later died. In other words, a crime is depicted that seemingly does not warrant any emotion, not to say any investigation. Even when the stinking corpse is exhumed from the cemetery, there is no post-mortem, i.e. no autopsy, investigation or full report leading to the perpetrator's identity. The viewer has to assemble various elements of the puzzle to come up with a conclusion: as suggested by Samba to MP Fall, in all likelihood Guelwaar was assassinated because of his opinions. In the unfolding of the plot, the most important aspect of the crime, namely its commission, is absent. Although there is an investigation, it is really a misguided investigation into nothing, as it deals with the disappearance of the body instead of the reason for its taking place to begin with. Generally, in crime films, a detective finds a body and has to investigate a murder; in *Guelwaar*, an investigation concerning a body actually covers up the commission of a murder.

The drama that unfolds in *Guelwaar* paints a good picture of postcolonial socio-political landscapes where murder has become normal. In this case, one can understand Pius Ngandu Nkashama's and Jean-Pierre Bekolo's concern that crime fiction has a different resonance in Africa, because the State, notorious for its authoritarianism and corruption, would be subject to examination. Any such investigation on the part of a filmmaker would be suicidal. As Wendy Knepper (2006) puts it in her study of postcolonial post-mortems, examining the body of the victim and the body politic are inseparable gestures; she writes, 'the body of the victim is transformed into a site of multiple investigations and subject to many, often overlapping or intersecting modes of analysis and meaning' (39). The risk associated with a close enquiry may account for Sembène Ousmane's cinematic subversions of the conventions of crime fiction. Ousmane exposes crimes without investigations and structures his films in a way that may make a murder, however central it might be in other films, a peripheral element in a larger unfolding social drama. Such constructions speak to the authority of Mbembe's triumphant postcolonial *commandement,* which is nothing but 'a series of corporate institutions and political machinery that, once in place, constitute a distinctive machine of violence' (2001, 102), all too notorious for its 'systematic application of pain' (2001, 103). The right to kill, the 'biopower', characteristic of postcolonial domination and arbitrary discipline, becomes the most significant driving force behind crime fictions without investigations, where the murderer, the criminal, is the State. However, things have begun to change; the *commandement* is cracking.

3   Flawed investigations and the decline of the *commandement*

The interrogation of the relationship between postcolonial subjectivity, government, and the political economy of death as exposed in detective narratives requires a completely new epistemology given contemporary transformations in African society as well as the new aesthetic innovations in fiction. The previous analysis of Sembène Ousmane's film illustrates not only the banality of death in the (post)colony as persuasively analysed by Achille Mbembe, but also the absence of criminal investigations. Recent productions do not provide any significant evidence the *commandement* is able and willing to address coherent concerns about untimely death. Although the economy and the modalities of death are different in Moussa Sène Absa's *Madame Brouette* and Jean-Pierre Bekolo's *Les Saignantes*, investigative work is shoddy in both films, leading viewers to question the legitimacy of the forces of justice. The murder in *Madame Brouette* leads to incarceration whereas the death in *Les Saignantes* results in a complicated process whereby the disappearance of a minister goes undiscovered by the police. Beyond expressing a cynical and hopeless disillusionment with society, these two films complement that of Sembène Ousmane in another sense, using other aesthetic and discursive strategies. While the investigation in *Guelwaar* should have established that the suspicious death is the result of a crime, in *Les Saignantes,* Jean-Pierre Bekolo establishes a 'fake,' flawed investigation, which allows a girl to cover up an accidental death and enables the subsequent crimes she commits.

Bekolo's film opens with the sexual encounter of Majolie and an old high-ranking official, the Secretary General of the Civil Cabinet (SGCC), during which the latter suddenly dies. The unexpected situation to be dealt with is that Majolie has become responsible for the death of a top official who was about to give her a government contract before collapsing 'on (sexual) duty'. Interestingly, the 'emergency number' Majolie calls is not that of the police but of her best friend Chouchou, whom she enlists to help her get rid of the corpse. The rest of the narrative construction traces the adventures they go through in order to dispose of the body, rebuild it, and determine strategies to advance their own careers.

While it would be an overstatement to say that Majolie committed a murder, it is fair to say that the corpse requires a post-mortem, at the minimum. Majolie and Chouchou subsequently undertake a series of macabre initiatives to 'manage' what thus becomes a veritable crime. Under Chouchou's initiative, they try to make the corpse disappear. They take it first to the local butcher, who accepts money to chop the 'SGCC prime beef' and mix it with the meat sold to the public. The butcher breaks down in tears when he miraculously realizes, after tasting a piece, that the 'meat' is the SGCC. He continues rendering the meat after being bribed further, but in order to avoid any suspicion, he chops off the head and gives it back to the two women; this does not dispel the danger, for they still have a 'piece' of the SGCC. They head to Essomba the mortician and pay him to attach the SGCC's head to a new body. Although what he is doing is clearly illegal, Essomba is compelled by his love of money.

As Majolie and Chouchou try to find their way out of the situation, there is a general awareness in the official circles about the disappearance of the SGCC, which leads to some suspicion and eventually an investigation. Two policemen, Mamba and Rokko, do not pay special attention to the enquiry; in fact, the two officers argue about the very need for an investigation. Mamba asserts that the face of the 'enemy' has changed from a savage beast to a more 'sophisticated' self. Refusing to abandon his duties, the naïve and optimistic Rokko proceeds to Chouchou's house and continues the investigation. When he introduces himself to her mother and asks about her whereabouts, Chouchou and Majolie are alerted to his presence and escape through the window. He searches the house and retrieves a piece of meat in a plastic bag. Ghostly women wearing red headscarves suddenly surround Inspector Rokko. He fires his weapon, disappears, and is next seen at the hospital. The crime remains unresolved and the policemen are defeated. The 'investigation', which is a futile, unprofessional search, continues until the funeral, where the widow of the SGCC discovers that the body in the casket is not her husband's. Even this discovery does not create the reaction that might have been expected. Every initiative to understand the macabre reconstruction by the two girls is thwarted because they get involved with the minister in charge of security. The cover-up is never revealed in spite of the complaints and near hysteria of the SGCC's relatives. Chouchou and Majolie hence appear to be 'perfect' lawbreakers, for they use their physical attractiveness to prevent any investigation. Although Majolie did not kill her sexual partner deliberately, she and Chouchou subsequently break the law in many ways, remaining unpunished at the film's conclusion.

Unlike *Les Saignantes*, Moussa Sène Absa's film is, from a narratological perspective, less fragmented, and structured like a more conventional crime film. It starts with an actual murder. In the very first shots, Naago enters his residence to find his wife Mati facing him with a gun pointed directly at him. After convincing her to lower the gun, he forcefully removes it from her and proceeds to beat her. The camera moves outside, and shots are heard from within. Until the final moments of the film, the audience does not know exactly what happened. Naago is shown stumbling out of the bedroom, bleeding, and immediately dies. As in many traditional crime movies, a murder has just occurred and the task of the viewer is to fill the gap, answering the crucial question that the police investigation must resolve: who is the killer?

The first 'investigator' is not a policeman, but rather a television journalist who comically covers the story, promising the audience full in-depth coverage of the death. The police later show up, but instead of undertaking a systematic enquiry, the chief, Colombo, asks Mati to recount what happened. From here on, Mati's flashback recounts how she became involved with the boyfriend who has just been killed. The journalist seems more active than the police; both 'investigators' are featured in the same or consecutive sequences that show how their strategies to discover the facts either complement or compete with each other. The journalist appears in four scenes, always surrounded by a crowd seeking his opinions on the matter. The first significant police intervention occurs toward the end of the film, when Colombo arrests Boy Che and London Pipe for having burned down houses in order to develop a local business. In one of the very few scenes not presented in flashback, Mati admits to having killed Naago. However, a sequence near the end of the film reveals that she and her little daughter Ndeye collaborated in shooting Naago. After the police announce Mati's arrest and take her away, a group of children are shown running ahead of the cruiser containing the unrepentant woman after an investigation that is anything but by the book.

The conclusions of *Madame Brouette* and *Les Saignantes* raise important questions about the cinematic discourse and strategy of contemporary postcolonial subjectivities. Are African police and other institutions doomed? What does it mean to represent African institutions, especially the police, in the twenty-first century? How should the murder of a police officer, Naago, be interpreted? Why does Bekolo first use captions to put forward metaquestions that stress the impossibility of shooting a crime film in postcolonial Cameroon and then direct a film in which crimes go unpunished and the police remain largely ineffectual? Is there a link between the fragmentations of both narratives, their striking directorial techniques, and a discourse on death (or, as a matter of fact, life) and the inefficiency of the police 'investigation' in both films?

The formula of conventional detective films consists of the commission of a crime, followed by the identification of suspects, leading ultimately to the death or arrest of the outlaw. When such a conclusion occurs in *Madame Brouette,* it is less the result of investigative expertise than that of thwarted and half-baked imbroglios. It is equally clear that the policemen in *Les Saignantes* are not at all interested in following proper procedure for the enquiry. Several factors contribute to its ultimate failure. Mamba, who questions the validity of any interrogation and keeps discouraging his younger colleague Rokko from taking any initiative, is jaded and refuses to investigate the disappearance of the SGCC, which he does not consider his business. Rather than work, he prefers to drink on the job. The minister who is supposed to cooperate with the police dismisses all the concerns presented by officer Rokko. When Natu presents Rokko with evidence that could damage the minister's reputation, a flash-forward shows the minister attempting to bribe the officer. The incompetence of the police is further exaggerated by magical human apparitions. The women in red headscarves who symbolize the *Mevungu*[7] regularly interrupt the investigation when officer Rokko searches Majolie's house. His gun, symbolic surrogate of the phallus, is nearly taken away from him, magically moving in and out of his purse in ways beyond his control. When he tries to shoot the female apparitions, he realizes he has shot into a vacuum and is transported to the hospital. A similar situation happens in an earlier sequence when a woman passing by steals his weapon and he powerlessly watches the movements of his gun in and out of his pocket. The police in this film, notably Rokko, it is clear, are made hopelessly impotent in *Les Saignantes* by women seeking to fulfil their plans.

The mystical impotence of the police in Bekolo's film is further illustrated by a key formal feature: lighting. Literally, *Les Saignantes* is a 'film noir' not simply because of the macabre constructions that correlate corruption, cannibalism and sex. It is shot from beginning to end in a continuous night, with very high contrast lighting of its dystopian African setting. The colour scheme of the film evokes mystery, danger and tension. Some surreal colour tonalities accentuate the 'noir' nature of the narrative: white flashes/moon, red hue, extravagant make-up, etc. The chilling lighting effects give the film a sombre atmosphere. Death is everywhere;

we are unsure whether characters are dead or alive, a fact compounded by a voice-over's announcement, 'We are all dead'. The mysterious women at Chouchou's house, apart from their frightening voice-overs throughout the film, are physically present to help the mother make dinner, but intermittently appear and disappear to embarrass the police or talk to the girls. We are thus meant to inhabit a supernatural, dreamlike world where death, sex and corruption govern, as emphasized by the relentless hip hop soundtrack in the background. The sequences, usually fast-paced, are purposely slowed down to highlight either the protagonist's dialogue or the film's sexual and erotic elements. As in his earlier films, Bekolo makes regular use of rapid, jump-cut, music-video style editing.

The most striking commonality in *Les Saignantes* and *Madame Brouette* is the incompetence of the police. Moussa Sène Absa's film is certainly a crime film insofar as it portrays a murder mystery with investigators. Nevertheless, from the beginning, the efficacy of these authorities is questionable. Instead of having the detective uncover the events and details, the motive for the crime is portrayed through flashbacks detailing Mati's life and occurrences that led to the crime, thus allowing an understanding of the characters and setting. We see the police arriving late on the crime scene, after the entire neighbourhood has gathered and the reporters have set up their equipment. Further, the reporters seem keener about the investigation than the inspectors themselves. This scene demonstrates the incompetence of authorities and questions their effectiveness. Naago, the deceased, was himself a corrupt police officer. He is surrounded by many shady people, including prostitutes and the local pimp and gangster London Pipe. The police officers conducting the 'investigations' are rather comedic characters. Colombo's humorous details parallel his outlandish theories and his inability to conduct a proper search. The only 'professional' demonstration is a humorous segment in which he relates his theories to the chief. Colombo concludes that Naago must have committed suicide because the weapon belonged to him. The most insightful informants about the crime are witnesses interviewed by the journalist to whom the police chief expresses his frustration.

One fundamental element that outlines the flaws of the police and the decline of the *commandement* is the role of sex in the narratives. While *Les Saignantes* displays the classic models of the femme fatale – that is, cynical, double-crossing, conniving and dangerous subjects – *Madame Brouette* also offers proof that 'the postcolony is a world of anxious virility, a world hostile to continence, frugality, sobriety' (Mbembe, 2001, 110). Majolie and Chouchou take advantage of their sexuality to advance their careers and get contracts. When the SGCC succumbs, they succeed, partly with the help of the *Mevungu,* in annihilating any investigation. They seduce another minister whose attention is completely distracted by them even during official funerals. Most importantly, they succeed in escaping from any control and remain free at the end of the narrative. In *Madame Brouette,* in addition to his corruption, Naago is a lecherous, incompetent officer. Not only does he entertain multiple simultaneous relationships, but he also covers up for London Pipe, a smuggler and a pimp. Apart from his comic theories, Colombo cannot keep the city secure because his institution is infiltrated by organized crime: the money Naago owes London forces him to be silent about his creditor's shady businesses, to which he also substantially contributes. Early in the film, Naago is on duty when he suddenly leaves his post after seeing Mati. In *Les Saignantes,* two ministers are involved in sexual distractions, and the two investigating officers are professional failures because of corruption. All these characters offer evidence that 'the mouth, the belly, and the penis constitute classic ingredients of *commandement* in the postcolony' (Mbembe, 2001, 126). With the death of the SGCC and Naago, these films also reveal that the lure of bodily pleasures causes the postcolonial *commandement* to become vulnerable. It is significant that a top-ranking official collapses during sex and that the murder of an officer is perpetrated by his abused lover; that all such dramas are set forth in non-linear, labyrinthine, at times chaotic ways clearly indicates that postcolonial regimes are not immune from unusual cataclysms. After mastering the carnivorous 'biopower', postcolonial institutions are in turn devoured. Unlike some other unconventional crime fiction, the films of Bekolo and Absa do not stop with caricaturing investigations. They investigate the dealings of a top-ranking official and a police officer rather than those of ordinary citizens. The *commandement* is under attack, infiltrated and weakened, if not defeated. The socialization of pain is reversed, and death now becomes a signifier that can infect the postcolonial state, which consequently loses its power to choose which citizens are entitled to life or death. That is a major transformation of the genre which speaks to the innovations and 'indigenization' of detective narratives.

One final point concerning the aesthetics of crime in both films is the postmodern dissolution of categories and boundaries, or the ways status shifts in a new context. Although both narratives have been examined as crime fiction, they clearly contain elements drawn from several different genres. *Les Saignantes* combines elements of science fiction, action and even tragedy. It is in fact possible for these films to belong to all the categories the captions in the film state are impossible for African cinema. In *Madame Brouette,* the investigation turns into a farce and ultimately into musical comedy.[8] The crime in fact occurs largely in self-defence, as Naago was killed when he was about to further abuse his partner. Mati's own admission of guilt, which would have been mitigated by details revealed if an investigation had taken place, seals her fate. Because there is rarely a 'good' enough reason for a citizen (unlike the State) to commit a crime, she is arrested. However, by releasing the birds from her tree and giving it to her daughter, she ends the narrative in an almost victorious manner, with no remorse. To make her status even more complex, although she is a murderer, she is a criminal in the same sense as Naago. Mati and her lover both break the law, but in different circumstances. In the postcolonial context where the institutional apparatus is the prime criminal, it becomes difficult to agree with Thomas Leitch that the 'contradictory double project' according to which 'the central function of crime film' is 'to allow viewers to experience the vicarious thrills of criminal behaviour while leaving them free to condemn this behaviour, whoever is practising it, as immoral' (2002, 16, 306). It would be abstruse, in view of the films just discussed, to establish a dualistic description of crime. Considering the language, the names of characters, the anecdotes and the situations, which are clearly targeted at African viewers, one can comfortably state that apart from *Guelwaar,* these viewers probably identify with the criminals of the other films because they successfully set out to crack the postcolonial *commandement* that has made Africa so rife with crime. Contrary to the type of identification that Nicole Rafter discusses in *Shots in the Mirror* (2006, 11) regarding mainstream crime films, the African viewer cannot feel reassured that the society and the criminal justice system are salvageable. Given the state sponsored murder in *Guelwaar* and the rampant corruption in the other films, 'criminal' behaviour becomes an existential urgency, and private justice functions as the only successful challenge to the carnivorous *commandement.*

The aim of this chapter was to examine the emergence of crimes in African films, which shape the construction of new postcolonial subjectivities. In these films, killing has escaped the purview of institutions and become privatized. The result has been a radical transformation in the way the *commandement* is perceived. Because of its own weaknesses, especially with regard to its corruptibility and its propensity to fornication, ordinary people are now able to seriously destabilize social institutions. The fragility of the *commandement* is visible in *Madame Brouette* and *Les Saignantes,* where the state-sanctioned right to kill demonstrated in *Guelwaar* has disappeared. From now on, in postcolonial settings, the moral and social significance of crime changes.

These films also illustrate how African cinema interrogates the paradigms of crime, truth and guilt, the notion of a foundational or universal Western rationality, and the possibility of its representation. It is generally subaltern and peripheral productions that have radically undertaken the transformations of crime fiction, mostly by deconstructing state authorities. In such a case, the definition of justice, a conceptual precept of modernity, becomes obsolete and must be reinvented by individuals whose supposedly criminal actions actually protect them from the corrupt system. This 'neo-crime fiction' is, for Rafter, an 'alternative or critical tradition of crime films' (2006, 51; 213–233) because it challenges the canons of mainstream crime films and is typical of a new narrative and rational order in which semiotic roles and legal categories are destabilized. Instead of a happy ending, stereotypical heroes, and clear-cut morals, filmmakers working in this genre opt for ambiguity and irrationality. All these transformations in African films are also present in subversive non-Western critiques of 'modernity' as a social or theoretical project and its attendant discourse on rationality and truth, of which the detective fiction is an extension.

Notes

1 French original: '*la production des vingt dernières années ne révèle à aucun moment l'épanouissement d'un type de composition inédit. La très grande majorité des créations tant soit peu originales de cette période investissent le modèle narratif du roman noir: un enquêteur privé ou fonctionnarisé, en même temps qu'il élucide un crime, dévoile les aspects d'un milieu et / ou d'une problématique sociohistorique spécifiques.*'

2 Original: '*Le roman policier est, de tous les tests et de toutes les enquêtes, le livre le plus lu ou le plus consommé en Afrique. Le plus disponible aussi …*'

3 '*La fiction romanesque du policier ne peut nullement évoluer sur deux plans contradictoires; à savoir, la quête de la vérité et la dénonciation du système dans lequel*

est menée cette quête, ou qui fonde le principe de la vérité. Il apparaît constamment comme un sentiment de frustration, dans la mesure où la relation au sujet et à la thématique qui le porte est souvent décalée, énonciativement, par rapport à la méthode de narration'.

4 *'La croyance à la vengeance du mort qui revient hanter son meurtrier par-delà la tombe ... suffit à elle seule pour prédisposer à des attitudes non-romanesques 'policièrement'. Si l'esprit du défunt peut tirer vengeance, s'"accaparer de l'âme de son meurtrier", poursuivre en fantôme ses rêves, ses hallucinations, éparpiller ses facultés mentales, il devient superflu d'entreprendre une recherche d'indices. Celui-ci est déjà condamné à lui-même sans qu'il soit nécessaire de recourir à d'autres juridictions' (Ibid).*

5 'Dissident' is a very imperfect translation of the French 'élément incontrolable' which best describes the personality of the deceased rebel.

6 'in the upper hierarchy'.

7 The *Mevungu* is a female mystical cult in Southern Cameroon. It performs specific social roles and holds power beyond male control. In this film, they succeed in frightening the police and making all their action impossible.

8 For more on that, see Sheila Petty, 'The Rise of the African Musical: Postcolonial Disjunction in *Karmen Geï* and *Madame Brouette*', *Journal of African Cinemas*, Volume 1, 1 (2009), 95–112.

14 Sembène Ousmane, *Guelwaar*

15 Moussa Sène Absa, *Madame Brouette*

16   Sembène Ousmane, *Guelwaar*

17   Mansour Sora Wade, *Ndeysaan*

18   Jean-Marie Teno, *Clando*

19   Moussa Sène Absa

Chapter 4

Myth, tragedy and cinema

Postcolonial films are now starting to portray different types of individuals, with personal rather than collective agendas that they implement by all means available, and who do not hesitate to use sexual desire or 'bottom power' to achieve their goals. The teenage girls in Jean-Pierre Bekolo's *Les Saignantes* are young femmes fatales: cynical, double-crossing and conniving, they use their corporeal bodies to realize selfish goals. Mati's fate in *Madame Brouette* is sealed by the 'curse' of a beautifully framed body on which the camera and Naago's gaze insistently focus. The viewer is accordingly not surprised that an affair starts between the woman and the lecherous policeman. The crimes and murders examined in the previous chapter have sexual components: even Guelwaar, the village hero, is all too human in his penchant for fornication and extra-marital affairs. Another prime example is in *Yeelen* (Souleymane Cissé, Mali, 1987) where the main protagonist, Nianankoro, ends up having sex with Fatou, the king's wife, whose infertility he was supposed to cure. After a quick shot of her attractive breasts, the next scene shows both characters at the palace, where the young boy is apologizing because 'his penis has betrayed him'. Perhaps these examples explain Achille Mbembe's reduction of postcolonial male subjects and *commandement* to 'perpetual erection'. In any case, these narratives reveal at least one thing: sex is a curse, with tragic consequences. Historically, especially in Western societies, *desire and virility* are mythically associated with the Fall, fatality and destruction. Although the films just mentioned emerge from different social and historical contexts, a common theme arises from them, namely the dangers of (unfulfilled) desire which, according to Kenneth Harrow (2010), is one of the causes for the irreversible abatement (and fall) of the domineering, dangerous, authoritarian and patriarchal postcolonial authority.

This purpose of this chapter is to look at the interplay of myth and tragedy in films where overwhelming desire is the principal force that drives the plot. After looking at the possibility of African tragic forms, I will determine oedipal and other dramas at play in families that experience a severe crisis in situations reminiscent of Greek and biblical myths. There will follow an examination of the link between the power of oracles who, as forecasters of the future, convey messages of both terrifying judgements and unwavering hope. This chapter argues that postcolonial films depict cultures as porous, displaying unlikely affinities. It further shows how the hero, when present, no longer takes the form of the rebellious militant or freedom fighter; in the cinema of today, he or she is just an ordinary subject whose inability to master desire can be fatal.

1   On African cultural 'specificity' and tragic forms

In several of their studies, Nwachukwu Frank Ukadike and Manthia Diawara uncover connections between African films and indigenous cultures. Ukadike argues that films from the 1970s and 1980s are rooted in traditional storytelling strategies 'towards which *almost all* filmmakers now lean and to which *the level of [their] maturity* is attributed' (1994, 166, my emphasis). He further notes, emphatically (201), that 'black' postcolonial narratives are built around 'African traditions' and forms that utilize cultural associations 'in a unique fashion *no foreigner* is capable of providing' (202, my emphasis). As for Diawara, he compares filmmakers to the traditional bard, 'looking particularly at their reproduction of traditional modes of being, so as to show similarities and differences between their work'. He also examines how filmmakers import 'oral storytelling forms' (Diawara, 1996, 210) and popular culture in films for aesthetic, ideological and pragmatic purposes. For the critic and the artist, the task is challenging; Diawara elaborates,

> [t]o analyze African cinema, one must first understand that
> twenty-five years of film production has necessarily created an
> aesthetic tradition which African film-makers use as a point of
> reference which they follow or contest. An African aesthetic
> does not come merely from European cinema. To avoid making
> African cinema into an imperfect appendix to European cinema,

one must question Africa itself, and African traditions, to
discover the originality of its films. (1996, 209–210)

The views of Diawara and Ukadike, although relevant, are limited. Their
perception of 'specificity' is only true of a certain number of films,
especially those addressed in Diawara's typology: the 'quest for social and
economic justice' is mostly illustrated in social realist films; the search for
identity appears in films in the 'return to the source' category which rejects
colonial oppression through the rehabilitation of African cultures; and the
recovering of mutilated African histories is central to 'confrontation' films
(1992, 164). Sembène Ousmane's contention that the African artist is a
griot in his commitment to addressing social evils, in view of the recent
trends in African cinema, is, along with this idea of 'specificity,' reductionist
in several ways. The first, as indicated by Eileen Julien (1992), is that there
is something fundamentally 'oral' about African narrative praxis, a
consideration that would problematically allow orality to become a
metonym for Africa. The second is another kind of essentialism that would
imply that African filmmakers, like the novelist analysed by Mohamadou
Kane in his study 'Sur les formes traditionnelles du roman africain' (1974),
have probably only been exposed to African tales, and that the evening
story sessions are the only cultural experiences available to them. Such an
argument implies that these traditional narratives are the sole influences on
African productions. Finally, and most relevantly, we must note the
persistence of an essentialist, exclusivist and oppositional scholarship. Why
must postcolonial directors always refer to canons or norms that they
'follow or contest' (Diawara)? Can African films only be 'original' when
echoing indigenous 'traditions'? Is it not possible to come to terms with the
fact that, to borrow from Tommie Shelby (2005, 176), various forces create
an artistic dynamism and hybridity and thus foreclose the possibility of a
homogeneous cultural identity? Is Africa such an island, even after colonial
traumas? Must African subjectivities be situated only at one or the other
end of a cultural spectrum? Is there not on the contrary a point of
intersection, of mutual (and even beneficial) cultural gain?

Interestingly, neither Diawara nor Ukadike completely rejects the idea
that foreign influences must be downplayed in order to establish an
'original' cinematic tradition. Among the benefits of exposure to Western
education through globalization is the fact that African artists can borrow
from, or connect with, different cultures. They do not necessarily need to

leave their country in order to be global subjects. That was already the case with avant-gardist Djibril Diop Mambéty, who adapted the novel of a Swiss author for the screen. Joseph Gaï Ramaka also recently directed *Karmen Geï*, an African version of Carmen. In doing so these filmmakers illustrate Josias Semujanga's theory of literature as 'transculture' (1999), which considers art as a universal heritage, a sort of 'data bank' from which anyone can borrow. Furthermore, the features of current productions compel us to consider cinema in relation to other categories, cultures or genres that were not necessarily present in earlier films. Kenneth Harrow is right to state that it is time for 'a revolution against the old, tired formulas deployed in justification of filmmaking practices that have not substantially changed in forty years. Time for new voices, a new paradigm, a new view – a new Aristotle to invent the poetics we need today' (2007, xi). Why this reference to the Greek theoretician of tragedy?

For Harrow, the 'revolution' is suggested by recent productions that indicate that 'we have entered into the time when new voices can emerge in the crack of the text' (2007, 9). These new voices require original theoretical models that can breathe new life into overplayed ideological/cultural rhetoric, among which are conceptions of African storytelling and *cinéma engagé*. Most post-1990 African films do not fit into the aforementioned perceptions of 'specificity', and are directed by a generation of filmmakers who do not feel part of the 'Sembène School'.[1] These films explore in new ways questions of desire and the (sometimes dangerous) power of Eros. Myths and tragedies, coming from 'alien' contexts, are nevertheless present in the African context with films such as *Yeelen, La Genèse* (Cheick Oumar Sissoko, Mali, 1999), *Ndeysaan, The Price of Forgiveness* (Mansour Sora Wade, Senegal, 2001), *Adanggaman* (Roger Ngoan M'Balla, Côte d'Ivoire, 2000), *Tilaï* (1990) and *La Colère des Dieux* (Idrissa Ouedraogo, Burkina Faso, 2003). Oedipal motifs generated 'because of women' or hatred between brothers recalling the Biblical conflict of Cain and Abel are the main constructions that appear in these films, where clitoral power often proves disastrous. They are tragic narratives, describing a world of chaos, violence and destruction, where, in Etienne Souriau's words, 'any action whose sequence of situations signals the deadly progression of the central microcosm towards its own destruction'[2] (Souriau, 1970, 54). But what are myth and tragedy? How can they be imported in African cinema, especially today? Are these categories even 'African' at all and at home in film? If so, how?

It is always challenging to provide a generic definition of complex literary concepts like myth and tragedy. Isidore Okpewho's conception of myth best illustrates the plots in the narratives considered in this chapter: 'The word *myth* has ... frequently been used for describing a tale in which gods or divinities recognized by a community of people ... are the protagonists and which is therefore thought to have a sacred, serious, and authoritative character' (1992, 181). As far as tragedy is concerned, it appears to be more difficult to specify, and 'is nothing if not notoriously slippery as a concept' (Quayson, 2003, 59). In *The Death of Tragedy* (1980), after giving a series of explanations about this concept, George Steiner concludes that 'any neat abstract definition would mean nothing' (9). It is much easier to illustrate, following the Aristotelian conception, what constitutes a 'true' tragedy: the murder of a father, a brother or a son, or the narration of tragic situations which generally generate deep sorrow (Aristotle, 1990, 1453b–15). However, it is important to indicate, as will be shown in subsequent sections, that although they have social consequences, tragedies generally originate from the family unit, where the discovery of a secret results in a destructive outcome. In the history of tragic forms, the Oedipus complex plays an important role; although it is a prominent motif in much African cinema, doubts remain whether it is in fact applicable to this tradition.

After the release of his film *Tilaï,* Idrissa Ouedraogo made an interesting comment: 'I hadn't realized it, but it is a Greek tragedy' (in Barlet, 2000, 63). Although regularly mentioned in passing, the evident Greek intertextuality in this film has never been analysed by scholars. According to Manthia Diawara, *Tilaï* reveals a postmodern discourse with the 'Oedipus drama' it unfolds (1992, 164). Roy Armes writes that 'Most critics, both African and western, have experienced [*Tilaï*] as a tragedy in the Greek sense, dealing with universal human values and laws. Certainly the law is absolute here and the tale has strong Oedipal overtones' (2006, 126). David Murphy and Patrick Williams equally have described this film as 'an extremely complex tragedy, which explores the conflicting forces of family, social convention and love' (2007, 152–153).

In *The Athenian Sun in an African Sky*: *Modern African Adaptations of Classical Greek Tragedy*, Kevin Wetmore also highlights several reasons why African playwrights imported Greek tragedy into their plays. The main impetus is that it was much easier for them to use these 'canonical texts' as a vehicle for social and political commentary because they portrayed archetypal struggles. In this way, 'Greek tragedy becomes the vector by which the message of resistance to oppression is delivered to an audience' (2002, 35). The above references indicate that imagination is borderless, transnational and 'transcultural', that its scope is unlimited.[3] That is particularly true of the myth, as long indicated in Wole Soyinka's *Myth, Literature and the African World* (1976). Isidore Okpewho also clearly illustrates this fact:

> One interesting point about the mythic imagination is its tendency to appropriate material from wherever it may come, and perhaps the greatest boon to the oral tradition is the way it has transcended its own culture and swelled its repertory with material from the literate culture that steadily threatens to overtake it. (1983, 110)

It is within that framework that this chapter examines how postcolonial films position themselves within transnational circulations by constructing tragic narratives that illustrate, challenge or mirror some known foundational 'foreign' myths or tragedies. By involving ungovernable sons, doomed princes, enemy brothers, tragic oracles and, especially, by linking every conflict with an uncontrollable male *desire* to possess a rebellious woman, African directors show how myth and tragedy connect to reveal families in deep crisis.

2 Oedipal conflicts, enemy brothers and families in crisis

Discussing the possibility of an 'African Oedipus' generally raises a lot of 'anxieties' about cultural specificities. Although I would not state, like Marthe Robert, that 'the Oedipus complex is a universal phenomenon, [and] all fiction, invention and image making expresses it more or less explicitly' (1980, 31), it is nonetheless unmistakable that several of its patterns are transparent in African productions. However, in his seminal study *Black Skin, White Masks*, Frantz Fanon categorically indicates that because Sigmund Freud and other psychoanalysts never considered any African subjects, their findings do not apply to them. He writes: 'Like it or not, the Oedipus complex is far from coming into being among Negroes' (1967, 151–152). One other strong charge against psychoanalytic models is from Ibrahim Sow (1977) whose archaeology of the African subject involves a cultural and social component, unlike the Western one that is purely individualistic. In *Psychiatrie dynamique africaine,* he clearly dismisses the possibility of applying Freud's models to African people. Jacques Lacan also refers to the Oedipus theory in a Sudanese context as 'a rather thin joke … a very tiny detail within an immense myth' (1988, 86). Although he largely uses psychoanalytic categories, Neil Ten Kortenaar contends that 'The application of psychoanalysis to uncover African literature has also proven problematic when not disastrous. Those European scholars who have sought Oedipus in Africa … either ignore colonization or [make] it seem inevitable' (2007, 183). It is manifest that for these scholars, the Oedipus paradigm can only forcefully be associated with Africa. Psychoanalysis was born in specific social, political, cultural and economic contexts. This foundational narrative involves a relationship triangle, namely the ascension of a son who kills the father in order to take over the mother. The challenge for the critic is to determine if all components of the triangle need be in place to allow for a psychoanalytic interpretation. For instance, need the father be the 'real' father, and *must* there be a woman for a tragic conflict to occur with the son? Are the roles of father and mother the same in African cultures as in Western ones? Does the son have to *literally* murder his father? Must he *actually* be involved with his 'real' mother? In other words, is it possible to interpret the myth metaphorically?

In spite of the understandable discomfort with Freud's theories, one must mention the work of Edmond and Marie-Cecile Ortigues, whose *Oedipe africain* (1966) helped contextualize the Freudian paradigms. For them, father and son do not share the same relationship in Africa: 'In the European model of the Oedipus complex, the son imagines that he will kill the father. Here is the rather typical pattern: through the intermediary of the father the son relates to the ancestor, who is already dead and therefore beyond any attack, and constitutes his brothers as rivals' (106).[4] In *Le Regard de l'autre,* J. B. Fotso Djemo (1982) also advocates for this necessary contextualization. The author is very careful to neither completely reject nor blindly apply Freudian hermeneutics in the context of Africa. The father, who functions as superego within the contexts of many households, has different roles depending on his age and domestic situation. That recalls the 'collective phallus' (the father's peers) discussed by the Ortigues. Finally, Fotso Djemo, as well as the Ortigues and even Sow, clearly refers to the 'fathers' as 'inégalable/matchless' and 'inattaquable/indisputable'. With this idea of rivalry and collective political phallus, Hortense Spillers' comment becomes useful: for her, the 'African Oedipus' simply generates a new symbolic order, and the word 'father' designates *a function,* not a 'genitor' (1996, 732). In fact, her perception is close to Sow's, who does not completely dismiss psychoanalysis, but emphasizes the *context* in which it may appear. For him, the possibility of an African Oedipus can only be different from its manifestation in Sophocles's tragedy and be articulated *differently* around the mechanics of power. In all cases, the symbolic order survives through repression and reproduces itself through violence.

Some examples show how these contested categories may vary. In *African Experiences of Cinema,* Mbye Cham mentions 'father-son rivalry and fights for power' (1996, 11). Although they do not use psychoanalytic categories, one can reasonably contend that by referring to the tragic form, Diawara, Armes and Murphy and Williams allow for possible Oedipus formations that need attention, interrogation and possibly contextualization. Does the 'multiplicity of fathers' in African contexts, as acknowledged by all these scholars, not occasion confrontations that challenge the symbolic order? Given the proliferation of tyrannical 'Fathers of the nations' that have plagued African countries in the last fifty years, is their murder not a necessity? Although 'loving' the mother is not present in all cases, there are multiple occurrences of father-son violent confrontations in African literature or cinema. Although he emphatically argues that (social) 'tragedy is pushed on Africa', that Africa is purely 'manufactured' as tragic (in Ukadike, 2002, 220) and that he does not think a narrative form must inspire pity or fear as is the case with tragedy, Jean-Pierre Bekolo also illustrates some points that make the death of the father a social and historical necessity:

> many African filmmakers are rooted in this tradition of
> respecting the elders … but at the same time, you cannot
> respect an elder who is keeping you down or preventing you
> from moving with the times. You cannot respect a corrupt father
> who is selling your future. That is why I say the younger
> generation should eliminate all the dinosaurs …. (Ukadike,
> 2002, 235)

In Chinua Achebe's novel *Things Fall Apart,* Okonkwo is obsessed with the father he would not want to be or wishes he did not have. Similarly, in

Ferdinand Oyono's *Houseboy* the young Toundi, a little boy, wants to kill his brutal father, at least in a symbolic sense. In several parts of his *Violence and the Sacred,* René Girard points out many similarities between Oedipus and some African cultural archetypes. Although some take issue with the label 'Oedipus', one cannot ignore that the tragic desire for wish fulfilment is identifiable in multiple societies. Uzoma Esonwanne writes that 'psychoanalysis and African literature have long maintained a studious, if not wary, distance from each other' (2007, 140). Maybe, he further argues, it is time to end this 'mutual exclusion' and initiate 'mutually productive dialogue' (142) that would help better interpret cultural products. In his study of *Les Saignantes,* Harrow (2010) elaborates on the active degradation and loss of patriarchy. The fallen father has been replaced by an equally threatening female figure. Her use (and abuse) of clitoral powers humiliates degenerate, licentious and greedy elders. Whether because of male or female rebels, the father is therefore dead. Why, then, such a 'postcolonial resistance' to psychoanalysis on the part of Africanists like Fanon?

Perhaps Fanon has been inattentively read. At the very least, it is clear that critics have consistently failed to identify what appears to be a contradiction in his thought. For in spite of his reservations, Fanon states:

> There are close connections between the structure of the family and the structure of the nation. Militarization and the centralization of authority in a country automatically entail a resurgence of the authority of the father. In Europe and in every country characterized as civilized or civilizing, the family is a miniature of the nation. As the child emerges from the shadow of his parents, he finds himself once more among the same laws, the same principles, the same values. ... There is no disproportion between the life of the family and the life of the nation. Conversely, when one examines a closed society – that is, a society that has been protected from the flood of civilization – one encounters the same structures as those just described. (141–142)

The latter statement is more 'political' and does not exclude Africans from theoretical frameworks. Fanon's point intelligibly relates to Sow and Girard's discourse about the eruption of conflicts and regicides in traditional African societies. This point is particularly relevant to the films under consideration, which involve many fights between the male central character and his father. These conflicts, which ultimately entail revenge and death, reveal the centrality of tragedy in the postcolonial experience as formulated by Ato Quayson.[5] In addition to the sexual fatal ingredient earlier mentioned, *Yeelen* would equally appear as a partial illustration of the Oedipus crisis, given the irreconcilability of the relationship between Nianankoro and his father Soma. The reason for the fatal rivalry is not a woman, but the possession of power and knowledge (the *Nkomo*) which the son has taken away. Nianankoro's irremediable defiance enrages Soma, who promises to kill him, until he himself is ultimately killed by his son in a ferocious combat. Likewise, when Saga openly challenges his father's will in *Tilaï*, he brings about a full-blown 'Oedipus drama' (Diawara, 1992, 164), although it is not described as such in postcolonial scholarship.

After a two-year absence from the village, Saga comes back from the city and finds that his father has married Nogma, the same fiancée he had promised Saga. In fact, Nogma was forced to marry the old man. Saga feels betrayed and decides to leave the village, establishing himself at its periphery. Nogma regularly meets him at his hut and is seen by some villagers who report back to the whole community, to the dismay of her family. In keeping with local tradition, Saga's involvement, which is considered incest, must be punished. A ritual is organized in order to determine who will deliver justice by killing the offenders. Kougri, Saga's brother is randomly selected to enforce the law, but instead of killing his brother as required, he wounds himself and allows Saga to run away behind the flames of his burnt hut. When Saga hears that his mother is dying, however, he decides to come back in spite of the fact that he had promised the brother who saved his life never to return. Because he was thought dead by the villagers, when they see him they are scared and run away thinking that they have seen a ghost. They realize that Kougri, the chosen dispenser of justice, did not perform his duty towards his community. Feeling betrayed by his brother, Kougri fatally shoots Saga.

The Oedipal topos is without a doubt present in *Tilaï,* which portrays the suffering and the tragic destruction of the cultural order. By opposing his father, Saga refuses to bargain his way into an oppressive society that controls desire. By helping his brother run away, Kougri tries to reconcile his love of his brother with his abhorrence (maybe) of the 'incest' that has been committed. As he says himself, his loyalty is torn between the right of his brother to act on his desire, and his father's wishes. He also has a good deal of sympathy for Nogma, his brother's ex-fiancée, who has in a strange turn of events become his mother after being forced to marry his father.

The tragic element lies in the conflicting situation that does not allow the son to challenge his father in a community where respect for elders, parents and local cultures is an obligation. On another front, it is clear from the film that Nomenaba, Saga's father, can forgive his banned son after he runs away. But as he says to his wife, that can only happen if Saga makes the first step. The matter is more than that of a 'criminal' incest: it is a matter of honour, *authority*, strong will and respect. Tenga, Nogma's father, commits suicide out of humiliation. His daughter not only dares disobey him by challenging a choice he makes for her, but further humiliates him by sleeping with a banned son. Although the crisis in the community is about something as simple as a marriage, it is the metaphor for a more profound weakness, namely *desire and power*, a theme at the heart of many tragic narratives where death is usually the only resolution. From tragic death may come a new life or order, but Saga, whose desire transforms him into his father's rival, demonstrates that the absolute need to control or to satisfy one's wishes is a tragic curse in modern societies. By making love with Nogma, Saga performs a major transgression. For Terry Eagleton, desire is a human curse:

> it is an affliction which was lying in wait for us at the outset, a
> perversion into which we were plunged almost from birth. What
> makes us human subjects is this foreign body lodged inside us,
> which invades our flesh like a lethal virus and yet which ... is
> closer to us than we are to ourselves. Since desire in
> psychoanalytic thought is always bound up with death, a death
> which the lack at the heart of desire prefigures, not to give up
> one's desire means to maintain ... a constant relation to death,
> confronting the lack of being that one is. (2003, 233)

However, as Eagleton also indicates in *Sweet Violence*, the fact that myths and tragedies are so common in the modern world shows that we are 'homesick for the primitive and archaic, in thrall to spiritual absolutes which spell the death of liberal enlightenment' (206). According to him, 'In the modern era, mythical destiny shows its face again in the guise of vast, anonymous forces – language, Will, power, history, production, desire – which live us far more than we live them' (206). Eagleton's words ring true in *Tilaï*, where all these elements interact to generate conflicts in a traditional African village.

In Idrissa Ouedraogo's *La Colère des Dieux*, the transgression that creates chaos in the social fabric is not incest, but rather power control. As in the previous example Ouedraogo depicts the powerlessness of the father; here, however, the father, who in this case is a king, dies, and is unable to prevent his ambitious son from taking over power by force. The film is a more direct reflection on political power and tyranny, as explored through a son's unquenchable thirst for domination. Tanga challenges all the rules and imposes himself upon the community as the new king simply because he is the commander in chief. The dying father can do nothing but leave the matter in the hands of the gods; as in ancient tragedies, the transgression can only be punished by 'angry gods'.

However, when Tanga uses his new power to force Awa, the fiancée of Rasmané, to marry him, he does not know that she is pregnant with Salam. This boy is initially anointed prince. Later, when his illegitimacy is revealed, an oracle stipulates that Tanga must kill him lest he usurp his power. The son, whose own tyranny rivals that of his adoptive father, commits suicide when he realizes that he has also offended the very gods that offered him the protection and the strength he needed to fight the despotic Tanga. Apart from the Oedipal metaphor present in *La Colère des Dieux,* one can also note the issue of illegitimate power as illustrated by Nero in classical tragedies.

What is interesting about these films is that in all cases, a son's strong will has to confront the authority of his father in a society where social cohesion is not compatible with *individual desires*. Apart from *Tilaï* where the father has two sons, Kougri (Saga's brother) and Saga himself, the fathers in the others films have only one son. The tragic suffering these sons undergo and the repetition of the Oedipal cycle in these films are indicative of the persistence of the conflict between the individual and his community and, especially, between father and son. The particular case of Tanga confirms René Girard's opinion that

> Behind the pageantry of the African monarchies lurks the specter
> of the sacrificial crisis, suddenly resolved by the unanimity arising
> from the generative act of violence. Each African king is a new
> Oedipus, obliged to play out his own myth from beginning to
> end, because ritualistic theory sees in this enactment the means

of renewing and perpetuating a cultural order that is constantly at the brink of destruction. As in the case of Oedipus, there is a charge of incest associated with the original act of mob violence and serving its justification, an accusation seemingly confirmed by the effective results of the collective action. (1977, 106)

More importantly, these films illustrate Girard's observations that in many tragedies the son functions as the double of the father, the father is an obstacle to be eliminated, the best or most loved son always appears to be the worst, this most loved son is the easiest door through which misfortune enters and destabilizes the cultural order. In the Bible, it is Jacob and not Esau. It is Oedipus, Tanga, Salam and Saga. In all these cases, the families, then the community, are involved in reciprocal destruction in an environment where death always results. These films furthermore illustrate Marthe Robert's point that murdering the father is an obsession for all illegitimate sons: 'The Bastard is never done with killing his father in order to take his place, imitate him or surpass him … Guilty by nature, not by accident, he has no choice […] condemned by the source of its inspiration, into a cycle of transgressions' (1980, 31).

The tension in these films is not only between fathers and sons, but also between brothers. All these films are haunted by what can be called 'the spirit of Cain,' the original example of disaccord between brothers. A family can become very fragile, especially when brothers become competitors; the fraternal relationship should no more be taken for granted than the paternal. As argued by Girard, the proliferation of enemy brothers has always haunted classic texts: Cain and Abel, Romulus and Remus, Eteocles and Polynices, Richard the Lion-Heart and John Lackland, Jacob and Esau. In most cases, these enemy brothers are divided over some issues that can only be explained in terms of a general political economy of desire, namely the desire to dispossess the other brother from an object. Tragedy, which results from the desire to dispossess, occurs because of competition and the inability or the refusal to share. Although the Ortigues, Sow and Fotso Djemo do not agree with 'mainstream' psychoanalysis regarding the role of the father, they accept that the brother, on the other hand, is a dangerous rival who permanently faces death. This family dynamic is present in *Genesis, Ndeysaan* and *La Colère des Dieux*.

Cheick Oumar Sissoko's *Genesis* revisits the conflict between Isaac's two sons, Esau, the elder, and Jacob, the younger. Esau gave away his birthright to his brother: after a hunting expedition that proved futile, the starving Esau came to his younger brother Jacob and asked him for some of his lentil soup to ease the hunger pains. However, Jacob would only provide him with the food if Esau gave him his birthright, to which Esau agreed in his desperation for food.

It is worth noting that the myth of the 'enemy brothers' is a recurrent theme in many cultures, regardless of their link to the biblical narrative of Jacob and Esau. Although it is clear from the names and locations cited in the film *Genesis* that the story being told is the biblical one, what is most imaginative about the film is the large number of flashbacks used to tell the stories of past deeds that have brought about the current realities to each of the characters, as when Jacob explains to his young son why Esau wants to kill him. It is important that the flashback show the audience how Esau's birthright was taken as opposed to merely telling the audience. In the film, it is both the showing and the retelling of past actions that make the film transcend cultures. What is interesting to note, however, is that in the retelling of the biblical narrative, an old story takes on a relevance as it resonates with current twenty-first century issues. Although it is not located in so identifiable a time and place, Mansour Sora Wade's *Ndeysaan* is thematically similar to *Genesis*.

In Wade's film, Mbanick and Yatma live in a small village near the ocean where fishing is the main activity. Although they are not 'real' brothers, they were born in the same village and were circumcised together, which explains why they are usually referred to as brothers. They unfortunately fall in love with the same girl, Maxoye, who happens to prefer Mbanick, the brave and successful fisherman. Their relationship, which later degenerates into outright enmity, is made explicit in a tale of their origins, magnificently expressed in a colourful flashback where animated cartoons replace real characters. One evening, as their peers relax under a tree during one of the mysteriously cloudy nights, a young man promises the most beautiful girl of the village (the camera zooms on Maxoye) to whomever would restore happiness and brightness in the village between the King of the Savannah (Yatma) and the Lord of the Sea (Mbanick). On the symbolic level, this is the first confrontation between the two rivals, who declaim their respective genealogies, emphasizing particularly the heroism of their ancestors. Bama Ndoye, Mbanick's ancestor, was the strongest and most successful fisherman of the region; he won the ocean battle against the monster that was preventing him from attaining his prey.

Mbanick Ndoye is the descendant of successful fishermen and wrestlers. Although for his part Gol Njaay, Yatma's ancestor, fought a lion, it is not clear he actually won the battle. The lion hurt Yatma's ancestor, leaving a mark on his shoulder. The victory was never decisive.

Although the superior tale clearly positions Mbanick Ndoye as the winner, Maxoye jocularly congratulates Yatma, making Mbanick visibly jealous. He gets angry and leaves the scene. After this sequence, Maxoye and Mbanick meet and make love. Yatma literally goes crazy when he witnesses the scene. The director dedicates many shots to Yatma's self-mutilation as he screams in the dark, kicks the earth, and hurts himself on the sand. There are a few close-ups on his darkened wounded face. On his way from Maxoye's place, Yatma waits for Mbanick on the sandy land and fights, then kills him. He then burns his rival's pirogue and throws his body in the ocean.

The motif of the illegitimate son occurs here again as Maxoye is pregnant when she accepts Yatma's marriage proposal. She later tells her new husband that by accepting to marry him, she wants him to pay for his crime by looking after Mbanick junior, the son of his victim. For several years, she refuses to make love with him. As time goes by, Maxoye finally gets used to her husband and eventually gives birth to a second son. But because of his defiant will and monumental lack of judgement, which characterize any tragic character, Yatma steps into the ocean to follow little Mbanick and his friend Amul in spite of the fact that he was warned against ever coming close to the village waters. The revengeful spirit of Mbanick reappears in the form of a big whale and kills him in the middle of the river. His body is never seen again[6], thus bringing about the punishment always incurred by the villain in tragedies.

In Idrissa Ouedraogo's *La Colère des Dieux*, Tanga and Halyaré are not exactly brothers. Halyaré is Tanga's uncle and has been waiting for the king's death to assume power. Without much effort, Tanga forces his uncle to give up on his dream and be made an elder in the kingdom. Although he apparently accepts this new position, Halyaré never forgets the numerous humiliations of Tanga. He becomes very close to Awa, who tells him a terrible secret: the newborn prince is not Tanga's son, but Rasmané's. When the king discovers the truth and decides to kill Salam in order to protect his power (as stipulated by the oracle), Halyaré runs to warn Awa, who escapes with his help.

It is worth noting that in this community where the king's wishes are law, Halyaré is the only person to overtly challenge Tanga or to request that he behave in a more responsible way. Although it is clear that Halyaré's behaviour is morally correct, this righteousness is actually nurtured by the reciprocal hatred between the uncle and his nephew. When the guards catch Halyaré and take him to Tanga, who requests that he be immediately killed, Halyaré spits on his nephew and insults him; he faces his death without the slightest remorse. Halyaré seems to have attained a goal: ruin his rival brother who will move from failure to failure until he dies like his victims, killed by his own (adoptive) son.

Whether depicting nobles or ordinary characters, victims or agents, brothers or parents, these films similarly use mythical imagination or metaphor to reflect on the metaphysics of evil, desire and power in a family and a society in crisis. The reproduction of both the oedipal cycle and the biblical myth reminds us of the persistence of cultural archetypes in human societies because, as Kenneth Harrow writes, 'the difference is never so great as to justify the notion of Otherness, or radical essentializing difference. … texts are culturally permeable' (2002, xxiv). These films also explore the place of self/mutual destruction in cases where the ego is pushed to the absolute. Families and communities are scattered, historical values are challenged and destroyed. The expulsion or death of the father, cousin or rival brother is the only guarantee that the protagonist will avoid a similar fate. The violence is both fatal and inevitably reciprocal: the community kills Saga before he destroys the cultural order; Yatma kills Mbanick before he can continue to humiliate him by his various successes; Tanga tries to kill Salam before finally being killed by him as announced by the oracle; the gods abandon Salam, who commits suicide after realizing that he is only a pawn and does not have as much free will as he imagines. The only certainties are tragedy and death; most characters come to realize this at their own expense, weakening the family through hatred, envy and desire. The tragedy worsens according to the extent to which the characters are deprived of knowledge. Oracles are present in many of these stories because in order for the tragic to erupt, warnings must be ignored. When the full meaning of their message comes to light the disaster is more evident and devastating. This will be explored in the proceeding section.

3   Absolutism, oracles and the tragic

There are concerns in African feminist criticism about the way women are portrayed in societies where they have to obey first their father and, later, their husband. To take just one example, Farida Hayari writes that 'nine times out of ten, female characters in African films meet a sorry fate. [...] There are almost no positive heroines' (1996, 183). This is the case in the films I have discussed that represent women according to the cliché of the *femme fatale*, where their sexuality is correlated to the Fall, banishment, exile and moral decadence. Apart from Safi Faye, who will be discussed below, all directors considered in this chapter are men belonging to societies that subject women to various abuses. This is not a phenomenon particular to Africa, but what I am trying to stress is that women here again appear to be the most perfect channel for the tragic. This pattern is not really new in African cinema, but simply appears to have been previously interpreted in terms of the tradition/modernity dichotomy, or included in the discourse surrounding forced marriage.

In Souleymane Cissé's *Finye* (1982), for example, the openly political nature of the film belies the emotional tragedy of two young people, Bah and Satou, who cannot get married because they belong to different social backgrounds. Beyond advocating the need for political change, this film also depicts the intimate drama of impossible love and friendship. This same dynamic is present in Safi Faye's *Mossane* (1996), a film that clearly portrays woman and beauty as a social curse, a *beauté fatale*. The fourteen-year-old main character, Mossane, is an exceptionally beautiful girl whose existence disrupts the social order as everybody, including her own brother, either desires or falls in love with her. Even the gods are visibly disturbed by her presence. In fact, her name is derived from *moss,* the word for beauty in the Serere language. When she refuses to marry the man her parents have chosen, she flees to the city where she eventually commits suicide. In Kramo Lancina Fadika's *Djeli* (1981), another pair of young lovers, Fanta and Karamoko, likewise cannot get married because they belong to different castes. Like Mossane, Fanta reacts to her parents' unbearable pressures by committing suicide. The same motif is present in Bassek Ba Kobhio's *Sango Malo* (1991) where Ngo Bakang's father hangs himself after being humiliated by his peers at a men's assembly. The reason is simple, but serious: his daughter has married a Marxist without informing her family. Worse, the husband refuses to pay a dowry and/or organize a ceremony, hence depriving the whole community of celebrations demanded by the culture.

The suicides, murders, violent deaths and tragedies in the diverse films just discussed as well as in *Tilaï, La Colère des Dieux* and *Ndeysaan*, allow us to draw several important conclusions. First and foremost, apart from a few cases, these narratives all primarily involve young people, who, whether male or female, pay a high social price for transgressing cultural and political norms. Significantly, it is the youth who thus bring about social transformation and reform. Second, these texts are all about impossible or tragic love, which inevitably results in murder or suicide. Writing about *Finye,* Férid Boughédir (1987, 121) suggested that it is an African *Romeo and Juliet,* because the plot (students rioting against a tyranny) is a simple pretext for the expression of more complex issues. The social order (and even the cosmic order in the case of *Mossane*) is disrupted, hence generating a sort of cataclysm. The characters' ideals are incompatible with the empirical environment with which they have to cope. Because they are unable to live in the world around them, unable to handle reality, because their desire and will are much stronger than experience, death becomes an inevitable fate; these tragic characters are driven to challenge a postcolonial system that is determined to reproduce itself. Individual flaws lead to social tragedies when the collective fabric becomes doomed and calls for destruction.

The other factor that exacerbates tragic flaws is a lack or surplus of knowledge. Tragedy usually occurs when a secret is made public, or when characters fail to make good use of the knowledge provided by those forces, for example oracles or witch doctors, that control it. One may actually say that women are so powerful that in *La Colère des Dieux* the oracle is unable to predict the threat. Tanga, at least at the beginning of the film, is totally incapable of evaluating the danger that Awa poses to him. However, his most tragic flaw is the hubris that provokes him to dismiss the prediction about his son. Because he challenges and rebukes any information that does not match his wishes, he makes himself vulnerable, especially as the elders of the community know what is awaiting him. In *Tilaï,* Saga has to be killed because there is evidence people know that he has committed incest. Knowledge and the lack of it provoke tragedy. The suicides in the films discussed are committed because information is *shared* within a community, even though the tragic hero is usually the last to know.

In *La Colère des Dieux*, there is a more damaging truth that Tanga is forced to discover after persistently dismissing it. Several years after the birth of Salam and after ignoring all advice, he finally agrees to meet the village priest in order to face the 'calabash test,' which would tell him the truth about his son. After emphatically asking Tanga if he really wants to know this truth, he finally tells the king to look into the calabash full of water. What he sees is devastating and almost makes him insane, as he immediately begins to wander like a drunkard: what appears in the water is Rasmané's face. In other words, he has just discovered, after more than fifteen years, that he had been raising somebody else's son, a 'son' that has actually ruined his usurped tyrannical power. He feels completely betrayed and realizes that the power that he took by force has devastated his life. The most tragic element, for Tanga, is that such disappointment could have been prevented if he had not dismissed the terrible knowledge. Would there be a tragic narrative, however, if the knowledge of a priest were really taken seriously by the fully-conscious tragic hero?

The same scenario occurs in *Ndeysaan,* where, after Mbanick's death, Yatma is constantly tormented by supernatural forces. When he goes fishing, the waters which host the spirits of his victim (who belongs to lineage of fishermen) become angry, blowing waves in all directions and turning as red as blood. More humiliatingly, he does not catch a single fish. In order to reverse the curse, Yatma consults a priest who tells him that his crime will not be forgiven and his remorse will not be accepted until he stays twelve moons without approaching the angry water. But Yatma, like Tanga, dismisses the priest's words. The oracle is what Girard calls the 'infallible and omniscient prophet, the sole possessor of an indubitable verity, long ripened in the keeping' (1977, 70). The main characteristic of this figure is that he knows and bears a truth that is essentially ignored, unwanted, and which completely transforms the social as well as cultural fabric. This knowledge becomes crucial for the narrative because it is forecasted for characters that can do nothing but suffer from the tragic *fatum*.

In fact, *La Colère des Dieux* starts with a prediction[7], a curse from the dying monarch. When Tanga's father realizes that his son is determined to force his way into power, the last words he says are that the will and the anger of the gods will prevail. From the very first shots of the film, the few words expressed by a dying father are those of violence. This speaks to the predominance of cause and effect; the prediction is the first of a series of warning signs that the tyrant will refuse to consider.

Immediately after the birth of Salam, there is a change of scene which takes the narrative to the compound of a man who looks at the sky and predicts that something terrible will strike the community. He then goes directly to the palace and requests to speak in private to the king about this.

Tanga defiantly asks him to reveal the secret in front of everybody. He tells the population that the newborn will bring misfortune to the community, which is precisely what happens. From the day the new prince breathes, there is famine, drought, poverty and diseases in a once-prosperous village. The plague lasts for fifteen years, as Tanga refuses to make the necessary sacrifices to stop it. When he eventually decides to do so, it is too late and the gods refuse the libations. Salam grows up and kills his father as predicted. When he meets a supernatural protector who gives him a potion against danger, he becomes as power hungry as his father and kills the benevolent protector. Before dying, however, the protector curses him and tells him that white men will humiliate him. When Salam, having grown up and become a tyrant, realizes that his fellow villagers are being cruelly killed and raped by colonizers, he prefers to commit suicide instead of living as a slave.

The previous examples illustrate how stubbornness can make rulers blind to the fact that oracles can intercede between them and gods. Although they are invisible, they are present and their anger is felt in various ways. Their presence is first felt through the violence of the knowledge and the language of the oracles whose logos exerts a sort of tyranny over the destiny of tragic subjects, as in all sacred texts. What the prophecy knows and conveys is the power of the violent word, which itself is the message of *transcendental beings* that control collective destinies. From Tanga's father's original curse, it becomes obvious that in this context, the word predicts, manipulates, threatens, and even acts. Due to a fantastic religious narrative logic, speaking implies future action.

But before they can get to that stage, there is always a tragic mistake: the refusal or inability to listen, or the denial of the power of a sacred word. In *Ndeysaan,* Yatma defiantly steps into the sea to rescue his son in spite of the warning of the oracle who had instructed him not to come close to the ocean for twelve moons. As soon as he takes his pirogue into the sea, the whole village is suddenly aware that fatal events are about to unfold. As soon as he gets there, the spirit of Mbanick, in the form of an ocean whale monster, comes out and kills him. In *La Colère des Dieux*, Tanga defiantly ignores the warning of the priest who emphatically tells him that the gods are angry and that something needs to be done to appease them. In the religious societies represented, these mistakes are fatal and must be punished; the gods are always present and do not tolerate insubordination. The only possible way of staving off their vengeance would have been to make a sacrifice which, we know, Tanga refuses to do. In all these films, the tragic characters seem to be following a predetermined itinerary, beholden to their fate. The irony is that, as always, the protagonists who are confidently moving toward self-destruction are always the last to realize what will happen to them. Their self-determination causes them to perform the fatal transgression that destroys their own life and the lives of the members of their community. By refusing to make a sacrifice or by making it too late, the tragic figure (as we saw with Tanga), condemns himself to be sacrificed by the supernatural guardians of the cosmic order. Tanga's fate is an illustration of how Aristotle described tragedy: gods must intervene to avoid chaos and prevent men from taking themselves for what they are not. The order of the world is only re-established after the tragic resolution, namely, the death of the offender. Yatma's case, on the other hand, is different. Justice is not re-established by the gods, but rather by the spiritual world that is reincarnated in the soul of Mbanick. In *Tilaï*, social justice is reintroduced through a public sacrifice, which is the way power usually comes to light. This restitution is reminiscent of Michel Foucault's words on the role of spectacular punishment.

Tragedy in African cinema involves both noble and ordinary characters. Tanga, Salam, Saga, Mbanick and Yatma are all representatives of a disenchanted world where tragic death is demanded. Although in most of these cases death is brought about by specific human actions, Tanga's and Salam's cases are illustrations of tragic hereditary misfortunes. Tanga in particular is reminiscent of Oedipus. Like the Greek hero, he defies the gods, who later take their revenge. The unfortunate prediction is announced and every attempt made to avoid it is either late or actually leads to its coming to pass: he eventually kills his father. Although there are certain variations, all the films discussed illustrate the inevitability of tragic death when it is ordained by fate and man does nothing to alter its course. In that respect, these narratives have stayed very close to the structural construction of most tragedies, where violence and death are the forces in control.

One final point that deserves to be mentioned is that although *Ndeysaan* deals with destiny and inevitability, it also has a very modern undertone in the depiction of characters who are not fixed and determined *for ever*. The murderer, Yatma, for example, does not stay a violent and jealous character, but develops contradictory feelings. Although the ending is tragic and gives a feeling of impossible hope or redemption, there is a sense of a possible mutability. Yatma, who was rightfully vilified after the murder of Mbanick, almost seems to become a 'true' hero in that he gives his life to save his children. His heroic sacrifice is sharply different from Mbanick's blind, bestial vengeance, which could be regarded as evil because he cannot forgive even after his death. Yatma takes on certain qualities of the epic hero in that he faced destiny and knew he would die if he went into the sea, as he was warned by a *marabout*. At the end of the movie, the village powerlessly watches the tragic end of a former murderer who was almost forgiven by everyone in the community. The biggest loser, it must be pointed out, is Maxoye, who has lost two husbands and is left with two orphans. Her fate is arguably more tragic than that of her two dead husbands. At the end of the film, she has become the most popular widow who causes men to kill each other. In that sense, one can state that *Ndeysaan* is not particularly feminist.

It was the purpose of this chapter to explore the various facets of tragedy in several African films. In spite of fundamental differences between Africa and the West, in spite of some profound dissimilarities in purpose, scope and structure, it is still possible to use some foundational Western archetypes to evaluate a different cinematic tradition. The exclusionist and reductive notion of cultural specificity fails to appreciate that while it is problematic to categorize Africa according to generalities, it is no less incorrect to believe that its productions belong to another planet unknown to anyone and completely autonomous. Wole Soyinka's plays, as well as the films analysed in previous sections, illustrate the transnational and transethnic potential of myth. In the preface to *Myth, Literature and the African World,* Wole Soyinka notes,

> Nothing in these essays suggests a detailed uniqueness of the African world. Man exists, however, in a comprehensive world of myth, history and mores; in such a total context, the African world, like any other 'world' is unique. It possesses, however, in common, with other cultures, the virtues of complementarity. To ignore this simple route to a common humanity and pursue the alternative route of negation is, for whatever motives, an attempt to perpetuate the external subjugation of the black continent. (1976, xii)

It is therefore within this dialogic framework that one can interpret the similarity between the structural or discursive constructions of the films analysed and some famous Western narratives. These intertextual connections reveal a tragic universal human experience, namely our vulnerability in the face of physical desire. Desire has the power to transform subjects into larger-than-life figures and thus create a place for the epic within the context of postcolonial experience.

Notes

1 Jean-Pierre Bekolo and Idrissa Ouedrago openly reject Sembène Ousmane or Férid Boughédir's perception of cinema. In fact, Bekolo's perception is actually radical: according to him, there is no such thing as 'African cinema' and he does not feel part of this concept. Idrissa Ouedraogo thinks that 'Africanity' is a reductive ghetto. For more on that, read Alexie Tcheuyap (2006) and Jean-Pierre Bekolo's interview (217–238) in Nwachukwu Frank Ukadike's *Questioning African Cinema: Conversations with African Filmmakers* (2002). Finally, it is worth noting in addition to the arguments put forward in this book against the intellectual labyrinth of nationalism, Harrow's book also vigorously questions the concepts of authenticity and *cinéma engagé*.

2 '*toute action où l'enchaînement des situations montre une marche fatale du microscosme central vers son propre anéantissement*'.

3 In *Introduction à la poétique du divers,* Edouard Glissant states that believing in a monolithic identity is actually a creation from the West: '*Car en fait c'est de cela qu'il s'agit: d'une conception sublime et mortelle que les peuples d'Europe et les cultures occidentales ont véhiculées dans le monde, à savoir que toute identité est une identité à racine unique et exclusive de l'autre. Cette vue de l'identité s'oppose à la notion aujourd'hui "réelle", dans ces cultures composites, de l'identité comme facteur et comme résultat d'une créolisation, c'est-à-dire de l'identité comme rhizome, de l'identité non plus comme racine unique mais allant à la rencontre d'autres racines* / Because that is indeed what it signifies: a sublime and ephemeral conception of identity that the people of Europe and Western cultures conveyed to the world, an idea which holds that every identity is single-rooted and exclusive of any other. This view is at odds with today's 'real' notion of composite cultures where identity is considered as factor and product of creolization, as rhizome, not as a single-root entity but rather as a root that stretches out to meet other roots' (23). In *Imaginary Homelands,* Salman Rushdie also seriously questions the concept of national 'authenticity' in the case of India where he says it is 'fallacious' to believe there is something like a 'pure tradition'. Finally, I would like to raise one point on which social sciences have elaborated at length: the idea of 'purity' has historically been at the root of several genocides, including in Africa.

4 '*Dans le modèle européen du complexe d'Oedipe, le fils s'imagine tuant le père. Ici la pente typique serait plutôt: le fils se référant par l'intermédiaire du père à l'ancêtre déjà mort donc inattaquable et constituant ses "frères" en rivaux*'.

5 It is worth noting that Quayson does not use the Oedipus complex in his psychoanalytic critiques.

6 Although it would be a somehow forceful interpretation to say that Mbanick's son has killed him, it is nonetheless true that the death of this other father is linked to the son he tries to save.

7 Set in the late seventeenth century, Roger N. M'Balla's *Adanggaman* also reproduces the parallel between the political and the family structure where opposing the father or expressing free will in a conservative society is synonymous with opposing the state or the social superstructure, a situation that can only result in destruction. In this film, Ossei, the protagonist, is a warrior who refuses to marry the woman imposed on him and prefers a girl of 'lower caste'. The first shot of the film shows an old woman lamenting about the world falling apart with children not obeying their parents any more. Ngo, Ossei's father, tells his wife that 'ancient law must be obeyed' and he cannot endorse the involvement of his son with a 'slave' simply in the name of love. He tells his wife that it is his authority and the survival of traditional rules that are at stake. Also interesting here is the power of divination and prediction, as all that happens in the narrative, the horrors of colonization, is announced to Ossei by a priest: after slave traders, colonialists, invade the village and kill every living being in the community. Looking at this film, one is left to wonder if it was not actually a pessimistic forecast of the destiny of postcolonial Africa.

20   Mansour Sora Wade, *Ndeysaan*

21   Idrissa Ouedraogo

22   Mansour Sora Wade

Chapter 5

Epic constructions

In the previous chapters, I have argued that because of the blatant and multiple failures to which various liberation movements led, an aesthetics based on nationalist political agendas is today less viable. The contemporary cinematic landscape has witnessed the emergence of post-resistance texts that are not in line with the authoritative prose of FEPACI. The analysis of myths, crimes or comic forms strongly illustrates that postcolonial subjects are not just passive consumers in global cultural networks. Contrary to those of the pioneering phase, several contemporary African directors seem to have built an acute sense of conviviality and connivance with contemporary 'foreign' and global categories. In so doing, they refuse to take a stance against the state, invisible global capital or cosmopolitan cultural forms. These generic and discursive experiments, I have equally emphasized, do not in any way signify the end of the nationalist project or its dilution into an abstract universalism, because liberation is an *ongoing process*. Today the nationalist project is one among many, with various filmmakers now positioning themselves in transnational settings without necessarily abandoning their local culture.

Such new cultural polygeneric configurations distinguish films like Souleymane Cissé's *Yeelen* (1987), Mansour Sora Wade's *Ndeysaan, the Price of Forgiveness* (2001) or Idrissa Ouedraogo's *La Colère des Dieux* (2003). These works borrow motifs from classic tragedies, and it is additionally possible to detect echoes of the epic saga in their larger than life figures and gigantic battles that establish a new order, protect a vanishing power, revisit a lost past or solve a devastating crisis. In addition to such characterization of superhuman roles, the films previously mentioned, along with Dani Kouyaté's *Keita, the Heritage of the Griot* (1995), open textual lacunae where *oral language*, as in the Biblical world, triumphs over the written. More importantly, *the word, la parole, orality,* as well as the *performance* that accompanies it, is narrated by an archetypal character central to traditional African narratives: the griot or storyteller. Generally a male in these films, he specializes in narrations of wor(l)ds and events concerning the metaphysical and supernatural realm.

This chapter therefore reconsiders the concept of orality and determines one of its fundamental, yet unexplored, relationships to African cinema, namely the formal relationship of various narratives to the epic genre in which *the past* and *memory* become indispensable to identity formation.[1] It will examine the aforementioned films in connection to the tradition of the epic, focusing particularly on the ways in which directors use strategies like hyperbolic characterization, temporal manipulations or supernatural codes to reinvent a vanished past. Unlike Manthia Diawara (1992, 1996, 2000), Nwachukwu Frank Ukadike (1994), Josef Gugler (2003) and Melissa Thackway (2003), I will not take up what Achille Mbembe calls the 'burden of the metaphysics of difference' (2002a, 240) by limiting the interpretation of oral structures to cultural illustrations of 'authenticity'. Neither will I, as Diawara does in his reading of *Keita,* marginalize the elements of epic by reducing the films under consideration to 'a very simple story about the education of young children in contemporary Africa [which only] takes an epic dimension when the director connects the life of the protagonist to that of Soundjata Keita' (2000, 88). Apart from the structures to be investigated, I am interested in understanding why postcolonial narratives turn to myth and epic in order to search for *new meanings.* More importantly, considering the irreversibility of time, the 'scientific' denigration and repudiation of African historical experiences, why do directors search *other truths* in the past without falling into the pitfalls of an uncritical celebration of it[2], or lapsing into unquestioned appropriation of dated forms? How relevant is the past in comprehending the present? Although we know national liberation movements drew their ideological sustenance from the past (Nkrumah inventing Ghana for example) how do epics reposition national allegories without an aggressive, increasingly less relevant, nationalist discourse? Where do we find *new answers* to *contemporary* postcolonial predicaments? Is the present ethos best represented in the realist documentaries of Regina Fanta Nacro or Anne Laura Folly, in the futuristic sci-fi narratives of Jean-Pierre Bekolo and Sylvestre Amoussou elegantly analysed by Taiwo Adetunji

Osinubi (2009), or in a 'fixation on the past' (Mbembe, 2002b, 635) mediated through oral prose? And what is the place of epic forms in this enquiry? Subsequent sections will address these issues by examining how epic narratives are translated into film. I will first look at the devices that constitute the filmic oral performance and then consider how the strategies elaborated in narratives create epic heroes originating from a social crisis. Before proceeding, it is first important to locate the epic genre within the context of African cinematic and literary theory.

Like crime fiction, the analysis of an epic film in the contemporary postcolonial reality may at first sight be considered an impracticable theoretical investigation. According to Paul Zumthor, modern technological civilization has developed 'repugnance for the epic' (1990, 95) and has made mediation by poetic forms 'useless'. It has however 'recuperated' the principal epic function: the elevation of the hero by genres like the western. In his conversations with Osvaldo Ferrari, J. L. Borges (1988, 168) also deplores the fact that modern cultures have lost what he calls '*la saveur fondamentale de l'epique*/the fundamental flavour of the epic'. He rightly points to the fact that instead of lamenting personal matters, ancient poets first celebrated epic bravery and public successes. For him, the loss of this 'epic duty' has resulted in Hollywood's taking control over such responsibility and creating the myth of the American Far West, with its questionable values. In addition to Borges' and Zumthor's concerns, two remarks by Walter Benjamin (2000, 122) may make the possibility of an African film epic seem purely speculative. Benjamin deplores that the art of telling stories, so central to the epic performance, is disappearing. He further mentions the fact that modern fiction often lacks 'remarkable narratives,' in other words those with heroic characters. Borges's, Zumthor's and even Benjamin's complaints however appear compatible with a general modernist nostalgia for the grandeur of the past. The 'classic' definition of the epic, which heavily emphasizes spectacle and entertainment (concepts which for a long time have been absent from African film theory) may likewise be incompatible with African cinematic traditions.

In *The Epic Film: Myth and History*, Derek Elley (1984) writes that 'The chief feature of historical epic is not imitation but reinterpretation [of the literary epic]. *Spectacle* is the cinema's own transformation of the literary epic's taste for the *grandiose*, realised *on sufficient scale to impress modern audiences*' (1, emphasis added). According to Elley, cinema is the most likely art form to effectively handle the epic due to the presence of speech, image, sound, music and colour, whereas in other art forms these elements often appear individually. For Steve Neale, any operational definition, categorization or understanding of the epic film needs to include historical and logistical considerations:

> Epic is essentially a 1950s and a 1960s term. It was used to identify, and to sell two overlapping contemporary trends: Films with historical, especially ancient world settings; and *large scale films of all kinds which used new technologies, high production values and special modes of distribution and exhibition to differentiate themselves from routine productions* and from alternative forms of contemporary entertainment, especially television. (2000, 85, emphasis added)

In a similar perspective, James Russell (2007, 10) stresses the spectacle and prestige of historical epic films which are exceptionally expensive, shot in locations with a massive cast and crew. In addition, Russell emphasizes top of the line technologies and processes like Cinerama or Cinemascope as important features. He further elaborates,

> Stylistically, epic films were defined by a sense of scale that exceeded the Hollywood norm. The wide screen allowed for expansive shots and landscapes, lavishly constructed sets and the thousands of extras facilitated by the vastly increased production budgets. An exemplary epic scene involves the positioning of the individual subject within massive landscapes, huge crowds, or in the forefront of sizable and opulent sets. [...] the epic of the 1950s was usually *bigger* than other releases in almost every way. These opulent production techniques helped to stress the cultural importance of the events being depicted. (11, original emphasis)

In *The Epic Film: From Myth to Blockbuster,* Constantine Santas (2008, 3, 13, 17, 23) likewise considers technology, special effects, large casting, spectacle and money for production as central characteristics of the epic.

From the above theorizations, it stems that production values are key to the generic designation of Hollywood epics. However, if we consider Neale's argument that they are also marked by 'a dramatic and thematic concern with political and military power, political and military rule, and political and military struggle [which] found articulation on national, international and sometimes global and cosmic scales' (2000), the incorporation of narrative contents becomes very valuable in understanding African films where, because of the extreme scarcity of financial resources as well as the usually rudimentary technological equipment, the African epic necessitates a different rubric. As such, it is crucial to turn our attention to narrative strategies, character specifications, performance dynamics and content archetypes.

David Bordwell once argued that no strict definition of a single genre can be generic and remain uncontested (1989, 147). That is certainly true of the epic, which is notoriously variable and intertwines with myth, heroic narratives and legend. In the case of African oral literature, the groundbreaking work of Isidore Okpewho has significantly contributed to a better comprehension of epic as a narrative genre that is performed in specific social and historical contexts. In *The Epic in Africa,* he defines the oral epic as

> A tale about the *fantastic deeds* of *a man and men* endowed with *something more than might* and operating in something *larger than normal human context* and it is of significance in portraying some stage of the cultural or political development of a people. It is usually *narrated or performed* to the background of music by an unlettered singer working alone or with some assistance from a group of accompanists. (1979, 34, emphasis added)

Okpewho's *African Oral Literature: Background, Character, and Continuity* proposes a similar conception of the epic genre as 'the story of *extraordinary* personalities (i.e. heroes) achieving *unbelievable* feats under equally *extraordinary* circumstances' (1992, 182, emphasis added). In *Oral Poetry: An Introduction* (1990), Paul Zumthor proposes what he considers a 'prudent definition':

> As an action story, concentrating its effects of meaning in the action and sparing ancillary ornamentation, the epic poem stages *virile aggressivity* for the sake of some grand venture. Basically, it narrates a combat and selects from its host of protagonists one *uncommon character* who commands our admiration, although he

may not always come out a victor in every test. (1990, 81, emphasis added)

For John William Johnson, Thomas A. Hale and Stephen Belcher (1997, xvii), African epics involve prestigious heroes who move through an essentially mythical landscape. Apart from describing in detail some core features of epic oral performance, Jean Dérive also emphasizes specific stylistic traits: 'another major feature of the epic style often underscored is the hyperbole. Whether it concerns the representation of actions, feelings or qualities of a person or an object, all is taken to the extreme' (2002b, 127).[3] How does this help in comprehending African films?

A few conclusions can be derived from the definitions just cited. The first one is the *gendered*, we might go as far as to say, sexist, nature of the African epic, which is clearly a male genre. While Okpewho explicitly refers only to male characters, Zumthor mentions the 'aggressive virility' of epic figures. Dérive hardly mentions women in his book and John William Johnson et al. likewise fail to account for a gendered division that is probably reflective of the societies under consideration. Such theorizations, especially from Africanist scholars, are disappointing. At least one female historical figure has in fact been celebrated: Sarraounia, from the Niger region, whose decisive role in challenging and defeating French invasion is the subject of a novel by Abodulaye Mamani (1980) and a film by Med Hondo, *Sarraounia* (1986). As I will show, women usually play a purely instrumental or manipulative role when they appear in epics.

The second element is its *oral* nature: epics are reproduced orally, which could reinforce the myth of Africa as a fundamentally 'oral' society. The third consideration is the exceptionality of the epic hero, the extraordinariness of his performance and his superlative attributes. All these features can help us to better approach African narratives like *Keita, the Heritage of the Griot* that evoke the historical epic, or others like *Ndeysaan, Yeelen* or *La Colère des Dieux* which display heroic conquests and mythic clashes. Most importantly, all the films to be discussed below bear important relationships with the idea of the epic; apart from *Yeelen* and *Ndeysaan*, which both have high production values, the other films under consideration are technically rudimentary when compared to the standard of the Hollywood epic. Subsequent sections will first describe oral performance as a principal feature of these films, and then will establish the stylistic specificities that constitute the epic.

1   Narrative performance

In an essay, François Jost (1982, 115) poses crucial questions whose answers are at times contradictory: Whose voice is heard in a film? Who is the *real* narrator? The answers are not always straightforward in 'classic' texts. The complexity of narrative voices and representations is best illustrated by Emile Benveniste, whose description of the 'objectivity' of *story* in opposition to *discourse* is deceptively subtle. Such 'objectivity', he implies, is strategic, manufactured and stylistically built. As such, in the story, 'The events are set forth chronologically, as they [occur]. *No one speaks here; the events seem to narrate themselves*' (1971, 208, emphasis added). Christian Metz goes even further in suggesting that under the guise of innocent stories, narratives are strategically discursive and manipulative:

> the traditional film is presented as story, and not as discourse.
> And yet it is discourse, if we refer it back to the film-maker's
> intentions, the influence he wields over the general public, etc.;
> but the basic characteristic of this kind of discourse, and the very
> principle of its effectiveness as discourse, is precisely that it
> obliterates all traces of the enunciation, and masquerades as
> story. (1982, 91)

Indeed, it is common in film for there to be *no audible voice*; the story, as Benveniste points out, can thus appear to be *self-generated* in third person prose. In such contexts, understanding narrative strategies leads to the analysis of *filmic enunciation,* that is, the ways in which filmic discourse is hidden under the guise of film story.

However, several African narratives that incorporate epic figures openly position the narrator as a both audible and visible figure. The question about 'who speaks', as will be seen below, is virtually non-existent in epic African narratives where there is *always* a narrator. Benveniste's construction of objectivity in these cases becomes irrelevant. That is why Manthia Diawara goes as far as to equate the camera with the griot because 'In oral tradition, it is through the griot's point of view that one sees and realizes the universe around one. In film, the camera replaces the griot as the director's eyes and constructs the new images of Africa to the spectator. It is in this sense that one says that the African filmmaker has replaced the griot in the rewriting of history' (1996, 216). Jean Dérive rightly attributes the existence of the epic to its oral delivery by a figure in charge of chronicling historical events. For him, 'a narrative will be considered an epic only if interpreted by a specialist (affiliated or unaffiliated with a caste, initiated or uninitiated but recognized as such) in a diction which sets it apart from other forms of discourse and which brings to fore a specific rhythmic structure' (2002c, 81). Instead of considering the griot as an external, non-diegetic instance as Diawara does, I will look at the figure of the griot as the central part of the *internal* narrative performance of the *oral* epic in Dérive's perspective.

There are close similarities between the three films where the griot operates mainly through voice-over narrations. In *Ndeysaan* and *Keita,* the voice-over narration has a *direct* relationship to the events, sounds and dialogues. In these two films, it is used as an *expository* feature that helps set the background of the story to be narrated, hence situating it in time and space. This contextualization gives the film the flavour of a first-person point of view by introducing the vocal, and subsequently physical, presence of a character, the griot, who announces the hero's glorious exploits and genealogical lineage. *Ndeysaan* opens (before the credits) with a word that becomes a leitmotif throughout the whole narrative, namely 'ndeysaan', which means sorrow or pity in the Ouolof language. This exclamation, repeated by either the griot in voice-over or another character, can clearly be identified as a part of the 'epic formula,' an essential component of oral performance. Because of its recurrence, this word operates as a narrative indicator, signalling the hopelessness that is plaguing the village of Timbering, in desperate need of a heroic 'saviour'.

After the inaugural alert, the griot of *Ndeysaan*, then a young boy, sets the background of the present crisis in the village. The narration begins with broad metaphorical statements, which express the concerns of the desperate populations: 'The world moves on/Time goes by and human beings change/Yesterday is not today'. In this opening scene, the voice-over chronicles the history of Timbering. The story is chronological, beginning with 'those days' when every villager thought the community was approaching an unavoidable apocalypse. From the thick fogs that covered the village and prevented people from fishing, to the irruption of Mbanick as the new hero, the early sequences detail this original crisis. Mbanick challenges the violent weather, sails into the sea and comes back with a boatful of fish, thus liberating the community from its suffering. The griot explains Mbanick's journey from ordinary boy to community leader.

He also relates the character's misfortune and tragic fate, and it is crucial to mention that his voice also concludes the film when, after the tragic destruction, 'the waves have swept away their stories to far-off oceans and the sea itself has learnt to forgive'.

In *Keita,* the narration is conducted in a similar mode. As in *Ndeysaan,* the narration of various deeds is proclaimed by way of a set of creative words, as in the Bible. In the opening sequence, a voice-over offers a history of the Mande kingdom:

'From chaos a new world was born/The darkness and obscurity of pre-life had just been dissipated/Wagadu was the theatre of the first reunion/In those days, no one commanded men.'

Contrary to *Ndeysaan, Keita* is not chronologically narrated. However, what both films have in common is the presence of a character who guarantees that the hero's deeds will be narrated. The griot Djeliba Kouyate is called by the spirits to 'initiate' Mabo Keita into the history of his name and, by extension, his secret identity; in order to do so, the griot has to tell the young boy how the kingdom was founded by his ancestor. His story is told by way of flashbacks, which help Mabo fully understand the importance of his family history. The narration is regularly interrupted by Mabo who asks questions and thus makes Djeliba Kouyate's performance interactive: he is invited to guess the subsequent parts of the epic of Soundjata Keita. In so doing, Mabo ensures the continuity of a narrative that cannot always be presented dramatically. However, in both *Ndeysaan* and *Keita,* the 'physical' character often withdraws from the camera and at times allows only his voice to continue the oral performance; the social dynamic and the story then become more important than who relates them to the audience. There are several instances where the griot is actually off screen and mute, although he is identifiable in the background. In these instances, according to Benveniste, the story is still 'being told'. It is however clear, at least in these circumstances, that an instance delivers and controls the narrative content. The story of Soundjata Keita is so well transmitted by Djeliba Kouyate, with the smallest details, that at the end of the film Mabo takes over the role of the griot. Having learned from Djeliba for so long, he in turn is now capable of entertaining his friends with the story of his ancestor. Djeliba's concern with the past here is not the kind of fixation with bygone events Mbembe deplores. On the contrary, it is an attempt to cure a profound cultural wound provoked by colonial education, which taught postcolonial subjects that their ancestors were monkeys in order to substantiate institutional racism. The spiritual voyage of Soundjata Keita and Mbanick finds a new historical narrative. The past invoked in this epic is in stark contradiction with an ugly present that must be wiped out. In such circumstances, the mythical past becomes the only referent for a lost glory in its characters and worlds dominated by absolutes and superlatives. For Mikhail Bakhtin,

> The world of the epic is the national heroic past: it is a world of 'beginnings' and 'peak times' in the national history, a world of fathers and founders of families, a world of 'firsts' and 'bests.' The important point here is not that the past constitutes the content of the epic. The formally constitutive feature of the epic as a genre is rather the transferral of a represented world into the past. The epic was never a poem about the present, about its own time. [...] The epic, as the specific genre known to us today, has been from the beginning a poem about the past, and the authorial position immanent in the epic and constitutive for it ... is the environment of a man speaking about a past that is to him inaccessible, the reverent point of a descendent. (1981, 13)

In spite of fierce resistance from Mabo's mother, the boy's oral performance at the end of the film is indicative of the success of the mission Djeliba had to undertake in a hostile urban environment. When he left the village to go and meet Mabo, Djeliba had pedagogic, ideological and aesthetic objectives assigned to him by supernatural powers. His task was to inform Mabo of his origins and the real meaning of his name so as to help repair what Manthia Diawara rightly called 'a split in the identity of modern Africans' (2000, 89). He so thoroughly teaches the boy about his ancestors and the hardships surrounding both the birth of the kingdom and Soundjata's ascension to power that at the end of the narrative Mabo becomes the new oral performer. He takes control of the narrative authority and continues where Djeliba had left off, securing the survival of the figure Borges and Zumthor suggest is in danger of disappearing in Western cultures, while remaining vibrant in African narratives. As the new narrator performs before a young audience, one can see how satisfied and even proud he is of the knowledge and the ancestry he has been privileged to discover. It is clear, then, that the past is being validated by oral performance. However, this genealogic anxiety is marked by a sense of the absolute which makes temporal sequences timeless, immeasurable and even chaotic.

As argued by Bakhtin, epic tales are centred on past foundational and heroic actions that determine the present. The films considered in this chapter are not only organized around the rediscovery of such heroic past, which is modulated in a formal organization where time is mythic and immeasurable. Although these films are not epic because of the much longer running time that characterizes 'classic' Hollywood models, there is obviously, on the part of Mansour Sora Wade, Idrissa Ouedraogo and Dani Kouyaté, a temporal organization that positions their films in the epic realm. In these narratives, the time spent on any action, from the most trivial to the most important, can expand over an eternity. Very early in *Keita,* Djeliba tells Mabo Keita that it can take a day, a year and even a whole life to narrate the epic history of his ancestor Soundjata Keita. When the new king meets Sogolon, who it has been prophesied is the bearer of the future leader of the Mande, it takes him a seven month fight for the opportunity to impregnate Sogolon, who will give birth to Soundjata Keita. The pregnancy itself lasts seventeen months, and Djeliba tells Mabo that other versions of the same epic say it actually lasted seven years. When Soundjata is finally born, he does not walk for fifteen years, until he miraculously instructs the smith to build a solid iron rod which he then uses to stand, walk and, ultimately, rule. All the above speaks to one of the main features of 'oral narratives', namely, the contraction of time. A three-hour film cannot follow the details of a whole life, and perhaps this is why these films employ the voice-over (an integration of the griot and the realism of cinematic time-image), which we do not sense in Hollywood epics like *Gone with the Wind* or *Ben-Hur.*

In *La Colère des Dieux,* Idrissa Ouedraogo equally significantly extends the length of the story through various features. Although there is no character in this film who plays the role of the griot, subtitles relay the sequence of events. The film opens with the death of the king, the events unfolding over several years. The succession of disasters that plague the kingdom occur after two set periods of time: nine months, that is, when the prince is born, and twelve years, which is when the king decides to kill him in order to save his power. There is one interesting feature used by Ouedraogo to express the epic construction of time. When the king discovers that Salam, the boy he has brought up, is actually somebody else's, he decides to kill him. Awah, the Queen, runs away with him; eventually, Tanga kills his in-laws and the family that hosted the illegitimate son. Salam is left with a girl named Sana. In a supernatural mode characteristic of the epic, Salam meets a white eagle from whom he requests a magic potion for his future life challenges, and the eagle instructs Salam to run after him. It is at this point that the director successfully employs a cinematic device to represent the passage of epic time.

Salam is twelve when he starts this marathon with his wife. As both characters, beginning as children, run in search of spiritual and political power, we see them metamorphose into teenagers and, finally, into fully grown adults. Sana becomes a beautifully dressed woman, and Salam a virile man. Every new shot reveals the transformed faces of the couple. This is another example of the kind of contraction of time mentioned above. These physical transformations are mediated through the use of dissolves which slowly tell us that a temporal manipulation is taking place. More importantly, when at the end of the marathon Salam has acquired all the attributes he will use to kill his tyrannical father, we are told he is now twenty-seven; the marathon has lasted fifteen years. When these characters are running, the moving camera closely focuses on their legs, their backs, and then gives a close shot to fully document their biological maturation. In this performance, the epic gender gap is clearly marked again, as Sana eventually gives up the Herculean undertaking. She only reappears when her husband has acquired the attributes promised to him by the mystical bird. In any case, this sequence, which lasts a few minutes but covers fifteen years of marathon, is a clear depiction of the ways epic narratives stylistically express performances that can only be achieved in a universe where the absolute and the superlative prevail. It is even more so with Mansour Sora Wade's film *Ndeysaan,* where visual effects function as expressions of temporal hopelessness and are more pronounced.

As in previous narratives, several characters are involved in attempts to challenge uncompromising temporalities or to rediscover a lost, albeit glorious, past. Postcolonial experience, therefore, is represented metaphorically, with unrealistic portrayals of time. It is evident African filmmakers working in the genre depict collective salvation as requiring alternative temporalities. In *The Theory of the Novel,* Georg Lukacs identifies the hazards of temporality within the context of the novel:

> Time, consequently, can only become constitutive when all links
> with the transcendental fatherland are severed. In the novel,

sense (direction) and life part ways and, with them, essence and temporality; regarding the most intimate aspect of action, one could almost say that *action in the novel is nothing more than a battle waged against the forces of time*. And [from the resignation of the individual], ensue some authentic epic experiences of temporality: hope and recollection. (quoted in Benjamin, 2000, 136, emphasis added)[4]

Lukacs' analysis is relevant to the films considered here, especially Mansour Sora Wade's, where the story and plot are organized around challenging epic temporalities. *Ndeysaan* is not only a film about a tragic love story; it is also an epic in which it is virtually impossible to identify a coherent temporal structure. Contrary to previous narratives in which time was distended but measurable, in Mansour Sora Wade's film time is an abstraction. The story of Mbanick and Yatma can only be fully understood if one goes back to ancient times to 'the year of the locusts, the year of the great drought'. When Yatma and Mbanick recite their respective genealogies, they begin with 'one day' or 'a long time ago'. Is this perhaps because while *Keita* makes an epic into a story, *Ndeysaan* makes a story into an epic? In other words, does this difference have to do with the fact that the former film is historical while the latter is essentially mythical? In any case, the most interesting characteristic of *Ndeysaan* is the unique visual texture, which perfectly suits the tragic story told and the disaster that the fishermen are facing.

Although this film is in colour, Wade's visual design clouds the screen in a pervasive white fog. *Ndeysaan* opens with a dark and cloudy sky. The camera captures several silent and isolated subjects whose facial expressions illustrate the despair of the community. The characters blend into the foggy, often hardly visible, background. They are generally shot in (extreme) close-ups which, in this specific context, strongly reinforce the dramatic situation. When the villagers make offerings to dispel the fog and allow normal life to resume, we hear a violent wind blowing in the background. After a few sequences, we see sunset, dark trees, and we also hear violent waves beating the shore.

To add to the sombre atmosphere, we are introduced to Baye Sogi, the village elder, who is in tremendous pain, spending his last moments on earth. The camera shows a group of wretched people gathered at his home, expecting the fatal last breath, the announcement of his death. The camera focuses on their non-functional limbs, capturing their devastated faces, folded arms and crossed legs. The unusually bad weather and uncooperative times have reduced them to misery. The image background is either very dark or almost white with clouds, obscuring the human faces. Even at the tea party where Mbanick and Yatma tell their respective heroic family narratives, the weather remains aggressively cloudy. In spite of the fact that they are having fun, the friends assembled are aware of the environmental threat under which their village has been living for months. They repeat the word 'ndeysaan' on multiple occasions during their conversations, trying to both infuse hope into their outlook and express their powerlessness.

Interestingly in *Ndeysaan,* Mansour Sora Wade maintains this grave visual design for more than thirty minutes, until Mbanick reveals himself as the community hero by defying the aggressive weather and the fears of villagers who had sought help from a charlatan. Supported, guided (and manipulated) by his father's spirit, Mbanick brings back a boatful of fish, which no one has seen for years, from the sea. When he does so, the visual aesthetic of the film completely changes. As people watch him from afar as his boat returns, the previously cloudy screen begins to brighten. As prosperity and happiness come back to the village, the shadows and clouds that previously clouded the screen disappear. The sun shines again and everybody rejoices. Even the soundtrack becomes livelier as the previously afflicted community enters a more optimistic phase. The editing becomes faster and the frame begins to encompass more people. The costumes, as well, alter in keeping with the newfound celebration of life: the villagers, women in particular, don bright yellows, reds and whites. At Mbanick's return, as he comes closer to the camera, the griot's announcement that 'the pure light of truth has emerged' is reflected in the actual light portrayed on screen. Although darkness returns again when Mbanick is murdered by his best friend, this event is not of the same scope as the visual affliction that dominated the first third of the narrative. Such transformation is evidence that in epic narratives, 'every temporal reference has a function. Time signifies and punctuates an important event from its beginning to its end. But every signal of time comes especially from the sky in general, and from the sun in particular' (Soro, 2002, 162).[5]

2   Epic magnification

Keita, Yeelen, Ndeysaan and *La Colère des Dieux* portray, as most epics do, characters who belong to an elite class (Dérive, 2006b, 137). Soundjata and Salam are both princes. Mbanick's father is a respected spiritual leader in the village. Yatma's father is very powerful and people are afraid of him in Timbering. Clearly, all these figures hold special places within their communities; although they are thus predisposed to social importance, they must nevertheless overcome significant difficulties.

In *Keita* and *La Colère des Dieux* the protagonists usually have to overcome a childhood misfortune before they accede to heroic greatness. Such affliction is common to many folktales where young heroes are often victims of ill-treatment. Their marginalization is generally due to a birth defect or other physical affliction; ugliness and genetic calamities are thus distinct features of the epic. Sogolon is the ugliest woman in the village. Another case in point is Soundjata whose mother endures an exceptionally long pregnancy. She gives birth to a child with a severe physical handicap. He crawls for several years, practically until adulthood. There are also some other defects that significantly marginalize his adult life. He has an enormous head, with eyes said to be as red and wild as red coal. He is also very heavy. Not only does Soundjata speak from within the womb, he is moreover born with many teeth. As the camera pans on huge rocks at the announcement of his birth, audio and visual effects are used to attest to the importance of the new life: lightning and thunder accompany Sogolon's cries of pain.

Salam's childhood in *La Colère des Dieux* is not substantially different. He is born with an outgrown tooth which makes him ridiculous to the other children, who systematically humiliate him. They constantly remind him that he is the cause of all the distress affecting the village since his birth, and some children even regularly request he smiles so that the ugly tooth becomes even more apparent and they can laugh at him. His two nicknames are in that sense significant: Salam Big Tooth and Rhinoceros Tooth. When Halyaré teaches him to ride a horse and he proudly takes one to the river where his peers and other adults are doing their laundry, they all burst into laughter. The camera then shows several close-up shots of his face with the disfiguring, protuberant, tooth. After crying silently, he tries to extract the tooth with a tool before being interrupted by his mother. She then immediately takes him to the blacksmith who performs the dental surgery with rudimentary equipment. Only after enduring this anguished childhood and a repulsive physical appearance does the protagonist become the epic hero, more powerful than other human beings and only slightly less than gods.

However, in order for a character to achieve great things, a particular situation must set events in motion. *Keita, Yeelen, Ndeysaan* and *La Colère des Dieux* are not only narratives about the glorious exploits of singular individualities; rather, these figures emerge in specific social and historical contexts which make their emergence possible. Not every situation is conducive to epic accomplishment and that is why the presence of a hero speaks to a particular social context. According to Gabriel Soro, a *crisis* is always necessary, if not indispensable, to reveal an epic hero:

> in the epic emerging within a society in crisis, the hero is a
> symbolic subject, the main character who offers a positive
> answer to the concerns of the people. If in the epic people take
> delight in exalting the central figure, it is because such a figure
> better embodies and crystallizes the moral values, the virtues of
> the entire community: in this regard, the hero is a popular hero.
> (Soro, 2002, 265)[6]

While the epic hero does not always necessarily embody strictly positive values, his emergence is necessarily predicated upon a social crisis. In *Yeelen,* such a crisis has already erupted at the film's opening. Nianankoro has already run away with his mother after stealing the forbidden *Nkomo,* the Bambara secret knowledge and power. A terrifying figure, the deprived father promises to kill the son who has dared take up a power to which he is not entitled. The entire film is centred on Nianankoro's flight and his father's mission to find him, until they finally meet in the last sequence for the deadly confrontation. In *Keita,* although some people challenge Soundjata's constitutional right to rule, the crisis is more private than public. The only obstacle to Soundjata's ascension to power is his half brother, whose mother is unable to come to terms with the fact that her own son has been disinherited for the benefit of the handicapped Soundjata. The other crisis that requires epic grandeur is the fiery buffalo that terrifies the land of Do, killing ten hunters daily, causing famine as well as anxiety in the community. The last and, probably, most important conflict which allows the rise of the epic hero, is personal. When his mother asks for some baobab leaves from the queen, the latter sarcastically refers to Soundjata's disability. Having witnessed such humiliation, Soundjata summons the blacksmith to make him a huge iron rod which he instantly uses to make his first steps as a new and extraordinarily powerful leader.

La Colère des Dieux takes place in a different setting. When the king dies, his son Tanga imposes himself as the new monarch because he is the commander-in-chief. As is the case with *Keita*, the crisis in Ouedraogo's film is politico-institutional. Although the film is set in a distant past, it seems to suggest that the entitlement to govern as well as the thirst for political power is not a novel postcolonial experience. The narrative opens and concludes with a death. Although Salam kills his tyrannical father who has systematically terrorized populations with his despotic authority, he fatally reproduces exactly the same autocratic ruling patterns. In that sense, Salam may not be Tanga's biological son, but is truly his political heir as they both practise the same despotic trade. However, Salam proves not to be that heroic after all; although he kills Tanga and thus delivers the community from a ruthless tyrant, his own thirst for absolute control ultimately destroys him. The severe drought, famine, diseases and mass catastrophes that the kingdom experiences after the birth of Salam do not allow him to emerge as a true epic hero who will successfully deliver the community from disaster. When he challenges the spirit which gave him the magic to destroy Tanga, he fails to realize, although he was warned, that there is a more important power which this spirit conceals. When Salam discovers his fatal mistake, it is already too late and he prefers to commit suicide instead of experiencing inevitable (and forecasted) defeat. In this respect, there is a sense of *repetition* and *reproducibility* in the epic structure of *La Colère des Dieux* where two political and social crises follow each other. Tanga's atrocities do not prevent his son from repeating the same political choices. In fact, Salam's reign is so short that one can see that his emergence as a personage, in view of the running time in which he is involved and his tenure in power, appears like a simple prolongation of his father's fatal epic extravagance. Given their defiance, these characters are, as Isidore Okpewho argues (1979, 97), obsessed with the need to express superiority and inspire fear. They lack modesty, claim precedence over everyone else, gods and elders included, and demand to be revered.

The above narratives depict epic figures that are distinct from one another. Although it is clear that Soundjata appears to be the only 'nation builder', Mbanick, Nianankoro, Tanga and Salam illustrate themselves by their ability to carry on specific, at times selfish, agendas. While Gabriel Soro (2002, 166) argues that epic heroes serve as models to future generations and are meant to convey specific values in the communities where they emerge, it is rather obvious, as Olivier Barlet (2000, 164) and Manthia Diawara (1996, 210) suggest, that the purpose of incorporating oral storytelling techniques is not to promote a set of reproducible, generally conservative values. The stereotypes that generally characterize the epic world are more nuanced in the contexts at hand. In spite of the fact that the typical epic protagonist remains moved by courage, bravery and determination, the social transformation Gabriel Soro believes he enables is absent from *La Colère des Dieux* and *Ndeysaan*.

On the other hand, these characters do not always appear to be the best model for the society. Mbanick, for example, is extremely vengeful and there is an implication at the end of the film that he could and should have forgiven his friend. While Yatma is marginalized and vilified, time passes and some learn to forgive his hideous crime. When he succumbs to Mbanick's revenge, there is a reversal in their respective roles of 'villain' and 'hero', categories which, in this narrative, are not correlated in the traditional Manichean way to good and evil. Mbanick's lack of forgiveness is far from ennobling. His reluctance to assume his destined role as spiritual leader and his refusal to lead the village healing procession at the beginning of the film both indicate a collective loss of faith in traditional methods. Social beliefs can therefore be challenged in oral narratives. Mbanick's success in assuming his role has consequences for the entire village, which he finally delivers from hunger and the fog. In *Yeelen,* Nianankoro illustrates, like Mbanick, the need to question tradition and accepted ideas. By taking over the knowledge and power from a tyrannical father and ultimately killing him, he paves the way for a new future where all can be shared and children respected.

Epic narratives examined here are not only characterized by an unfriendly temporality. If Mbanick, Soundjata, Salam and Tanga are more than just inconsequential anonymous subjects, it is not only because of their passion for danger or excesses. The challenges faced precisely allow various subjects to emerge as heroes. Within a very short time, under a cloudy sky, Mbanick chops down a huge baobab tree by himself, as the bewildered villagers look on. He then carves it and makes a canoe which he uses to go fishing, in defiance of sea and weather, which have for months antagonized the powerless population. The long thirty minutes of running time, during which the clouds are maintained on the screen to express Timbering's utter despair, is hyperbolic. So is the sound of waves which is often replaced by a funereal sound track. We are told that with his bare hands, Soundjata uproots a baobab tree in *Keita*. He subsequently carries it to his humiliated mother so that she is not without much-needed baobab leaves any longer. In this hypertrophy, Sogolon moves from total material scarcity to amplified abundance. If we add to all this the fact that Soundjata miraculously uses newly built rods to stand and make his first steps after crawling throughout his life, his subsequent achievements then become just epic narrative patterns. In *La Colère des Dieux*, the blacksmith expresses his astonishment at Salam's reaction to a dental extraction he performs without anaesthetic: Salam makes no noise. When he later runs after the mythical bird for seventeen years in order to get the power he needs, it is clear that we are operating within the realm of epic hyperbole. Such hyperbolic expressions are in several respects due to the influence of non-rational elements, which significantly contribute to the construction of a world of superlatives.

Epic exaggeration would not be possible without the extensive use of supernatural elements. According to Derek Elley, in dressing the epic action in noble style, the often mythic elements of the narrative allow a distinction from profane ordinary narratives. With 'the introduction of the irrational, the inexplicable, the magical' (Elley, 1984, 10), the epic gains its fullest dimension. In fact, Jean Dérive argues that no epic world is conceivable without supernatural components; the epic is simply nonexistent if various characters do not, at any given time, deal with some transcendental mediator, a magus, a priest or a diviner, who appears as a necessary adjuvant (2002b, 139). For Isidore Okpewho, it is not possible to fully appreciate any epic story without focusing one's attention on its supernatural elements. African epic characters generally appeal to the gods for assistance, harnessing supernatural powers to accomplish deeds that would otherwise be impossible in the human realm. The idea of the 'invisible' represents a blurring of the distinction between the 'religious' and the magical:

> Whether the hero puts himself at the mercy of divinity and
> acknowledges his subordination to its will, or demonstrates
> extreme self-sufficiency and simply coerces otherwordly
> elements in ensuring his supremacy, the distinction between

what may be called the 'religious' and the 'magical' has always been a difficult one to establish. The essential mark of the heroic personality in many African folk epics is its reliance on supernatural resources. (Okpewho, 1979, 119)

The importance of supernatural powers is demonstrated in several films. In *Ndeysaan* for example, there is an explicit correlation between Mbanick's amulet and his tragic fate. Indeed, his father gives him an amulet before his death. As he leaves Maxoye, with whom he has just made love, it gets stuck to a tree branch without him realizing it, and there is a quick extreme close-up on this symbolic object. When he is attacked, there is another close-up on his face as he expresses his astonishment at having lost his crucial protection. His facial expression anticipates a kind of future disaster. After his father's death, his spirit takes complete control of Mbanick who then becomes cut off from the community. Everybody is afraid of him and he does not recognize anyone, including Maxoye. During those moments, he is a totally transformed individual whose actions are determined by a world beyond human borders. It is during the time when he is possessed that Mbanick fells the huge tree in the midst of chaotic and dangerous weather.

Characters in *Yeelen* make extensive use of objects that protect them from evil and perform other important functions. For example, Soma, Nianankoro's father, has a *Kolonkotani* or magic pestle which helps to find lost objects and punish outlaws; he and his brother use it to look for the rebellious son throughout the film. Nianankoro's special power is not only due to his possession of the *Nkomo,* for his mother also gives him an amulet that permanently protects him. When he arrives at a village where people are astonished by his magical abilities, the king realizes that he must rely on a young stranger, whose help he requests to defeat his enemies. He makes a potion from a horse tibia that generates a huge cloud of bees. The bees sting the enemies, who run for their lives, to the satisfaction of everyone now indebted to Nianankoro. Another scene makes the king and his subjects realize that Nianankoro has mysterious powers. When he is arrested stealing milk from cattle, he is brought to the court, where a punishment is required. When a guard tries to hit Nianankoro, his hand suddenly freezes and he stays still until Nianankoro decides to release him. The same thing happens when his uncle gets to this village. Outraged by the stranger's insolence, the king instructs that he be killed; his arm likewise is frozen in the air when the executioner tries to kill Nianankoro. In both instances, Nianankoro and his uncle make the simple gesture of spitting to release the guards. In the final decisive altercation between Soma and his son, it is again the spiritual forces that are at war. In this last scene, Cissé makes excellent use of audiovisual features to portray the confrontation towards which the entire narrative was leading. In a desert landscape, the two holders of the *Nkomo* clash, and the father is defeated. Extensive use of special sound effects and lighting are incorporated to indicate the presence of the occult. The last battle, clearly, is a battle to establish new temporalities because the tyrannical father is defeated, which paves the way for a new order.

Tanga, who has usurped power, has also received amulets in *La Colère des Dieux*. As one of the elders explains, the amulet has three principal powers: to create fires, to transform its bearer, and to render its bearer invisible. However, Tanga is reminded that there is a higher power, namely that of the gods, which is stronger than that of the amulet. Tragically, Tanga comes face to face with the amulet's limitations during the epic battle with his son. After running for years and achieving competence in magic from a spirit, father and son wage the war of their lives. The battle leaves Tanga dead in a desert landscape where light and dark, loud noise and silence, alternate. Thanks to his newly acquired capabilities, Salam provokes sudden darkness to kill Tanga, who in turn reacts by starting a huge wildfire. The screen erupts with red, yellow and orange. In response to Tanga's fire, Salam prompts a heavy rain which extinguishes the fire. The combat goes on for a long time; Salam, at the height of his performance, feminizes Tanga by instructing him to run away in defeat like a woman. Because both opponents have the ability to metamorphose, Tanga becomes a rabbit and begins to flee. He is transmuted back into his human form when he is shot in the leg by Salam, who cold-heartedly kills the despot.

A similar episode takes place in *Keita*. When the two hunters go to the bush looking for the buffalo that has been terrifying the village of Do, they come across an ugly woman, Do-Kamissa, who informs them that she is the buffalo who has killed and wounded many men. Because the two brother hunters are courageous and friendly, she decides to surrender her life and instructs them how to kill her. Most importantly, she shows them a distaff, a stone and an egg which she instructs them to use when they wage the crucial battle with the buffalo. The woman leaves the scene until the desert landscape is introduced as the site of the final epic confrontation between the brother hunters and the woman-animal. As the buffalo charges at the hunters, they run for their life, look back and first throw the distaff which becomes a thick field of palm trees. This allows the hunters to hide for some time and continue the marathon. When they later hear the buffalo roaring closer to them, the younger brother throws the stone. Immediately they find themselves on a mountain of rocks where the buffalo, stuck below, cannot harm them. The final ammunition is the egg, which becomes a deep muddy swamp in which the buffalo sinks before being shot by the two hunters. Although *Keita* is limited to portraying Soundjata's adolescence, the intervention of invisible forces we see here in the confrontation between the woman-buffalo and the two brother hunters is an essential part of Soundjata's future trajectory. That, for Gabriel Soro, is an indication of a religious syncretism which reconciles Islam and African beliefs (2002, 159). Such syncretism is mediated through *objects* to which specific *forces* are attached. They have a strong spiritual and symbolic influence that is found in the spoken word which is a vehicle for *knowledge* and *prediction*.

Keita and *La Colère des Dieux* provide ample evidence that '[p]rophecy is characteristic of the epic, prediction for the novel. Epic prophecy is realized wholly within the limits of the absolute past (if not a given epic, then within the limits of the tradition it encompasses)' (Bakhtin, 1981, 31). The dramatic irony of these narratives is very sharp in that the epic (and tragic) hero is usually the only one unaware of his fate. Although the prophecy is not always announced by an oracle, in the epic it is always fulfilled. *Keita,* for example, opens with a hunter who silently waves a horse tail on Djeliba's face, without saying a single word. Djeliba immediately wakes up and leaves without telling even his family anything about the miraculous mission he has been instructed to fulfil. Do-Kamissa, the woman-buffalo who terrorizes the Mande land, predicts exactly what is going to happen to the people of Do. Her prediction comes to pass in the subsequent sequences of the narrative. Because they have given her *their word*, when the king offers them a bride they go for the ugliest, Sogolon. She later will indeed give birth to the future leader of the Mande, Soundjata Keita. One should equally mention that the hunter who appears at the beginning also predicts the birth of a mighty king who will bring pride, honour and success. He also miraculously emerges when Mabo has taken up his role as the new storyteller, and then vanishes. If one adds to this the fact that even when Soundjata goes to request that a solid iron rod be built the blacksmith is not surprised at all, saying he knew that would happen, a picture emerges regarding the power of the prophecy in epic tales.

In *La Colère des Dieux* the ability to foresee essentially applies for tragic events. Shortly after Tanga imposes himself as the new king, a villager sees a star in the sky. Everyone, including the emerging tyrant, looks at the strange star with circumspection. The animals become strangely aggressive and nervous, and the screen becomes almost white with bright light. Although no explanation is given for these phenomena, an element of uncertainty seems to characterize the new regime. This puzzlement is confirmed soon after the birth of Salam. A priest goes to the palace and informs the king that the newborn will cause terrible things to happen in the village. In spite of Tanga's violent dismissal of the warning, the nameless priest warns Tanga that he holds knowledge and that if nothing is done, his reign will be disastrous and fatal. He illustrates his prophecy by pointing to the unusually aggressive sun, with a strange star shining alongside it during the day. No one seems to pay attention, and Tanga, like any tragic hero, dismisses him with utter hostility and scorn. Unfortunately, everything that was prophesied comes to pass very soon after. The village is suddenly inflicted with a severe drought, hunger and disease. The failure to pay attention to advice is a central feature of Tanga's character. Love for danger and arrogant defiance are imperative constituents of epic and tragic destinies. As Bakhtin puts it, 'Outside his destiny, the epic and tragic hero is nothing; he is, therefore, a function that the plot fate assigns him; he cannot become the hero of another destiny of another plot' (1984, 36). The same applies to Salam, who is his father's double. When he gets the magical power from the white eagle, he is warned that there are more powers than the one he has just acquired, and that failure to respect them can only lead to destruction. Like Tanga, he realises his mistakes too late and takes his own life. Destiny and inevitability are central to epic constructions.

It is interesting that all the films discussed have two particular commonalities, namely the presence of the animal world and the exaggerated efficiency of liquids. It is a truism that African epics break down the borders between human beings and animals. In *Keita,* Do-Kamissa is a woman-buffalo. Her dual existence speaks to the importance of the totem in African settings, where a human being can have a double identity. Later, when Mabo Keita takes over as the narrator, he sees a white bird in the sky which the camera tracks. As promised by Djeliba, this bird, which equally appears toward the end of the film, is his double and is in charge of ensuring his protection. In *Ndeysaan,* Mbanick and Yatma are descendants of a lion and an ocean monster, respectively. In the case of Mbanick, Yatma, Mabo and Do-Kamissa, the animal association originates from a family history. As Isidore Okpewho (1979, 114) sugggests, such totemic doubles derive from past favourable encounters between the characters' ancestors and these animals. In *La Colère des Dieux,* there is a flying bird in the early sequences of the film. The camera then shows animals that become uncharacteristically aggressive as soon as Salam is born. He later meets a white eagle/human being from which he gets the supernatural powers to kill Tanga. As previously noted, in *Yeelen,* Nianankoro uses a horse tibia to manipulate bees and send them to defeat enemies. During the ultimate showdown, there is a dissolve which transforms Nianankoro into a lion and his father into an elephant. These animals, which act as protecting forces, can also turn against the epic hero, and are bearers of what Okpewho calls 'the magic of counterforce' (1979, 114).

Another similarity of the films considered in this chapter is the prominent use of liquids, especially water. Water does more than purify or harbour fish for the people of Timbering. The first shot of *Yeelen* offers an acute illustration of the irreconcilable difference between Nianankoro and his father. He looks into a calabash of water and sees Soma, his monstrous double. It is after looking several times at the ugly face he tells his mother that what he foresees for the near future is horror and war. In several instances, Nianankoro spits on people in order to cure them from a disease or free them from a misfortune. It is also in a river that Nianankoro's mother goes to purify herself with milk. In *La Colère des Dieux,* another calabash full of water reveals a different double, or, rather, a new rival. When Tanga finally decides to consult the priest about the disasters afflicting his kingdom since the birth of Salam, the water in the calabash shows him the face of Salam's real father, Rasmané. All these examples suggest that water is a vehicle for truth as well as an agent of purification and liberation. It is, definitely, an important touchstone for the epic hero.

This chapter has suggested alternative meanings for old myths being explored by new narratives in which the most important values seem to be found in past mythologies. The epic form provides African directors with a means with which to re-examine the past without necessarily falling into an uncritical glorification of it. It is interesting that in *Keita,* Djeliba does not seek to oppose the new teaching he offers Mabo to alienating Western education. While the boy's mother and the schoolteacher, typical alienated postcolonial subjects, dismiss Djeliba's initiation and practically abuse him, the old griot, a supposedly traditionalist and conservative figure, proposes that Mabo go to school during the day and take his informal lessons in the evening. This film offers a hybrid, non-patronizing cultural formation which reconciles Africa and the Western world. Epic forms do not magnify the past, but rather lead to a better understanding and also, crucially, an improvement of the present, which in turn offers hope of a better future. The narrative process in *Keita* goes beyond contestation of the Western abasement of African history and cultures. It shows reconciliation between history and the *contemporary experience*. And it is interesting to note that in that process, a teenage boy takes over the hybrid identity of traditional storyteller and Western-educated subject; as such, the film positions itself far beyond the narratives of victimization or nationalism.

Another important element that needs to be mentioned is the way epic narratives offer mythical interpretation of historical military defeats and humiliations. In all the films examined, an oracle predicts the future. In *Yeelen,* Digui Diara does not only reveal to his nephew Nianankoro that his wife will give birth to a boy with a bright future. He also predicts the future decline of the Bambaras, who will renounce their faith and be reduced to slavery. This forecast is similar to the one in *La Colère des Dieux* where the white eagle curses Salam and informs him that his ungratefulness will result in severe humiliations by white men. Indeed, in the last scenes of the film, one sees a French officer giving specific instructions to his men to fire on the enemy in the recently-invaded village. Instead of experiencing such indignity, Salam prefers to commit suicide.

This mythical interpretation of colonial domination is quite interesting. It basically provides an alternative metaphysical understanding of a historical Western military superiority. Such metaphysical elucidation of African subjugation is facile, and is reminiscent of Kwame Anthony Appiah's critique of Wole Soyinka's Yoruba ontology. According to Appiah (1992, 176), Soyinka's metaphysics is not only useless but damaging in that it attributes African unity to gods, who, Appiah argues, have not been useful in the continent's interactions with the world. For him, Soyinka fails to account for the reasons that, in spite of their power, Yoruba gods have almost been wiped out by Christianity and Islam. In revisiting the past through the lens of mythology, these films appear to portray what Achille Mbembe calls a 'reified vision of history' in which '[c]ausality is attributed to entities that are fictive and wholly invisible, but are nevertheless said to determine, ultimately, the subject's life and work' (2002a, 243). These films succeed in replacing historical accuracy and rationality with an alternative epistemological apparatus. However, does fiction have to be accurate or rational? It is the hegemony of rationality that is in itself challenged by these films.

Another important aspect of the films just analysed is the way in which they not only portray the hardships and challenges of the contemporary world, but also speculate as to future possible worlds, without necessarily providing clear clues as to the exact outcome. *Yeelen,* for example, clearly ends with the inception of a new world, a new order of things born at the death of the autocratic father. Although *Keita* narrates a mythical origin story, the narration is deliberately incomplete, as if the past has become endless or subsumed the present. The film's conclusion suggests that Mabo will wait for or will bring about this new departure, this new era. *Ndeysaan* equally ends with a sort of peace and a new order, as a hideous crime ends being forgiven by everyone in the community. One is left to wonder if these films undertake a genealogical archaeology in order to prepare for a new future. Is the mythical the key to challenging the status quo and suggesting possibilities for the future? Mircea Eliade, one recalls, once said that a nation without a myth runs the risk of self destruction.

One final point concerns the role of cinema itself as a medium. When considering the case of *Keita,* one can state that modern media serve as alternatives to conventional oral transmission. As is well known and as argued above, oral performance is only possible when a griot undertakes the massive task of transmitting a vanishing history. Whether they overtly incorporate storytellers or not, African films seem to play a crucial role in the preservation of an endangered memory. What is more, it compensates for the modern lack of exposure to oral tradition and performances. In that sense, one can comfortably admit that in order to protect an oral heritage in danger of disappearing because the griots destined to transmit it have become rare, modern technology can play an important role.

Notes

1 In 'Film and History in Africa: A Critical Survey of Current Trends and Tendencies', (2004), Mbye Cham offers a very brief reading of *Sarraounia* which he describes as 'the very first truly African cinematic epic' (64) without

further illustrations of the ways in which this epicness is conveyed in film, which is not the purpose of his essay anyway.

2 K. Martial Frindéthie's *Francophone African Cinema* (2009, 88–113) typically uses *Keita* for elaborations on the Mali Empire, technological inventiveness, occupational specialization, pharmacological knowledge or administration of justice in ancient Africa.

3 Original: '*un autre grand trait du style épique qui a souvent été mis en avant est sa prédilection pour l'hyperbole. Qu'il s'agisse des actions ou de l'expression des sentiments, des qualités d'un individu ou d'un objet, tout est représenté à l'extrême.*' (2002b, 127).

4 '*Le temps, dès lors, ne peut devenir constitutif qu'à partir du moment où toute liaison avec la patrie transcendentale est rompue. Dans le roman, sens et vie se séparent et, avec eux, essence et temporalité; on pourrait presque dire qu'en ce qu'elle a de plus intime, toute l'action du roman n'est qu'un combat contre les puissances du temps. Et [de cette résignation de l'individu] procèdent les expériences authentiquement épiques de la temporalité : espoir et souvenir*' (quoted in Benjamin, 2000, 136, emphasis added).

5 '*chaque évocation du temps est fonctionnelle. Le temps est destiné à marquer un événement capital dont il ponctue le début ou la fin. Mais chaque manifestation de ce temps provient surtout des éléments du ciel en général, et du soleil en particulier*' (Soro, 2002, 162).

6 '*symbolique, le héros l'est dans la mesure où, l'épopée naissant dans un état de crise de la société, le personnage principal est l'individu qui apporte au peuple une réponse d'ordre positif à ses préoccupations. Si dans l'épopée les gens se complaisent dans l'exaltation de la figure centrale, c'est parce qu'elle incarne, mieux, elle cristallise les valeurs morales, les vertus de toute la communauté : en ce sens le héros est un héros populaire*' (Soro, 2002, 265).

23   Souleymane Cissé

24   Mansour Sora Wade, *Ndeysaan*

Chapter 6

(Un)masked sexuality

The previous chapter has laid out the ways in which some narratives make extensive use of epic devices to shape new subjectivities as well as to create superhuman figures within communities in crisis and in need of a new hero. In spite of their power, these figures nevertheless remain extremely vulnerable and maintain a fatal 'weakness' that in the end humanizes them. This 'flaw' is inherently related to social disasters brought about by issues of sexuality, and the analysis of myth and tragedy clearly addresses that issue. The purpose of this chapter is to look at the textual strategies used to *represent* sex and classify it as a signifier of the (decadent) nation, as well as a discrete social commodity. More specifically, the following sections discuss how African narratives reveal sex in films and in spectators' minds with strategies other than explicit nudity or penetration, thus developing imagined rather than direct viewing. Following this analysis of the theoretical articulations of African sexuality, the subsequent section examines the link between sexuality, the nation, and the 'trouble' with representing 'it', that is, sex. The next section will explore the formal strategies used by various directors to frame desiring bodies in limit texts that border on pornography, one of several categories deemed 'un-African'.

1   African sexuality as category of analysis

In *Les Couples dominos*, her pioneer essay on African sexuality, Thérèse Kuoh-Moukoury (1977) analyses the forms of sexual politics in traditional African society and in mixed (black and white) couples. One of the key points she makes is that in Africa, the enjoyment of sex is very private; because intercourse is regarded as intended for reproduction, female pleasure is not culturally considered to be a priority. It is very 'conventional' by Western standards and certain practices, among them homosexual relations and '*manœuvres anales*/anal manoeuvers,' are regarded by many as immoral. Africans, Moukoury argues, do not see any sense in enjoying the 'dirty' parts through which all the stinking, unpleasant substances are evacuated. In another work, Kuoh-Moukoury and other African theorists such as Pius Ngandu Nkashama and Massa Makan Diabaté acknowledge the radical metamorphosis that African societies have experienced since independence with regard to the explosion of sex and discourses of sexuality, as well as the transformation of sex into a *public* topic. In the introduction to Gérard Clavreuil's book *Erotisme et Litératures* (1987) these theorists and others investigate new forms of sexuality. They identify a kind of social hierarchy in sexual practices: eroticism is regarded as the 'human' and decent part of sex, while pornography is the 'dirty', 'immoral' and wild part of it. It is in this sense that Kuoh-Moukoury (in Clavreuil, 1987, 50) contends that 'At present, we are witnessing an explosion of sexuality, and furthermore of pornography, without having experienced the *belle époque* of eroticism'.[1] According to her, the explosion of the consumption, discourse and representation of sex is unprecedented. The most compelling evidence of this explosion can be found in the openness of the African literary discourse on sex, demonstrated in the books of Sony Labou Tansi or Calixthe Beyala for example. Both authors' representations of sexuality are radically different from those of people like Mongo Beti or Camara Laye who are more subtle in their social perception of sexuality. The praxis of new generations of African writers and filmmakers corresponds to Michel Foucault's (1978, 32) analysis that sex has become 'something to say, and to say exhaustively in accordance with deployments that [are] varied, but in their own ways compelling. Whether in the form of a subtle confession in confidence or an authoritarian interrogation, sex – be it fine or rustic – [has] to be put into word.'

The emergence of discourses pertaining to sex and sexuality as the cultural, political and aesthetic fabric of everyday postcolonial experience is compellingly theorized in Achille Mbembe's *On the Postcolony* (2001). This text, which provides a sort of African 'history of sexuality,' theoretically and chronologically follows Frantz Fanon's definitive conceptualizations of Black sexuality in *Black Skin, White Masks* (1967). Mbembe shows that the slave trade and colonial adventures were not only assaults on specific values but, moreover, were first and foremost violent 'phallic' undertakings that both feminized and subjugated African peoples. The territorial conquest was both literally and metaphorically a *sexual* rape. Accordingly, Mbembe (2001, 175) argues that 'Without a phallus, the colonizer is nothing, has no fixed identity. Thanks to the phallus, the colonizer's cruelty can stand quite naked: erect. A sliver of flesh that dribbles endlessly, the colonizer's phallus can hardly hold back its spasms.'

Although at times excessive and nearly essentialist, it is also obvious that in Mbembe's view there has been little change from colony to postcolony as far as sexuality and its dramatization is concerned. His depiction of Africans' attitude to sex at times borders stereotype:

> The everyday life of the postcolonial bureaucrat consists of the following: alcohol, amusement, lewd propositions, and bawdy comments in which the virtue of women comes under scrutiny through allusions to the sexual organs of office secretaries and prowess of declared favorites and young mistresses. (127)

In a recent study, while deploring the 'hypocrisy' of the public African discourse on sex, Célestin Monga (2009, 76) also expresses the difficulty of constructing a balanced and coherent representation of black sexuality:

> However, it remains a delicate exercise to speak about sexuality in Africa and in the black world. The subject is often obscured by phantasms and myths fabricated and peddled by ethno-political mythology dating back to the era of slave trade and black oppression. It is thus not easy to offer a reading of behaviors bereft of hasty generalizations. It is necessary to avoid the double pitfall of voyeurism and clichés, to stay at equidistance to the racialist discourse which feeds collective phantasms in the West on 'black sexuality', and to the reductionist and self-flagellating discourse of many African authors concerned with 'political correctness'.[2]

Surprisingly, this apparent saturation of sex in public discourse did not become subject to extensive representation for African filmmakers, whose characters up to this point remain exceptionally ascetic and discreet. In a continent fraught with social and political imperatives that heavily determine filmmaking, Françoise Pfaff (1996, 258) contends that African cineastes are 'more interested in analysing the forces at work in a given society than the amorous frolicking of romantic heroes'. To talk about sexuality corresponds to addressing individual subjectivities, which is a heresy for nationalist ideologies and political movements committed to the view that the subject is nothing but an instrument in the hands of the community. What matters most is material production and industrial efficiency, not obscene pleasures that uselessly delay social imperatives.[3] Such a conceptualization positions sex and sexuality as incompatible with revolutionary praxis; abstinence is accordingly represented by the authorities in power as essential to citizens who have other pressing priorities. Ethiopian director Haile Gerima (in Pfaff, 1996, 259) is very radical in his assertion of the absolutely inessential role of sex in African films:

> In our societies, sex is not the point of departure for everything.
> There is more to life than sex. In the West, it is the point of
> reference for everything ... In Africa people don't wake up for
> sex. They wake to find out where they are going to get their
> next meal. I think it has got to do with the nature of society. ...
> Sex is only one of the things you go through in the initiation of
> life. In the West, sex is a decisive factor. So every movie has to
> abide by that ...

Opinions like Gerima's are not only dated, but are also based on a relatively essentialist or static perception of cultures and societies that have undergone major metamorphoses.[4] Such scarcity of the obscene in films has reduced sexual imagination and its representations to a process of mystification or mythification whereby contemporary African sex(uality) has remained something of a mystery. It has thus actively generated curiosity in what is perceived to be its 'exotic' nature. It is therefore no surprise that the only African films with nude sex scenes and homosexuality have drawn crowds in all continents, while benefiting from the privilege of censorship on the continent. After its release, *Visages de femmes* was banned in Côte d'Ivoire. As Jean-Pierre Bekolo (in Romuald Nkonlak, 2007) explains in an interview, *Les Saignantes* went through multiple 'rigorous' preview sessions and was eventually allowed to air in

Cameroon almost by chance. It is no secret that although Joseph Gaï Ramaka's *Karmen Geï* (2002) was banned in Senegal by religious authorities (and notably not by the government), this film and Mohamed Camara's *Dakan* (1997) have gained significant attention in the West, especially among gay and lesbian cinematic and cultural communities. Labelled 'half-Western, half-African' by Nwachukwu Frank Ukadike (1994, 4), Désiré Ecaré's *Visages de femmes* (1984) is the first African narrative with active athletic sexuality and frontal nudity. It was also a major commercial success in France. In *Bal Poussière* (1988), Henri Duparc's most successful film because of its comedic appeal, the overt sexual content is likewise strategically masked by innovative formal interventions. Ukadike's charge against this film, however, is emblematic of a 'nationalist' and essentialist criticism as well as a tendency to dismiss certain practices as 'un-African'. The obsession in the West to emphasize they are not has now become endemic:

> [In *Bal Poussière*], Duparc's structure and his method of
> construction become *questionable* in view of his cinematic
> voyeurism. Consider, for example, his camera's *preoccupation with
> the conspicuous*, leering at Binta's features and contours, to expose
> them in close up – her bouncing breasts, and in full-screen
> close-up, her buttocks. *For Western viewers, these features may be more
> gripping and profoundly alluring, but for African critics, including
> feminists, Duparc's experimental interludes are simply jaundiced,
> misguided, and stereotypical.* (1994, 288, my emphasis)

Clearly, there is a chasm in Africa between the consumption and discussion of sex, on the one hand, and its (cinematic) representations on the other. Given that African oral literature is full of erotic tales, the absence of open sex in films is putatively, as Pfaff puts it, yet another consequence of the self-inflicted challenges of 'nation building' or 'development' which sought to avoid voyeurism and entertainment in film. However, as Pfaff (1996, 258) adds, 'increased film eroticism is to be expected in the forthcoming years in Africa because its societies are changing, and so are people's attitudes towards sex'. Contrary to what Abiyi Ford (in Pfaff, 1996, 258) believes, African films will not lose their chasteness as a direct result of the supposed Western desire for the exotic; more specifically, this change will occur as a result of local forces, both commercial and diversionary. African screens and streets are flooded with pornographic magazines and films, which probably fuel a local demand. An example that confirms Pfaff's prediction comes from popular culture, where the abundant market for sexual or erotic performances has been overlooked by filmmakers owing to moral, nationalist or ethical exigencies: the Mapouka dance, which originated, in Côte d'Ivoire. Notably, the surprising popularity of Mapouka video productions[5] among African spectators abroad and on the continent clearly indicates that attitudes to eroticism or sex as dramatized in media have completely changed. This transformation is due not only to the daring and provocative choreography in the footage, but to the high number of close-ups on the intimate parts of the 'devils'[6] illegally filmed in private houses in cities and sold in Europe or North America. Both pleasure and voyeurism now appear to reign in Africa, and several filmmakers seem to have decided to 'rehabilitate', if not to celebrate, the black body. Apart from the 'scandalous' *Visages de femmes* or *Karmen Geï*, in films like Jean-Pierre Bekolo's *Les Saignantes* (2005) or Moussa Sène Absa's *Madame Brouette* (2002), sex has become almost trivial; at the very least, it is clearly no longer taboo. Aesthetically, these directors have used features that resolutely celebrate the beauty of the obscene and break cultural codes in ways previously unparalleled.

Sexual attitudes and practices are now observable, be it live or off screen as is increasingly the case, especially because 'the postcolony is a world of anxious virility, a world hostile to continence, frugality, sobriety' (Mbembe, 2001, 110); nevertheless, apart from Kenneth Harrow's article (2010) on the rise of clitoral power and the collapse of patriarchal authority, very little scholarship has undertaken a systematic investigation of sexual politics and aesthetics in the limited number of African productions that 'dare' adopt it as a subject of analysis, representation and discourse. Central to this chapter is therefore an examination of the ways in which postcolonial films have addressed sex in a context where the elaboration of collective national imperatives and the influence of daily struggles were generally dominant theoretical and political frameworks. If one admits that sex needs to be represented and that it almost has to force its way into public representation, one must ask how such representations should be undertaken in a context where political and ethical disagreements abound. According to what rules? Considering that in films discourse generally operates through images, it is incumbent upon critics to examine how sex is explored in films such as the foundational *Xala*

(1973) to the more recent *Les Saignantes*. What are the modalities of this discourse? This chapter will use early and recent productions to explore the evolution that led to some recent critical insights, namely the place of sex in the nation, the implicit language of nudity and the temptation of what could be called 'African pornography'. If in Africa some people now enjoy homosexual or, more commonly, heterosexual, sex, critics often fail to take into account the conditions of articulation of a discourse of sexuality, as well as the strategies used by various filmmakers to mask or unmask it. Although sex remains, as it was originally, part of the discourse of a 'castrated' or failed nation, it has now moreover become a signifier denoting private happiness and challenges, unstable moral standards which have little to do with national anxieties. Stylistically, apart from a few notable exceptions to be discussed, the filmic dramatization of sexuality is mostly verbal and relies on *trompe l'oeil* strategies that prevent the viewer from actually seeing what is implied.

2   Sex in the nation and the trouble with representation

Achille Mbembe's (2001, 126) statement that 'the mouth, the belly and the penis constitute the classic ingredients of *commandement*' expresses the fact that postcolonial authority has consistently defined itself in terms of clichéd physical, reproductive and digestive attributes. An attention to such anatomic structures was long ago articulated in Sembène Ousmane's *Xala,* which established the equation of political and sexual deficiency in African films. The loss of sexual virility on the part of El Hadji Abdul Kader Beye, the main character, is associated with and followed by the decline of the freshly 'independent' postcolonial state. El Hadji's severe and unexpected sexual impotence signals the decline of nations that were supposed to quickly move forward after independence. The corruption of the penis, now reduced to a lamentably flaccid state, is the sexual replica of the political, economic and social decay dramatized in the film by characters who have relegated the most important challenges of young states to the level of nothingness. As phallic potency declines, so too does the postcolonial state and its fundamental structures. Clearly, the nation to be 'erected' in *Xala* is already in active decomposition and is about to collapse. Successful nation building therefore seems to be associated with fully consummated sex, raised penises, sexually satisfied subjects, 'receptive', 'open' and subjugated women in dominant heterosexual encounters. In aggressively assertive and nationalist films such as *Xala,* an efficient construction of the postcolonial state seems to develop from a problematic foundation, namely, pleasureful sex, the absence of which signals a decline. Why is sex so central to the representation of postcolonial experience?

This question would have remained rhetorical if other films produced several years after *Xala* had not performed similar interrogations. Fanta Régina Nacro's *Le truc de Konaté* (Burkina Faso, 1998) for example can be positioned within official policies on public health and in that respect, views undisciplined sexuality as a danger to the nation. The narrative follows Konaté's search to regain his virility after it is mysteriously stripped by what he perceives to be the curse of the condoms his wife Dieneba has brought back from the city. He is told by a 'healer' that he must find the tree that bore the condom, and so he sets out on a quest that ultimately leads him to a group of sexual health activists. Konaté is educated about the dangers of AIDS and STDs as well as the proper methods for protecting oneself against them.

In *Clando* (1996) by Jean-Marie Teno, the main protagonist's virility does not survive the endemic repression of postcolonial Cameroon. Sobgui is unable to satisfy his wife, who realizes that he has 'changed' (i.e. become impotent) since the day he was caught and tortured. In this broken family, sleep becomes her only consolation. *Les Couilles de l'éléphant* (2002) by Henri-Joseph Koumba Bididi reframes the same sexual and socio-political decadence addressed by Sembène Ousmane. In this film, Alevina, the incumbent Member of Parliament, makes a strikingly meaningful Freudian slip that speaks to the depth of his personal drama: he loudly and emphatically states in the middle of his campaign trail that he must win the upcoming … erection! The proximity of erection to election, the intended word, is not only phonetic. Lecherous metaphors and associations stress the need, throughout the film, to maintain active penises in a postcolonial stylistics of power which starts and ends with sex.[7] National (de)construction seems to begin, or at least to be associated with, impotent males and sexually frustrated women.[8] Simply put, sexual satisfaction has apparently taken a major role in the phallic order of nation building and development. Not surprisingly, Alevina's first scene in *Les Couilles de l'éléphant* involves a failed attempt at sexual intercourse that takes place in a bathroom. The devastated male, whose 'stick' has remained fatally flaccid, leaves behind him an unhappy and almost furious woman who says she hopes the impotent man will have a better performance at the meeting over which he is about to preside. The next 'urgent' matter he rushes to handle after this meeting is a trip to the countryside where he is seen dragging a woman behind his car with the intent of performing yet another ultimately unfulfilled act. In another scene, the politician comically struggles with a defeated and tragically flat penis that leaves another woman deeply frustrated. The drama is so devastating that Alevina bursts into tears and gets the woman, unsuccessfully, to caress his 'stick'. His party's motto, '*L'expérience aux commandes*/Experience in power' thus can only refer to multiple sexual experiences performed with lamentably weak phalluses.

The latest, and most tragic, representation of sex in the postcolonial nation is offered by Jean-Pierre Bekolo. *Les Saignantes* is unique not only because of Bekolo's now traditionally innovative editing, lighting and narrative techniques, but also because it is the first African film to start with a depiction of sexual intercourse. Significantly, this sexual act, though performed with an 'active' penis, involves a teenager, Majolie, and an old high ranking official, the Secretary General of the Civil Cabinet (SGCC). The man lies back passively, helplessly, watching the girl direct the forward and backward 'phallic' movements. In one of the first scenes in the film, he suddenly dies while on sexual duty. Although the penis is erect, it is subjugated and submitted to the female acrobatic sexual partner. Eventually, the SGCC's tale, like that of all other previous characters, is put to eternal rest because the Olympic performance exhausts and kills the nation's top official. Therefore, from *Xala, Le Truc de Konaté* and *Les Couilles de l'éléphant* to *Les Saignantes,* sexuality is transformed from a hopefully temporary flaccidity, with a frustrated living subject, to a permanent one, with the death of the SGCC. In all these cases, the intercourse is depicted as incomplete, negative, disastrous, and even fatal. The discourse of the decadent nation and the corrupt postcolonial administration is represented in terms of a flawed sexuality that is generally verbalized although not always openly dramatized; there can therefore be said to be a trouble with its representation.

What appear to be quite important to the sexual imagination in these postcolonial narratives are the strategies used by various filmmakers, with the exception of Bekolo and Ecaré, to (un)mask African sexuality, be it related to national or personal trajectories. In her analysis of the cultural paradigms that inform the representation of sexuality in African films, Pfaff (1996, 253) rightly indicates that '[t]he most common examples of *controlled* sexually suggestive postures in Sub-Saharan African cinema are shots of heterosexual couples walking hand in hand …; and/or couples kissing while standing and embracing […] *Bed scenes, though prudish, are much less frequent'* (my emphasis). Teresa Hoefert de Turégano (2004, 185) makes a similar point in discussing the 'lack of filmic representations of sexuality and eroticism' which, when they occur, operate within a strictly puritan environment. These observations are generally justified by the fact that in most African films, the phallus, erect or flat, as well as the empty or full vagina, is generally skipped, avoided, kept out of the frame or filmed with a purposefully distant camera. As far as the revelation of male sexual organs is concerned, Achille Mbembe (2001, 153) argues that systematically, '[f]rom what is shown, from what is visible, the phallus, erect or not, is omitted. But is manifestly legible, in regarding the subtext'. Permanent *trompe l'œil* and veiling strategies are used by filmmakers to move (copulating) genitals away from the screen. Sex is experienced in films, but implicitly rather than openly; it is present in the story, but absent from the plot. In this context, ellipses and cuts play a fundamental role.

In *Bal Poussière,* Demi-Dieu's first night with his fourth wife Binta takes an unexpected turn. As he confidently gets prepared to have a sexual encounter with her and the spectator expects lovemaking to be displayed on the screen, there is a very sharp cut and the film continues on a totally different track. What the impatient character tries to achieve is maintained out of frame as the images develop a completely new plotline. A few sequences later, Binta goes to her husband who is visibly exhausted by his activity with other wives. Demi-Dieu proudly welcomes the desiring wife. Knowing that he is exhausted, Binta claims her *séance* of marital pleasure. After using a typical language for the occasion, she approaches the exhausted man, and another cut interrupts the scene at the moment that sexual intercourse would follow. Later, when another spouse, Gnaoussi, arrives consumed by sexual desire, the film extensively depicts the woman engaging in foreplay. She wraps her African dress around her husband, and at the moment that the spectator would expect to see the couple in action, we rapidly move to a scene that is completely irrelevant to the intimate pleasure that preceded it. What becomes apparent and systematic in Henri Duparc's film is that it develops *aesthetics of deception* as does Jean-Pierre Bekolo's *Quartier Mozart* (1992).

Like many other African filmmakers, Bekolo metaphorically uses sexuality to address social issues such as gender politics and patriarchy. Sex acts are present, but not visible. The first of such relevant images shows Atango positioned on top of a young woman. Before this particular shot, we hear short laboured breaths suggesting that it is sexual pleasure that renders breathing difficult. Instead of the sex act, however, we witness a man who has almost lost his voice by trying timid moves on a woman who shows little or no emotion at all. The lower part of his body is covered, and the conversation is cut short by a dissolve that follows soon thereafter. Later in the film, while the character called Bon Pour Est Mort warms up to take over from his friend who is enjoying himself with a young woman, the action he undertakes is simply implied in the diegesis, but never revealed. When Mon Type meets with Samedi in a room, Bekolo's lighting strategically prevents the spectator from viewing the bodies of the lovers in action. In a dark shot, we only witness vertical movements underneath the sheets. The moment we hear the young woman asking for soap, we undoubtedly understand that penetration is about to occur and, moreover, that it is difficult.

In *Touki Bouki* (1973), Djibril Diop Mabéty offers different strategies to mask a sexual performance. As in the previous examples, the love scene in this film between Mory and Anta is continuously deferred by means of cuts and other repeated strategies of deferral. Set on the beach, the location par excellence for such encounters, the intercourse is merely suggested: when the young girl undresses and is about to lie down and offer herself to her lover, the scene is abruptly interrupted. What follows is the image of a bleeding sheep being slaughtered, then that of waves hitting rocks. How can this bleeding be interpreted? Is it the hymen being ruptured? In any case, the only evidence that something has happened is metaphorical, represented by the sounds of orgasm heard off screen and a shot of Anta's hand gripping a Dogon cross, the Malian symbol for fertility. A similar example of cinematic ellipsis is best illustrated in *Yeelen* (Souleymane Cissé, Mali, 1987). The protagonist Nianankoro is charged with curing the king's wife, who suffers from infertility. As he is working his trade and supposedly treating the young woman, the camera shows a quick shot of her breast, followed by her wanton heavy smile. Although nothing is ever shown on screen, the next scene moves from the bush to the palace where, after speaking in vague metaphor for an extended period, Nianankoro finally confesses his guilt, stating that '[his] penis betrayed [him]'.

Mansour Sora Wade also uses ellipses in full to mask sexual encounters. In *Ndeysaan, Le Prix du pardon* (2001), the first love scene between Mbanick and Maxoye does not involve intercourse. Exceptionally well shot like the rest of the film, the caresses take place on a village tree after the girl's water calabash suddenly falls as a result of strong emotions she experiences at the presence of her fiancé. What is striking in this sequence is the recurrence of (extreme) close-ups on Maxoye's ecstatic face and lips as Mbanick's hands navigate on her. Punctuated by very short, dark interludes, the camera slowly comes close to busy hands, lips and half-naked tops before stopping on Maxoye's hand preventing Mbanick from removing the *fèer*[9] around her waist. The extreme close-up on the hand interrupts an attempt the camera would probably not have shown in any event, as a quick cut moves the narrative to a completely different sequence. The other two love scenes, which infuriate Yatma, Mbanick's rival, are very brief and last just a few seconds. The viewer only sees the couple lying down and engaged in foreplay for a few seconds. The man is topless, and the woman has covered her body up to above the breasts. Yatma, who proceeds to murder his rival, does not have a better *actual* perception of the copulation than the spectator. In fact, unlike the viewer, Yatma does not even see the first scene. He guesses something is happening after he sees Maxoye's abandoned calabash on the street and knows something is going on not very far from the river where Maxoye went to fetch water. Although she becomes pregnant and gives birth in the film, the process by which this baby came is never *seen in full*. The viewer must therefore infer that certain secret events took place before these partners decided to protect at least the top parts of their bodies.

Idrissa Ouedraogo uses the same features to shield the viewer from witnessing sexual intercourse in two of his films. In *Yaaba* (1989), Koudi, a young woman, is married to a chronic alcoholic who is completely unable to satisfy her. In one of the very rare instances in African cinema in which a woman actually requests to have sex in order to fulfil a pressing desire, she is filmed in the dark trying to wake up a snoring husband who is in no way able to sexually satisfy her. Consequently, she has an affair with a local rogue in the bush. Again, the intercourse is always suggested: the voices of the lovers are overheard by children and other villagers who unilaterally condemn her infidelity and insubordination. The permanently frustrated Koudi only finds sexual satisfaction outside her marriage. Besides her smiles, and the obvious happiness of the lover, there is little evidence that intercourse has just taken place and their bodies hardly touch on screen. In *Tilaï* (1990), the scenario is identical. When Nogma runs away to meet with Saga, her fiancé who has to challenge his father's authority in order to be with the woman he has always loved, they go a small hut hidden in the bush. The camera does not come any closer to them as they are about to have sex. After a cut typical of African directors dealing with a sex scene, we hear Nogma express her satisfaction at Saga's performance. In her case as in Koudi's, heavy smiles and facial expressions are the only clues to an extra-marital sexual adventure undertaken by women who claim their right to libidinal happiness. Why is there such 'trouble' with the representation of sex? Why is there such mystification? Why is there so great a taboo and sense of the sacred?

The above examples illustrate that if sex seems impossible to be both 'successfully' represented and openly performed in African cinema, visual perception appears to be well controlled. Everything concerning sex takes place in front of a distant camera, or out of frame. The spectators are always placed in a situation of forced cooperation because they are compelled to undertake the hermeneutic task of interpreting the scene. Unlike conventional love or sex narratives, any vicarious or voyeuristic desire on the part of viewers is perpetually frustrated in African films. Intimate scenes are masked, delayed, almost censored. Sexual imagination is bound up with the logic of dissuasion as well as the idea that the fulfilment of desire is private and sacred. This ideology, as Pfaff points out, is based on conservative cultural orthodoxies: what is *viewed* is bad, forbidden, dangerous, *profane*, and moreover, indecent. In this sense, it is important to recall in *Quartier Mozart* Chien Méchant's warning to Mon Type who sees his daughter, 'I don't want to know if you see her; but if they come to tell me that they have seen you together, you'll ruin everything'.[10] In *Visages des femmes*, Nguessan, one of Kouassi's partners, expresses her fear of being seen, which again situates the discourse of sexuality in the realm of the forbidden: it is important that she not be *seen*. Sexuality means first and foremost privacy, not publicity, and these films all rigorously differentiate between what belongs to the public domain, that is, *the visible,* and *the invisible sex* which belongs to *private* settings. The body may be shared with another, but not in a showroom. This insight enables us to notice important cultural influences.[11] For many (African) critics, the act of displaying sexual organs stems from pornography, which is considered a Western practice that is judged in ethical terms. This 'limit of representability' is cogently expressed by Slavoj Žižek (1989, 33) for whom 'in a "normal", non-pornographic film, a love scene is always built around a certain *insurmountable limit*; "all cannot be shown"; at a certain point, the image blurs, the camera moves off, the scene is interrupted, we never see directly "that" (the penetration of sexual organs, etc.)' (emphasis mine). The ways (naked) bodies are framed in African films support Žižek's insight regarding what can be represented.

3   Framing bodies and the temptation of pornography

As one can observe in the films previously discussed, a specific conception of sexuality and its representation proscribes certain scenes, and selects what deserves to be shown. The viewer finds him or herself before a kind of censorship that is all the more remarkable for the way the body is framed. In fact, in African cinemas, the framing of the body involves two reoccurring characteristics: the upper part of the female anatomy, considered to be part of the digestive system, is depicted at times in a state of nudity, while the lower part is rarely revealed. Thus the body as a sexual object is rarely exposed in its entirety and *Clando* is a typical example: a close-up shot shows Sobgui and his wife Madeleine in bed, only half-naked. Both lower parts of their bodies are protected, and the temporary impotence of the husband simply makes any intercourse impossible. When Sobgui later goes to Cologne and seems to recover his lost virility with a German, a medium shot shows the white girl's naked upper part with firm breasts. As they caress, undress and kiss each other, Sobgui stops and moves back at the view of the wonders he says are as 'naked' as the plummeted Africa. A vertical pan later shows the girl kissing Sobgui downwards from the lips to his never shown lower parts. Filming half bodies establishes a sort of deconstruction and segmentation, which activate the imagination and the voyeuristic impulse. It is equally important to note that the body that is exposed on screen, either in parts or in its entirety, is often that of a young person, suggesting that all kinds of social mutations stem from youth, as further illustrated in several films.

In *Bal Poussière*, Binta's breasts form the first anatomical parts that the viewer sees. The aunt who sees her is scandalized. Notwithstanding the fact that the fastening of Binta's clothing is half-open, the framing is meticulously limited to the level of the hips. As with Samedi's body in *Quartier Mozart*, the consistent use of vertical panoramic shots describes the body of the young woman in a provocative way. In the scene where Binta washes herself before she overwhelms Demi-Dieu in a sexual encounter, the camera moves slowly to frame the breasts of the naked young woman, but comes to a stop at the hips. The rest of her body remains out of frame. When Binta's co-spouse approaches their partner to claim her 'turn,' her body is characteristically framed up to the point of the navel. The scene at the beach depicting the rivalry between co-spouses as to the firmness of their breasts operates similarly through this type of framing. At the end of the film, as the daughter of Demi-Dieu's foreman unties her *pagne* with fake innocence and exposes her chest to him, at which he looks with lust, this exposure is out of the viewer's gaze.

In *Clando,* the attempted intercourse between Sobgui and his wife is equally filmed in extreme close-ups where the enthusiastic wife tries to make the best welcome for her husband. The dark light, the laboured breathing bordering on suffocation, as well as the moving hands, clearly demonstrate that something intimate is happening. Here again, Teno, like other directors, makes his camera focus on the upper erotic parts: lips, chest, eyes and left breast for Madeleine. The interaction is interrupted when the wife realizes that her husband's penis is not reacting. At this point, Madeleine is not yet frustrated as she thinks it is a temporary accident. She even looks satisfied and hugs her man affectionately. In Mohamed Camara's *Dakan*, young Oumou's torso is similarly framed down to the hips, in order to reveal to the spectator the firmness of her wonders Manga refuses to appreciate on account of his homosexuality. Throughout the fraught sexual act between Oumou and Manga, the camera reveals in extreme close-ups the young man's big black lips receiving the young woman's, the crossing of their legs, and the fierce rubbing of their two chests until Manga's homosexual fantasies cut the sequence short. In general, in African cinemas, the ultimate depiction of female sexuality on screen involves showing the breasts, which represent a part of the digestive system. The freedom with which women publicly breastfeed their children in Africa proves the case in point.

Furthermore, the framing organizes what François Jost (1987, 67) calls 'internal ocularisation' (*'ocularisation interne'*), according to which what is being *seen* by the character is not seen by the viewer. When a director uses this strategy, he or she avoids the 'conventional' shot-reverse shot traditionally used in conversations in order to shield the genitals from the viewer. In fact, there is the question of regarding the reproductive organs as *sacred*; for instance, in *Clando,* when Sobgui's German girlfriend kisses him from lips to bottom, the framing of his body and his facial expression indicate that he is not in complete emotional control and that the lady is probably seeing or manipulating a body part which the camera never shows, but which she alone sees. In *Quartier Mozart*, Mon Type caresses his sex while washing himself. This becomes evident by his looking downward while the camera remains still, denying the viewer access to his genitals. A persistent rumour spreads in the film, which holds that a handshake with Panka makes male genitalia disappear. If, on the one hand, the spectator sees Chien Méchant touching himself to make certain that his genitals are in place, Mon Type, on the other hand, complains about the disappearance of his own. However, the camera frames Mon Type from the back, looking *all by himself* at the region of his body where his genitalia have now disappeared. This scenario is paralleled by Bon Pour Est Mort, when he bends over to inspect his genital apparatus fearing that it might have disappeared. The same type of framing from the back depicts Atango and Mon Type as they urinate on the wall. Though we only see the liquid running, this shot shows Atango expressing both his surprise and admiration at the size of his friend's penis. Because they do not have visual access, the viewers can only speculate and not verify that this is empirically the case; their trust guarantees the pact of reading. Only the characters have the visual advantage.

Additionally, in *Bal Poussière* Henri Duparc depicts Demi-Dieu's women from the back, especially when naked. For instance, this is the case of Binta when she approaches her husband to demand her weekly session of sexual activity. Across from Binta, we see an exhausted and desperate Demi-Dieu looking at her. Clearly, we can remark that African sex is maintained at a distance from the camera. In *Quartier Mozart*, the numerous layers of clothing that Samedi removes at the moment that she gets ready to offer herself to her lover have a twofold effect: apart from the fact that layers of clothing may in reality form a strategy of protection for young inexperienced women, they also reinforce the idea that sex is a trial for the gaze.[12] Although several films from other cinematic traditions do not always exhibit naked body parts, what appears here to be a systematic masking and veiling strategy is, as earlier argued, due to some cultural orthodoxies. According to the Togolese filmmaker Anne Laure Folly (in Barlet, 2000, 121), 'African culture is more discreet, less externalized, more modest and restrained. Every disclosure of the matter is a violation of the matter. In this sense, cinema is a transgression'.[13] The levels of this of transgression are variable, and recent productions have brought significant transformations to the ways in which the African body is at long last unveiled on screen. Such films fully display, if not celebrate, the beauty of the obscene in ways that move progressively from what Žižek (1989, 33) would call the 'light desire of eroticism' to what is clearly 'a vulgar groaning and fornication'. Some Africans have a similarly severe and conservative opinion of the matter of this film genre. According to Massa Makan Diabaté (in Clavreuil, 1987, 27):

> With pornography, mankind goes further than animality suppressed in the sexual act, like the drunkard that ingurgitates more than he can tolerate; the bird that takes such a quantity of grains that prevents it from flying. Briefly, pornography is a sexual addiction, the search for a frenetic and vertiginous sensation through sex. These frenetic and vertiginous conditions are perfectly useless to man's mental stability.[14]

The previous examples clearly demonstrate that African narratives gravitate toward eroticism rather than pornography. In the films mentioned above, genitals and bodies, especially female ones, often form the instruments and affirmation of power: they allow the domination of the other. The body and, more precisely, sexual organs seem to avoid and be avoided by the camera that shoots almost every part of the genitals in pornographic films in order to satisfy voyeuristic audiences. Within this context then, how pornographic are African films?

Neither open intimacy nor sentimental confession is popular in African cinema. The difficulty with which Mon Type conjugates the verb 'to love' to Samedi clearly recapitulates the difficulty of expressing sentimentality in some films. This recalls Thérèse Kuoh-Moukouri's statement (in Clavreuil, 1987, 24) that '*l'érotisme de l'homme noir : zéro. Ou le mutisme ou la pornographie/* the eroticism of the Black man: zero. Either muteness or pornography.' Apart from the exception of Mbanick in *Ndeyssan*, open sentimentality does not seem to be present in the sexual *rendezvous*, and the Black man comes off as a rigid and reticent lover who clumsily handles his emotions and sexual acts. We also note that physical intimacy between the characters is rare. Male and female bodies do not often approach each other; moreover, they are almost always covered. In order to expose the body, a number of filmmakers seem to have adopted a shared set of strategies of substitution. I now want to explore four distinctive cases: Med

Hondo, Moussa Sène Absa, Henri-Joseph Koumba Bididi and Ousmane Sembène.

As shown, certain parts of the woman's body, her sex organs in particular, are taboo to depict on screen. In extreme circumstances, it is the rear that is portrayed. In *Bal Poussière*, Henri Duparc deploys the same strategy of (un)masking, that is, showing with extreme restraint or just not showing sex scenes at all. However, when the naked body is depicted in a frontal shot, the camera keeps a reasonable distance from the genital organs, to the point that this technique can be regarded as a genuine form of censorship. Likewise, in Hondo's *Sarraounia* (1986), one of the first scenes that takes place occurs in a colonial camp, where there is a quarrel between two soldiers when one catches the other having sex with his concubine. Amidst giggles and laughter, we view in a very distant shot the unfaithful woman running naked, trying to escape. We catch a glimpse of her attempting to hold her breasts in order to be able to run faster. Her body, as in the cases discussed above, is banished from view. This act of showing by distancing from view almost equals the act of not showing at all.

There is the same method used in Sembène Ousmane's *Guelwaar* (1992), when Alfred narrates one of Guelwaar's wanderings in voice-over. Caught with one of his lovers, the deceased is also portrayed from a distance, with the reproductive organs hardly shown. In this instance, the camera appears to become more than ever devoted to the ideology of dissimulation. Whereas the scene of Guelwaar's escape is very short, Moussa Sène Absa's technique in *Madame Brouette* is a little different. In one of the very few public love scenes, Naago caresses Mati in public for a few minutes, accompanied by a romantic song in the background and shaky images that are transformed by multiple dissolves in order to express the tumultuous emotional state. When they make love in the next shot, the scene is very dimly lit. The couple kisses in a net in which one can see two black bodies moving in medium and close shots. What is important here is that *no* lower body part is shown, and the camera does not at any moment go below the waist. In *Les Couilles de l'éléphant*, the situation is no different: during all of Alevina's failed attempts at intercourse, his flaccid 'tail' is never shown. Although some extreme close-ups regularly show the breasts and thighs of his mistresses, for instance Wissi's when she is lying down, frustrated and pushed to masturbate as an alternative, there is hardly a shot with a bottomless Alevina. Alice, the other woman he snaps from his driver, is equally miserable: filmed from a high angle, with close-up shots on her breasts, she is also depicted masturbating to climax, her hands on her breast and clitoris. As these examples indicate, the uneasiness in the representation of African genitalia remains a reality.

To a certain extent, this also appears to hold true in *Visages des femmes*. In fact, Désiré Ecaré's long feature breaks with what is still considered the tradition in African cinema. Because it presents the nude body, the film is perceived as 'subverting moral codes in black Africa, where sexual explicitness is taboo in the cinema, whereas it is highly acclaimed in the United States' (Ukadike, 1994, 4). However, the modes of this unveiling situate the pornographic sequence of this film in the domain of clandestine and profane behaviour; in other words, in the domain of animality described by Massa Makan Diabaté. It is important to note first that the characters Kouassi and Afoué meet at the river as if by accident. In the previous sequences, although the attitude of the unfaithful woman indicates that she was tempted by the urbanite, there is no particular incident that would lead us to imagine that the two of them would meet in a sexual context. What follows, nevertheless, is the scene with the woman arriving at the river without underwear. It is important to consider here the coarseness in representation: the predisposition to fornication, the 'readiness' to do 'it'. In addition, the couple does not exchange a single word, which allows the hypothesis that this sex scene is included just as a 'pretext for introducing acts of copulation' (Žižek, 1997, 33) into the film. A sort of brutal magnetism seizes the senses and for ten long minutes, the first minutes ever of open sex in African cinema, the young man intensely engages in sex with the young woman, who lets herself be dragged into this situation like an animal. The cliché of the Negro as sex-machine, for whom sentimentalism and foreplay are useless, is well known. Indeed, the scene with the couple consummating their affair at the river proves this point; their breathing is hardly audible, whereas a Western hardcore would depict a boisterous brouhaha. This couple, however, is exceptionally silent, which is no surprise because 'In their large majority, the sexually intimate scenes in sub-Saharan African films are rather static and emotionless' (Pfaff, 1996, 254). Ecaré's *Visages de femmes* illustrates this exceptional lucidity, and gives us the impression that the lovers are like bulls thrown into the arena. Nevertheless, the representation of this long pornographic scene is rather distant from the 'hot' material of the pornographic film industry in the West. Variation in postures is certainly visible and efficient. But it is important to remark that the way the scene is shot privileges neutral full shot, *never close-ups on the reproductive organs in contact*. When Afoué's pubis is revealed, lighting almost hides it from view. We perceive Kouassi's impressive genitalia from quite a distance, and only for a very short time. We note here, however, that while the body is exceptionally revealed, the objective is to maintain a level of censorship by framing.

Moreover, the location where Désiré Ecaré opts to carry out this intimate scene is significant: the forest, the river. These are suspicious, *natural* locations, inhabited by animals. This is in keeping with the bestial nature of pornographic films, since these are clandestine locations of sexual vagabondage, and the relation that is being consummated in front of the camera is adulterous. In African films, there is the issue of *protecting intimacy from the gaze* by erecting walls where clothing is being removed. From all the intimate scenes discussed so far, only the one between Kouassi and Afoué takes place out of doors, in nature. Others are simply suggested and not shown. That is probably because it is an *illegitimate* affair. If in the West kissing in public is a sign of freedom, we notice that in this particular case such an exposure signals ethical decline, if not total moral degeneration. However, this 'traditionalist' moral standard has since changed. If Désiré Ecaré's film was considered a limit text, it is not any more when one looks at recent productions.

When the Zairian author Buabua Mubadité stressed that 'without the risk of being contradicted, I assert that [pornography is] a purely European institution. Africa has never seen any woman who, for the great pleasure of the public, offers the most private of her body parts as a spectacle' (in Clavreuil, 1987, 27)[15], it was probably overstated, if not naive. It was also too early. Although not exactly a 'conventional' porn film, the pre-opening sequence of Jean-Pierre Bekolo's *Les Saignantes* is not very far from a sophisticated hardcore x-rated tropical film. A film shot entirely in the dark, the opening shots, which precede the credits and the title, depict sexual intercourse that causes the death one of the partners. These 'sexual acrobatics' involve Majolie and a high ranking official, the SGCC. Solidly strapped into a leather harness, she performs phallic back and forth movements in the background of a silent hip hop music and a completely dark lighting. As in the previous examples, her body is also shot in fragments. First the legs, then the naked back, which takes up almost the full screen. It takes several shots before one can see her physical shape. When the old lover appears, he lies back passively with open hands, watching the sexual partner lead the actions, and waiting for her to finally descend from the strap and 'deliver' him. Although at times out of the frame, Majolie is also filmed from below, as the SGCC contemplates her in his eternally religious position. The girl makes herself most desirable, and his hands stay up for quite a long time like a Christian expecting his Messiah. When she eventually gets down to him, the SGCC lies still, and medium shots reveal Majolie performing on top of him with frontal nudity. Beautifully shot, the girl's body, filmed in parts or entirely, generally occupies the whole frame, and the quick cuts as well as the darkness add to the mystery and the dangers of an athletic sexuality. Contrary to other films, Bekolo does not hesitate to bring his camera very close those parts, like those beautifully bouncing breasts that Nwachukwu Frank Ukadike did not seem to like in *Visages des femmes*. Majolie's naked lower parts are filmed in their frontal, lateral and back positions, fully exposing the fatal beauty of the obscene. To show this body to greater advantage it is also framed in near close-ups between the thighs and breast. But contrary to Désiré Ecaré, Bekolo does not show the sexual organs in full contact. Here again, like in most films studied, it is the female body and sexual organs that are exposed *most often*. Women are permanently subjected to the male gaze. Reasons for this are yet to be investigated in African cultural productions.

In view of the above, it is possible to see that from *Xala* to *Les Saignantes* there have been significant transformations in the ways African directors reproduce and view sexuality as the everyday fabric of postcolonial experience. However, it is important to stress that the changes observed are mostly related to the *strategies* used by directors to (un)mask sex. *Les Couilles de l'éléphant* for example is another illustration of the central place of sex in the nation. The proliferation of flaccid penises and failed attempts at intercourse in decadent states is built on a subtle contradiction: while Mbembe believes that the (post)colonial authority is mainly determined by its tireless sexual attributes, if we recall that the Negro is generally reduced to a pathological virility, one could be tempted to state that a successful nation building heavily depends on erected phalluses and, consequently, sexually satisfied women. This hypothesis may seem contentious, and one must still consider it in view of the common association in African writings between political, economic and sexual deficiency. The image of Alevina weeping in the film over his lack of sexual performance in *Les Couilles de l'éléphant*, the number of aphrodisiacs he takes, Alice and his other lovers' open frustration in the film, Sogui's discouragement and his wife's subsequent despair in *Clando* all speak to the centrality of sex in an environment where guilt surrounds questions of the body and other corporeal pleasures.

One other important element in the dramatization of postcolonial sexuality is the way the few African porn 'limit texts' subvert traditional categories and gender roles. In the films discussed above, not only is sex brought back to *life,* in other words, transformed into something *normal,* it has also been made *public* by way of certain stylistic features. Furthermore, it is now becoming apparent in these films that African women are claiming and requesting sexual pleasure, be it from their husbands or lovers. To be sexually satisfied is now almost perceived and experienced as a *right*: Koudi tries several times to have her drunk and impotent husband make love to her before going to have an affair with the village charlatan in *Yaaba.* In *Les Couilles de l'éléphant,* Alevina's first and second wives, as well as his crew of lovers, are all experiencing such an intimate frustration that Alice simply makes it happen when she realizes her man cannot satisfy her: she decides to masturbate in front of her devastated weeping man. In *Quartier Mozart,* Samedi's 'independence day' involves first flirting and later the exploration of sexual pleasures. The rapidity with which Afoué makes herself available in *Visages de femmes* also speaks to this sexual laissez-faire and vagabondage. In any case, there is ample evidence that the search for orgasm has now become a decidedly female one in African films.

One final (and crucial) element that must be noted is the radical inversion of power structures in postcolonial African films. Many feminists have been very critical of the import of sex to film and, more specifically, of the role women are made to play in sex scenes. According to Andrea Dworkin (2000, 32), sexuality in film, and especially pornography, is built on the social and visual subjugation of women:

> In pornography, each element of subordination is conveyed
> through the sexually explicit usage of women: pornography in
> fact is what women are and how women are used in society
> premised on the inferiority of women. It is the metaphysics of
> women's subjugation: our existence delineated in a definition of
> our nature; our status in society pre-determined by the uses to
> which we are put. The woman's body is what is materially
> subordinated. Sex is the material means through which the
> subordination is accomplished. Pornography is the institution of

male dominance that sexualizes hierarchy, objectification, submission, and violence.

While such a charge may be relevant, three female characters in particular have an attitude toward sexuality that requires serious consideration and which could help question the clichéd image of the submissive, fragile, pitiful African woman: these are Afoué in *Visages de femmes*, Karmen in *Karmen Geï* and Majolie in *Les Saignantes,* who all aggressively reclaim agency through unrestricted and uncensored sexual pleasure. The carelessness with which Afoué has sex is literally unprecedented. A significant scene illustrates the control she has over her body and her awareness of the power she has over the equally lecherous male: after the beautifully shot romp in the water, they go back to the field. She lies down, opens her legs and, pointing to her vagina with consequent facial expression, *instructs* the lover to penetrate her. Although she is lying down, she is clearly in control. In *Les Saignantes,* as indicated earlier, it is Majolie who performs the phallic forward and backward movements. The SGCC lies down like a heavy bag, watching the teenager perform the acrobatic sex that will exhaust and kill him. In fact, Majolie never lies down, and there is an inversion of the 'traditional' lovemaking scene where the prone female is dominated by the man on top of her. This 'bottom power' gives Majolie all the pleasure she wants in the film. Things are even worse with Karmen, who seduces the lesbian warden, makes love to her and is subsequently miraculously freed from jail. She then causes a new marriage to collapse: Corporal Lamine literally goes crazy at his wedding and abandons his wife for the 'devilish' Karmen. With the skilful manipulation of their clitoral power, these characters seriously challenge the classic, overplayed image of the African woman who lamentably lacks any sort of sexual assurance and who unconditionally subjects herself to male pleasure. From now on, sexuality for these African women helps precipitate the decline of patriarchy and becomes, as Monga (2009, 75–76) puts it,

> an element of expression of truth on what one would like to be, on the kind of social positioning that one believes one is entitled to. In this sense, sexuality is the element which allows the woman to project the image that she wishes to impose of herself. It is an essential component of an accepted identity. Accordingly, it is part of the care of the self, of the self-subjectivation process.[16]

It is clear that their social role and status has taken an unexpected and original turn. The right to sexual happiness has become fundamental for women as well as men. The new discourse surrounding sexuality also points to a certain rejection of phallocracy in domestic life. Female spouses and lovers are demonstrating increasing sexual initiative. By divorcing women from hegemonic cultural norms and the self-abnegation that previously figured her as submissive, African filmmakers are stripping men of their dominant status. Not only are they denied mastery of the couple's sex life, they are moreover stripped of the exclusive power to establish and enforce moral precepts. Women are beginning to refuse men the sole right to sexual pleasure, the question of which is, in certain African societies, connected to female circumcision and other practices that deny woman the freedom to choose how to enjoy her body and her life.

Notes

1 In the original French: '*À l'heure actuelle, on est en train d'assister à une explosion de la sexualité, et même de la pornographie, sans être passé par la belle époque de l'érotisme*'.

2 '*Parler de la sexualité en Afrique et dans le monde noir demeure pourtant un exercice délicat : le sujet est souvent obscurci par les fantasmes et mythes fabriqués et colportés par la mythologie ethno-politique datant de la Traite des Noirs et la mémoire de l'oppression. Il n'est donc pas aisé de proposer une lecture des comportements qui évite les généralisations hâtives. Il faut éviter le double écueil du voyeurisme et des clichés, se tenir à équidistance du discours racialiste qui alimente les fantasmes collectifs en Occident sur la " sexualité noire", et du discours réductionniste et autoflagellateur de nombreux auteurs africains préoccupés par le "politiquement correct"*'.

3 One important element to be considered is the discourse on sex as a *health matter*. Several documentaries are funded in order to fight AIDS. Fanta Nacro's short fiction *Le Truc de Konaté* (Burkina Faso, 1998) can be positioned within this register. Contrary to what is apparent, the dichotomy the film sets up is not between traditional and modern ways, but instead between the secret and the public. Once AIDS and sexual health become a public topic, they can begin to be addressed and dealt with openly. As in most films discussed in this chapter, sexual relationships are *invisible*.

4 In *50 ans de cinéma maghrébin*, Denise Brahimi (2009, 18) makes a similar comment about 'Western' images as 'invaded' and saturated by sexuality. She contrasts to this conception of the role of sex the sensual, romantic and erotic features of Maghrebi films, in which sexuality is, paradoxically, experienced in the mode of … permanent frustration!

5 Mapouka is a popular and controversial dance developed from a traditional rhythm in Côte d'Ivoire. It expanded and was promoted very quickly during the military regime of Robert Gueï.

6 As these women are called.

7 Alevina is so notorious for his lechery that a member of the opposition party says in despair that '*Sa queue nous perdra*/his tail (i.e. his penis) will be the ruin of us'.

8 See 3 above. Due to cultural considerations, sexuality is duly 'repressed' in films from Maghreb, and characters experience permanent frustration.

9 In Senegal, the *fèer* is a sort of jewellery which most women wear around their waist. It is colourful and is said to have a very erotic function.

10 '*Je ne veux pas savoir si tu la vois. Mais si on vient me dire qu'on vous a vus ensemble, là tu vas tout gâter*'.

11 Nigerian video films are spaces of total freedom, as long as they are limited to violence and witchcraft. However, according to Pierre Barrot (2008, 49) when it comes to nudity and sex, their representability 'can raise questions about hypocrisy'. For him, although 'There are no shortages of sexy actresses [...] nipples are never shown on screen. The two puritanical movements of Evangelism and Islam are united in their rejection of female nudity' which he calls 'the only taboo' (47).

12 Also, in the case of Ngone in *Xala*, portrayed from the back, we see her rear in a sort of *plan américain* that was probably darkened on purpose.

13 '*La culture africaine est plus secrète, moins extériorisée, plus pudique et retenue. Tout dévoilement de la chose est viol de la chose. En ce sens, le cinéma est transgression*'.

14 '*Par la pornographie, l'homme va plus loin que l'animalité contenue dans l'acte sexuel, tel l'ivrogne qui ingurgite plus qu'il ne peut supporter, tel l'oiseau qui prend une quantité de grains l'empêchant de voler. Bref, la pornographie est une toxicomanie sexuelle, la recherche de la frénésie et du vertige par le sexe. Or la frénésie et le vertige sont parfaitement inutiles à l'équilibre de l'homme*'.

15 '*Sans risque d'être contredit, j'affirme que [la pornographie est] une institution purement européenne. Jamais l'Afrique n'a connu de femmes qui, pour la grande joie du public, offrent en spectacle leurs parties les plus intimes.*'

16 '*est surtout un élément d'expression de la vérité sur ce que l'on voudrait être, sur le type de positionnement social auquel on croit avoir droit. En ce sens, elle est l'élément qui permet à la femme de projeter l'image qu'elle souhaite imposer d'elle-même. Elle est une composante essentielle d'une identité assumée. Elle participe donc du souci de soi, de l'autosubjectivation.*'

25 Henri Duparc, *Bal Poussière*

26 Mansour Sora Wade, *Ndeysaan*

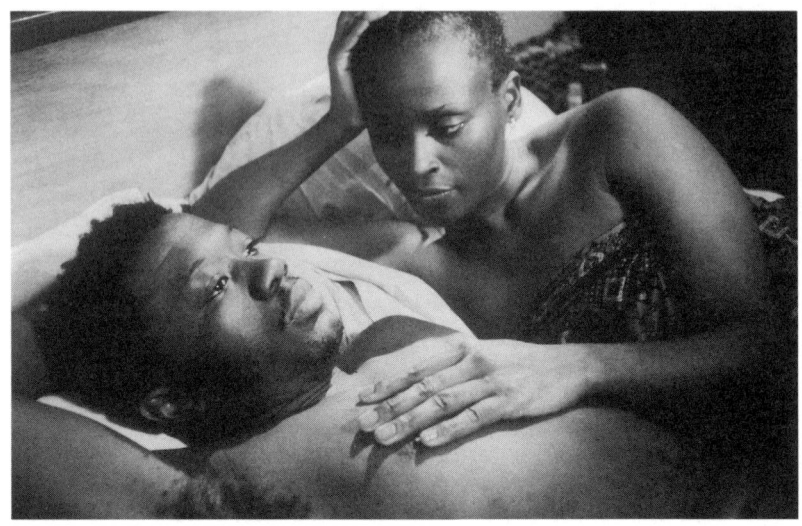

27   Jean-Marie Teno, *Clando*

28   Joseph Gaï Ramaka, *Karmen Geï*

29   Fanta Régina Nacro

30   Djibril Diop Mambéty

Chapter 7

Witchcraft and the postcolonial

I have just outlined the ways films invoke the supernatural to develop epic heroes with larger than life attributes. We have seen that characters can belong to both the human and the animal world; that fire, rain, smoke or vegetation can be started within a second, thanks to the use of specific magical fetishes. We have equally interrogated impossible or unsatisfactory sexual interactions attributed to invisible forces. These representations of the supernatural are part of a temporality and rationality that do not offer a 'logical' evidence for empirical facts, thus making any cause-effect relationship uncertain when the viewer is not familiar with cultural orthodoxies that allow her or him to realize that things may occur without a 'coherent' justification. For example, how can a distaff suddenly generate palm trees? How can an egg be transformed into a swamp? These examples from *Keita*, to which maybe added several others from various narratives, indicate that 'rational' explanations do not always account for objective phenomena.

Following previous discussions of the paranormal, the main objective of this chapter is to determine the strategies used by filmic discourse to offer cultural (symbolic) explanations for real (objective) phenomena. It focusses on the representations of irrationality, witchcraft and the invisible in African films. I will first map out the anthropological discourse surrounding witchcraft. I will then proceed to look at how certain films dismiss this social representation as imaginary in keeping with a colonial mentality. The last section will discuss a more balanced, less reductionist representation of the phenomenom. I will argue that it is hard to identify the components of any systematic nationalist discourse in the films under consideration because, as Teresa Hoefert de Turégano states with reference to *Yaaba* (Ouedraogo, 1989), these narratives offer 'clean, polished and poetic images [which] step into a universal world leaving the nation behind' (2004, 194).

African films contain many representations of mysterious phenomena on top of the pre-existing 'magic' of cinema. The extraordinary commercial success of Michel Ocelot's two films (*Kirikou et la sorcière*, 1998; *Kirikou et les bêtes sauvages*, 2005), as well as the release of S. Pierre Yaméogo's film *Delwende* (2005), clearly shows that African film is interested in the representation of the invisible, a representation whose nature sometimes varies markedly from one country to another. When we study the modes of (re)production and delineation of these phenomena, we must enquire as to what discourse African film is engaged in. In its ability to reduce matters to objects of study, scholarship can run the risk of perpetuating the exile of Africa to the margins of Hellenic reason. What are the relationships between Mama Thécla in *Quartier Mozart* (Bekolo, 1992), Napoko in *Delwende,* Sana in *Yaaba* and The Prince in *Le Cercle des pouvoirs* (Kamwa, 1998)? How can we interpret the persistence of the occult in film, which has been the case since the end of the 1970s? Does showing this phenomenon not create the risk of perpetuating the stereotype that African society is bound up in the paranormal? Moreover, is it possible to cinematically picture phenomena that are avowedly invisible? Would linking the paranormal to the quest for political power, as in Daniel Kamwa's film, or discrediting/denying it, as in other films, not amount to affirming a disembodied academic discourse? What variations can we observe in the proliferation of what Achille Mbembe (1988) calls 'symbolic narratives/ *narrations symboliques*'?

These questions are all the more important given that investigation in the realm of 'sorcery' has been important in academic discourse. Examining some films that are being created in Africa, Josef Gugler (2003) and Birgit Meyer (2003) show how, during evangelization campaigns and in prayers of deliverance in Ghana and Nigeria, prayers ensure the victory of faith over evil. In these films, narrative protocols echo 'mysterious' phenomena that are preoccupations of a people who are clearly in a completely postnationalist and postresistance mode, for the State is no more the main target. *Magical Interpretations, Material Realities* by Henrietta L. Moore and Todd Sanders (2001), and *Magic and Modernity* by Birgit Meyer and Peter Pels (2003) show that these preoccupations remain present in any human community that has to invent its rhetoric and its stories in a time of crisis. All these scholars confirm the fundamentally dual nature of postcolonial experience where, according to Achille Mbembe, the visible and the invisible are two sides of the same coin. For him, a representation of the real world is not possible without relation to the world of ghosts, masks, apparitions and phantoms because 'the visible [is] in the invisible, and vice versa, not as a matter of artifice, but as *one and the same* and as external reality simultaneously' (2001, 145, original emphasis).

It is this order of representations that colonial anthropology called 'witchcraft' in order to put a name on phenomena that did not fit a strictly Cartesian framework; following Peter Geschiere, I use instead the word 'occult', a less pejorative term that includes the good as well as the evil applications of spiritual practices. 'The occult' refers to unintelligible phenomena but does not try to attribute to them an empirically explainable mechanism; in other words, it concerns the 'why' and not always the 'how'. According to Francis Nyamnjoh, the occult breaks down facile dichotomies in that 'it builds bridges between or marries the so-called natural and supernatural, rational and irrational, objective and subjective, scientific and superstitious, visible and invisible, real and unreal; making it impossible for anything to be one without being the other' (2001, 29). We shall see that occult explanations, because they can bring contradictory elements together, rise up in situations of existential, ontological and material defeat, when hope is also defeated.

To date, scholarship in this field stems from a colonial tradition and is as such based on a monolithic concept of the world and of reason and science (Evans-Pritchard, 1937; Crawford, 1967 for example). Some critics, as Peter Geschiere (2000, 20) correctly emphasizes, consider the increased practice of 'sorcery' in societal life to be a sign of an exclusively 'African' modernity[1], that is, something happening exclusively in a backward continent. Despite the fact that the 'tradition-modernity' dichotomy seems to have been replaced by 'different temporalities which sometimes are telescoped into each other / *des temporalités différentes qui parfois se télescopent*' (Mbembe, 1988, 106), the continent remains outside of the modernity of the 'others'. This then calls for two observations: first, African modernity is incommensurable with the concept of modernity predominant in the Western world. This, at an epistemological level, is in fact the necessary condition for making any Western discourse about Africa possible; next, the 'occult', far from being a form of primitivism, shows itself to be the particular defining feature of a modernity that does not necessarily cut

Africa off from the cultural and discursive practices we see elsewhere, as has been extensively proven in studies by several scholars.[2] This indeed is the position defended by Geschiere and most vociferously by Jean and John Camaroff (1999) in their article on 'occult economies'. For them, the explosion of the occult is not a uniquely African phenomenon; it is global, appearing and growing in comparable contexts elsewhere in the world. The focus on the occult is linked to the implosion of capitalism and the desire to produce material goods.

This chapter will study the filmic discourse of the occult as another manifestation of a postnationalist experience. A concern with so-called sorcery is present in all societies, regardless of their social, political or economic structures. It will also be seen that in every period of its historical development, a society constructs new forms of the occult(ism) in which real or imagined aggression is central. The Sorcerer State (*L'Etat sorcier*)[3] is no more than the manifestation of a logic of conquest or protection of power; the figure of the 'witch' is in all respects similar to the scapegoat of which René Girard (1977) speaks in order to elucidate the growth of violence involved in the processes of social decontamination. This can be seen in *Yaaba*, *Delwende* and in *Wend Kuuni* (Kaboré, Burkina Faso, 1982), films in which representations of the occult recall what Maurice Duval (1985) says about a village in Burkina Faso whose paranormal phenomena he explores; for him, the perpetual violence and severe exclusions in rural areas constitute a kind of 'stateless totalitariansim'. But these three films whose discourse, as we shall see, can sometimes seem reductivist, echo the discourse of the Cameroonian Daniel Kamwa who represents the occult and problematizes it in a more dynamic and nuanced way; as a result, depictions of sorcery in Cameroon are very different to those in Burkina Faso.

1   From sorcery imaginary to the imaginary sorcerer

Without seeking to establish its geneology, we can note at least two films that ask the same questions as to an invisible evil agent. In Sembène Ousmane's *Xala* (1974), the main protagonist becomes impotent for reasons that are not understood by him, and this upsets him deeply. In *The Mad Masters* (1955), Jean Rouch describes the unlikely kinship of the occult, madness and colonial power. How then can we grasp the representations of these phenomena in films like *Wend Kuuni, Yaaba* or *Delwende?* What are the discourses that the directors employ in their films? Does their perspective seek to elucidate practices or condemn them?

In *Wend Kuuni,* which we should note takes place in pre-colonial Africa, a mother is expelled from the village for having 'eaten' the child of another woman, while her own son is sick. This expulsion produces the drama of little Wend Kuni, whose trauma causes him to become a deaf-mute when he discovers the dead body of his mother. In Idrissa Ouedraogo's *Yaaba,* Sana, an old woman, is likewise accused of witchcraft. In fact, her name is only rarely mentioned in the film; most often she is simply called 'the witch'. *Delwende* develops the same scenario: while an epidemic of meningitis is spreading that regularly plunges the village into mourning, old female 'devourers of souls' are accused. Following a fallacious 'test' ritual, another woman, Napoko, the mother of the protagonist Pougbila, is accused. She takes refuge in the city, in one of the many shelters that take in these old women.

But as opposed to *Wend Kuuni* and *Delwende,* in which the accused defends herself verbally and even tries unsuccessfully to flee, *Yaaba* reveals the innocence of a woman who has been held up for public calumny and condemnation. The women of the village indict Sana as the source of all the evils that have befallen the community, and two main charges are laid against her. First she is accused of setting fire to a house. At the start of the film, Sana appears in the cemetery where two children, Bila and Nopoko, are playing. When they return to the village and see a fire destroying a house, no one believes Bila when he says that he has just seen the accused woman and therefore she cannot have started the fire. It is in these circumstances that the first accusation is proclaimed throughout the community. Another incident occurs. Bila and a group of children develop a rivalry. During a fight that breaks out when Bila and Nopoko return from a walk, the little girl is wounded by a rusty knife. When she cries out, a close-up shows the metal object and then her bleeding arm. Sana appears in the next scene and looks at the knife. The expression on her face indicates that she has noticed something. After a few sequences, Nopoko falls ill and develops a fever which worsens daily. The village is gripped by panic and turns to a charlatan who, after securing payment, declares that the young girl's spirit has been 'eaten' by an old woman. Once more, things point to Sana. Despite many statements by Bila and Noaga, no one admits that Nopoko might simply be ill with tetanus.

In *Delwende,* in order to identify the person responsible for the ills that have befallen the village, a witch doctor named Raogo is called in. Since the 'ritual of the chicken' produces no results, the elders decide to use the ritual of the *siongho*, an enormous sledgehammer wrapped in raffia which, by means of a mystical force, is supposed to come down hard on the guilty party. Young virginal men are supposed to carry the hammer and while they are doing so one of them faints. He is replaced by Napoko's husband. After many turns through the little village, the hammer strikes Napoko several times, thereby indicating her to be the guilty party sought for so long. She flees and after much wandering about, rejected by her own family, she finds herself in the city shelter.

In a preceding scene, Pougbila informs her mother that she has been raped, but refuses to identify her assailant. Despite Pougbila's insistance, the girl's father refuses to speak to his daughter, forcing her instead to quickly get married. Pougbila flees to the city, where she too is rejected because she is the daughter of a 'witch'. Having returned to her village, where she is determined to reveal the truth about her rape, she succeeds in convincing the chief to re-open the matter of the test by the *siongho*. Another ceremony of expiation is convened during which the chief orders that any person who might know the truth about these deaths must reveal it. That is when Tiga, one of the young virginal men who had carried the *siongho* announces that Diarrha, Pougbila's father, had ordered them to strike his wife with the hammer; they thus learn how the village had identified its guilty party.

Kaboré, Yaméogo and Ouedraogo's films thus offer us this constant: the occult seems to be linked to women. Before Napoko is unjustly accused, all of the people involved say that these evils can come only from a witch, a woman, and all conversations on the subject held about the 'guilty one' are close to her, with camera movements and staging that point to her. Why such anti-feminine rhetoric?[4] Why are women always victims? These two films do not offer any straight answer.

It is also obvious that recourse to the occult, in rural areas, arises during social crises when central political power is absent, whence the concept of 'stateless totalitarianism' by which Duval defines the Nuna: the (post)colonial State does not even need to be challenged because it is missing. In other words, we are dealing with depoliticized communities in which, generally, people feel much more threatened by sorcerers than by established political power (Duval, 1985, 73). When a problem arises, people resort to the discourse of the world of spirits. In the case of Sana, the disappearance of her mother, then of her father, render her guilty from birth because, for the villagers, only an evil child can be responsible for such deaths upon her arrival in the world. Likewise, in *Delwende*, the terrible 'sickness that twists the neck' and which especially attacks children, can only be the work of an evil woman. The occult seems thus to be a permanent fact in this group that uses it to substantiate any phenomena it cannot explain. What can we conclude from this?

Idrissa Ouedraogo, Pierre Yaméogo and Gaston Kaboré take hold of this phenomenon in order to deconstruct it. Although set in different eras, their films demonstrate that the figure of the 'sorcerer' corresponds to a mythological construct rather than a factual phenomenom for which evidence can be provided. Simply put, the representation at work here is dismissive and sorcery is portrayed as mere irrational excuses for empirical anxieties. Starting with this 'invention' of the occult, these films equally shed light on the intolerant, outdated nature of certain practices in communities in which the power of consensus, and certain 'irrational' yet coherent convictions, remain solid. They can continue to provoke cruel marginalizations of people, suicides and even madness, but the unanimity with which a given matter is viewed allows a society to maintain its funtional coherence. Nopoko's tetanus and the deaths of Sana's parents in *Yaaba*, the meningitis epidemic that erupts in *Delwende*, and the fire in *Wend Kuuni*, all are perfect reminders of the 'persecution complex' of which Ibrahima Sow (1978) speaks: when something happens to an African, there is always a peception that there is a supernatural cause. Duval in fact notes, in his study of the Nuna, multiple depressions with deleriums of persecution (1985, 79) among young people, for whom the fear of poisoning and 'attacks from sorcery' is a 'permanent obsession'. There is always a spirit to be blamed. Moreover, as René Girard shows with respect to outbursts of violence, society always needs a scapegoat in order to exorcise its ills. Collective power is constructed at the expense of the victimized individual. In *Wend Kuuni* as well as in *Yaaba*, we see this mythical constant. Girard (1977, 102) argues that to heal the city it is necessary to identify and expel the impure individual whose presence contaminates the whole city. All must agree as to the identity of a single guilty party. In the cases just studied, there is a messenger-victim who, on the collective level, plays the role of that object that the Shamans claim to be able to extract from the bodies of their patients and which they then present as being the cause of all evil.

The two women represent an outlet which society needs in order to ward off evils for which no explanation can be imagined. We can also see that in these three films, beyond these women, no marginal person (elders, youth, drunkard) is listened to. The older people, especially older men, seem to be the only ones to hold the power to legitimize and decide: in effect, in African societies, with age comes authority, even when the elders are leaders of a deviant majority. Respect for elders, as we see in Sana's case, is lost only in circumstances in which the supernatural is in play. The old woman is driven to the brink of death while the other elders of the village are listened to and respected. If you are deemed a witch you lose the right to respect and life.

We must also note that, in showcasing the occult, these films, from the oldest to the most recent, perpetuate the view that Africa is a prisoner of aberrant concepts. This vantage is one that would be eagerly adopted by perpetuators of colonial agenda. The powers in the domain of the imaginary that are ascribed to women are based, in fact, on superstitions. It is fitting that, in *Yaaba*, Nopoko is saved from tetanus while an innocent woman is dishonoured. It is Pougbila's determination that ultimately proves her mother is innocent. In these films we see the need to turn one's back not only on the dictates of the group, but also on beliefs that prevent emancipation and the exercise of critical faculties. The films of Gaston Kaboré and above all of Pierre Yaméogo and Idrissa Ouedraogo constitute an intellectual endorsement for colonial anthropology in that they bring together all the elements of that discourse.

Yaaba, *Delwende* and *Wend Kuuni* suggest that the African is bound up in 'primitive' practices and beliefs. When the group faces a social crisis, a victim is chosen and violence is focussed on her in what Geschiere describes in terms of '*accusations montreuses contre de vieilles femmes ou des punitions imposées à de prétendus "enfants sorciers"*/ monstruous accusations against old women or punishment inflicted on alleged "child sorcerers"' (Geschiere, 2000, 27). Representation and (de)construction of the occult create a subject that is incapable of resolving the challenges Africans face because they are prisoners of an internal logic that borders on the absurd. A simplistic disqualification of the occult not only maintains cultural practices within the conservative arena of 'traditions', but also legitimizes the classic evolutionist and functionalist theses that have been and are deployed in order to justify the reckless imposition of 'progress'. Kaboré and Ouedraogo would likely agree with the agent of the colonial administration in Rhodesia who argued that '[t]he measure of the Native's progress from the state of savagery can be gauged to a large extent by their departure from or adherence to witchcraft beliefs. There is no doubt whatsoever that only a handful are completely free of the shackles of sorcery and witchcraft' (Rutherford, 1999, 98).

Yet *Yaaba* is not limited only to the (de)construction of the occult. 'Rationality' and, indeed, the questioning of certain certainties through the participation of two marginalized people – a young boy, Bila, and a 'fool', Noaga – make it possible for doubt to be spread within the community. In *Delwende*, another marginalized person, Elie, who is a Christian and whose abusive father and sexual predator Diarrha calls 'fool,' openly expresses his doubts as to the community practices in the matter of sorcery. Throughout the film, he holds to his ear a radio that keeps announcing the ravages of meningitis in Burkina Faso, and the sequences of the accusations sometimes alternate with those in which he is seen clinging to his radio. What is interesting here is that the 'healer' who, in *Yaaba*, sacrifices an old mother from the village, is revealed to be a charlatan and is ultimately arrested. We are not told exacly why the father asks the boys carrying the *siongho* to strike his wife Napoko in *Delwende* (we can guess that he has raped his daughter and wants her removed from the scene); however, the temerity of the young Pougbila allows her to re-establish the dignity of her mother. In both cases, the villagers ultimately recognize the error of their ways. By thus portraying the world of sorcery, film directors are able to demonstrate the falsity of certain supernatural beliefs. Classical anthropology based the construction of its object on examples such as these which frame sorcery as irrational inventions in supposedly backward societies where subjects are totally unable to distinguish facts from fiction. Evans-Pritchard notably writes as follows: 'Witchcraft is an imaginary offense because it is impossible. A witch cannot do what he is supposed to do and has in fact no real existence' (1937, 418).

Beyond the 'invention' of the occult at work in *Yaaba*, the film is above all a hymn to tolerance. A consensus is reached to indict a woman who is ultimately exonerated at the end of the film, and two young children try to re-socialize her. Clearly, an injustice is performed. Moreover, the members of the society refuse to listen to those people who do not possess any authority, namely two children and a drunkard. In *Delwende*, Elie the 'crazy' Christian seems to be the only lucid person, but he has no way to make himself heard. This blacklisting of marginalized people allows the group at the same time to magnify subjects that it tends normally to banish. Fortunately, a real healer from another village saves the sick person in *Yaaba*. Beyond the discourse of 'backwardness' and the invention of the 'sorcerer', Idrissa Ouedraogo shows us also that Africans possess all the resources they need to ensure their development. Self-doubt comes from inside. He also shows us that charlatans exist and that they exploit the fears of society; local healers can offer effective therapies where instead one might easily call up the forces of darkness. But what Mbembe calls '*le monde de la nuit/* the world of night' appears here in settings that are essentially rural and governed by no central political power. With an absent(ee) State, there is no collective project or resistance movement to rally around, nor nation to be built.

Another important point to make is that the imagined victim, as well as her or his executioner, does not come from the perpetrator's family circle. Geschiere has convincingly shown that witchcraft is always the dark side of kinship (1995, 275); the films we are studying, however, can also seek agents and patients of the sorcery event outside of the family, for although Sana is in no way related to Nopoko, the family crisis in *Delwende* is rather a pretext dreamed up by the father in order to hide his perversion. But although in this film, as in *Yaaba* and *Wend Kuuni*, the occult is part of a crisis of the imaginary and of the social conscience, things are not the same in Daniel Kamwa's *Le Cercle des pouvoirs* in which, from a more nuanced and, above all, less reductive perspective, the cannibalism of the universe of darkness is 'clearly' represented in motion, in all its 'reality' and even its 'truth'.

2   Occult side of power, power of the occult

There is a school of thought that links the outbreak of the occult in politics in Africa with post-colonial disenchantment (Jean & John Camaroff, 1997). However, as Bertrand de Jouvenel (1972) indicates, there is a very compelling aspect to the occult that is not necessarily reducible to something as negative as the Camaroffs' suggestion. Magical power serves to tame the invisible, rendering the powers of darkness not only ineffectual but even desirable. In a remarkable work on Cameroon (1995) and in many articles, Peter Geschiere demonstrates the mechanisms by which sorcery is integrated into politics. An important element of his work is that although it shows the role of the postcolonial Cameroon in the 'administration' of witchcraft, such attempt to manage the 'invisible' notably through court decisions does not necessarily serve nation building. In *Afriques indociles* (1988) Achille Mbembe portrays a 'pagan genius', i.e. the revenge of oppressed parties who invent languages to resist violence and interpret invincible 'material realities'. For him, 'sorcery' can best be understood in terms of the relationships between the forces of domination and their objects, relationships in which destitution, desire, and insecurity play a fundamental role:

> Faced with material and symbolic insecurity, it is felt, among the dominated groups, that there are many conditions that render attacks through 'sorcery' possible. This insecurity does not spare the dominant group. During those times when societies go through crises because they seem ungovernable, men and women set about seeking therapeutic strategies, rituals and prescriptions by which they might be spared death. (1988, 122)[5]

Another notable fact is the proliferation of 'symbolic narratives' in rumours, conversation and dreams, in written, oral, pictoral and musical texts. The narratives explore the theme of 'nocturnal violence'. Francis Nyamnjoh reports that, in some of these, the actors can be both those holding political power in Cameroon or their victims. These narratives illustrate at least one thing: both the State and its subjects concomitantly navigate in the same realm of sorcery. There also is a document circulating in the Cameronian diaspora and on the web, written by someone who once was among those in power there. This text, entitled *Blood: Biya's Power Lotion*, should be regarded as a subjective first-hand account rather than as a piece of scientific discourse. Nevertheless, Ebale Angounou's description of the practices that he alleges were common in the highest circles of the Republic under the supervision of French mystical brotherhoods is worthy of regard. These narratives on occult practices had been reported before through rumour, and in certain local newspapers. This text offers a hypothesis that is a constant in all stories having to do with the invisible: the occult is thus seen as being as much a condition for the acquisition and consolidation of power as it is a consequence of the exercise of that power.[6] With Daniel Kamwa's *Le Cercle des pouvoirs*, questionable manoeuvres for the acquisition of political and financial power through the use of the occult are set in play, mainly the cannibalistic structures involved in the ascension to political power and the further accumulation of material wealth in postcolonial Cameroon.[7] Further, the film once again engages the 'scientific' discourse on 'witchcraft', while at the same time going beyond it. In effect, we go from speculation about the occult, and from its 'invention' as represented in previous films, to its actualization and full dramatization. In other words, while in *Wend Kuuni, Delwende* and *Yaaba* we are dealing with a speculative, sacrificial, hermeneutic narrative in rural areas, involving an order difficult to 'describe' or which no one can witness, with *Le Cercle des pouvoirs* we move on to a different articulation of an urban story (with oral and visual 'evidence') that is able to 'show' and, thus, to interpret phenomena that, generally, are simply enunciated in terms of their relationships with political and economic power. This film also places us squarely in what the Camaroffs (1999) have called 'occult economies,' which illustrate both disenchantment with modernity and with economic rationality on the one hand, and on the other the implosion of capitalism as well as the emergence of nouveaux riches in postcolonial countries where nation building and orangized resistance against oppressive States are absent.

With *Le Cercle des pouvoirs*, Daniel Kamwa uses film to explore the relationships between the occult and the political, as well as the connection of the occult to the accumulation of wealth. Mbembe (1988, 2001) unflinchingly addresses questions of material and symbolic insecurity, the fear of dying and of the duty to kill, which all flow from the people's fraught relation to political power in the postcolonial era. What is interesting about this little-known film is not only the depiction of occult forces, which are invisible, but also the exposition of the limits of academic/scientific discourse on the role of the sorcerer in postcolonial settings. In Cameroon, popular belief maintains solid relationships between the accumulation of wealth or inexplicable socio-professional advancements and the occult. The nouveaux riches of the *grassfields* and other regions are suspected of having obtained their fortunes, often accumulated overnight, through the 'sale' or 'sacrifice' of close relatives on the mystical market of *Mont Kupé* or *Famla*[8]; it is rumoured that these relatives become slaves on the plantations and in other imagined businesses. The new capitalist bourgeoisie, which plays a crucial role in the unparalleled economic development of the province of Western Cameroon, is the permanent object of a mystical anthropological suspicion. The relationship between money and sorcery is in general easily established, as we see in the scholarship of Cyprian F. Fisiy and Peter Geschiere, who argue that witchcraft is linked to jealousy and wealth. In fact, for them, the accumulation of wealth is perceived to be possible only if one has, in one way or another, the support of the forces of the occult (1993, 99).

Kamwa's film is characterized not only by the presence of sorcery, the discourse of which occurs in everyday life (as studies by Geschiere, Fisiy or Nyamnjoh attest), but also by a discussion of the political. As we can see in Angounou's essay, since the arrival in power of M. Biya, there has been a proliferaton of French 'schools of philosophy' (Rose Croix, Franc Maçonnerie, CIRCES, etc.) which are generally perceived to be satanic cults that are supposed to guarantee that their adherents will have sucessful (professional) lives. Further, political power in Cameroon is in a certain sense 'occult' in that citizens do not know how it functions, what criteria it applies to government, nor where the centres of decision are located, be they with the party, the president, or ministers. Kamwa's film exposes the evil practices of its protagonist, Moni-Sam.[9] We will also see that anthropological discourse on the universe of the sorcerer can be put into question by the film because it also indicates that a character's fortune depends in the main on contraband. But, one of the interesting aspects of *Le Cercle des pouvoirs* is found in the use of the forces of the mystical. Through two priests/gurus, the Prince and Atchori, a distinction is established between evil occult forces and beneficial ones, between what Eric de Rosny (1992) identifies as the (evil) universe of sorcery and the (beneficial) universe of the 'undoing of sorcery.'[10]

One of the difficulties academic study faces is in proving the 'reality' of 'sorcery' phenomena, to the point that, despite the significant evidence provided in the work of Eric de Rosny, Geschiere vacillates as to the degree and manner of the occult's possible impacts on social experience. Despite the sometimes tragic consequences he mentions in the case of unjust accusations, he also notes that he does not want to disqualify this issue, nor does he want to 'emphasize too strongly the reality of these beliefs' (1997, 21). In other words, Geschiere neither wants to dismiss nor confirm 'too strongly' the verity and the rationality of the object of his study. The most compelling evidence behind his prudence is the lack of, or the difficulty of determining, clear, unquestionable and 'rational' evidence of occult practices. However, because fiction does not have to observe the same precautions as scientific productions, Kamwa's film offers a different perspective. As opposed to the two preceding films, *Le Cercle des pouvoirs* highlights (in fact, interprets) the 'reality' of sorcery. Such strategy allows the viewers to temporarily renounce their logical categories and embark into those of the universe of darkness in order to determine how the invisible world functions through the territory covered by Moni-Sam. The duo he makes up with The Prince establishes the occult as an 'axis of evil', but above all allows for the establishing of the fact that all of the mechanisms of the occult are based on 'real' and visible aggression.[11]

Le Cercle des pouvoirs begins with a banal tontine to which Moni-Sam goes. Because of the devaluation of the CFA franc, he sees a doubling of the cost of the products he imports, and this considerably increases the customs costs he has to pay. In need of cash, this businessman demands an immediate cashing out of shares in the 'Voeux et succès' tontine. Mamy Nyanga, the manager of the fund, declares Moni-Sam to be in a real fix, and offers to help him at a cost. She tells him, 'He who wants to win big must pay dearly. Since you have an urgent problem, I will arrange this for you. *But there will be an important gift that you will have to give*' (extract from the film. My emphasis). Moni-Sam replies that he can even make two such gifts. The fund manager indicates that just one is enough and adds: 'There are rules. We have to respect them'.

It is from this point that the construction of a project of the forces of darkness becomes obvious. A pact has just been sealed between an agent of Moni-Sam and an intermediary who knows better than anyone else the value of the oath. The pact is made between the fund manager and her disciple, who promises to produce the gift. The gift in question is the catalysing agent for the following engagement with the forces of darkness. This engagement will pave the way for many instances of aggression. For after recovering Moni-Sam's merchandise for him, Mamy Nyanga encourages him to offer a banal gift to a mysterious individual who has asked for it. After delivering the gift, the donor turns around and the expression on his face shows that he has been trapped by the 'beggar' known as The Prince.

In the following sequence, The Prince is taking part in an incantatory ceremony with, on his right, Mamy Nyanga and Moni-Sam facing them. The dark lighting is that of horror films. We also note some candles, generally considered in Cameroon to be the way to light satanic ceremonies. Three children then enter the circle. The Prince 'blesses' them and they leave the circle, then the camera fades back before the story takes up another, quite different, scene of incantation. Next we see Atchori receiving two women in his sanctuary. He announces to them that their little boy is sick. He divines the boy's future by looking in his canary, shakes his head, and pronounces a severe dignosis. A dissolve ends with a conversation between Atchori and Jisset, his protégé who has filmed everything concerning the preceding mystical scene and who has been touched by it, because he has seen things he is not prepared for. An act of aggression has thus taken place, rendered invisible by an ellipsis in the narrative that allows for the illustration of the act of sorcery.

The preceding syntactic disposition in *Le Cercle des pouvoirs* has, from the first sequences on, an anticipatory function. It brings together the first elements of the battle that will be played out between the two forms of the occult: a beneficial form and an evil one. The montage allows the director to announce the coming confrontation between these two factions. As opposed to *Yaaba, Delwende* and *Wend Kuuni*, in which the narrative organization leads to the exoneration of the accused and condemns the occult, placing it within the register of the social imaginary, Kamwa's film shows the accusation and establishes supposed witchcraft 'evidence' or 'reality', indeed the truth about the sorcerer's universe, at least as it is perceived within the social imaginary. It 'shows' without stigmatizing or encouraging, whereas other directors seem to be 'undoing' and discrediting. In the three films, the objective is to resolve a crisis, but in *Le Cercle des pouvoirs*, we *see* the protagonists resorting to parallel solutions in order to succeed. The occult is thus implicated in a plan of action, a conscious collaboration that materializes through the transfer of a *gift*, a permanent element in mystical exchanges. The action ends with a *visible* act of aggression, whereas it is of the imaginary with Ouedraogo, Yaméogo and Kaboré. The convention of the gift as well as its link to debt and aggression, as seen in Kamwa's film, is a constant in academic writings and in popular stories about the cannibalisms of the *Famla* or the *Ekong* of Cameroon. Personal ambition, be it an obsession with accumulating wealth, or political success, always seems to require human sacrifices to the powers of darkness. In fact, in analysing this question with respect to Nigerian and Ghanaian videos, Josef Gugler notably writes that 'Human sacrifice which brings great wealth is a recurring theme in such video films … Much wealth is ill-gotten by means that bring death. Violent crime, rampant in many cities, is the most obvious example, but greater wealth is amassed through schemes that kill many more' (2003, 178).

Indeed, if some researchers acknowledge 'the difficulty of establishing the proof of occult aggression' (Diane Ciekawy and Peter Geschiere, 1998, 8.), film, because of the means it has at its disposal, allows a director to *represent / construct* this proof and thereby identify those responsible. For the occult is in general characterized by its secret nature and is deployed in a space that excludes light. Cinema has the function of showing, and this makes it possible to resolve a question that the social sciences have always tripped over. Cinema can thus speak and 'present "the invisible" for us to see,' allowing us to see 'things of other orders'. Indeed, after the signing of the pact between The Prince and his partners, the subsequent sequences portray the forces of the occult, which start to destroy the characters: aggression on the move.

A child of Moni-Sam's is playing videos in the dark. Suddenly, we hear thunder claps, as if an electrical shock has occurred. When the child is taken to hospital, he appears to be dying, yet seems to recover. The next sequence shows Moni-Sam in the cemetery with the Prince. He wants to re-negotiate his 'contract'[12] and refuses to replace his son before the Prince reminds him: 'When you deal with The Prince, you must be able to pay the price for your ambitions'. We should note that during this nocturnal conversation, The Prince speaks while describing a circle, a symbolic imprisonment, around the stationary Moni-Sam. The master's movements demonstrate that the businessman has been caught in the 'circle'. The scene also reveals a principle of the invisible world, namely the importance of substitution. Debt and gifts have significant repercussions; the creditor can accept that the borrower offers a substitute as victim. In rejecting the role of victim, Moni-Sam refuses to become a martyr, an attitude that, in the Cameroonian cultural landscape, is said to conform to that of subjects who are involved in occult transactions and sacrifices. In order to survive, he must cause someone else to be killed. The death of the other, in this case his son, cancels the necessity of his own death. Mbembe explains the phenomenon in the following terms:

> In the postcolony, it is the power to delegate oneself that ...
> enables one to delegate one's death to another, or, at least
> constantly to defer it, until the final rendezvous. It follows that
> death, in its essence, can very well, each time, not be mine, my

death; the other can die in my stead. While awaiting the final
end, a Dasein may very well not, each time, take on itself its
own death (2001, 202)

The scene also allows for the machinations of the powers of darkness to be
demonstrated on screen. The power of the image moves this darkness into
the cinematic light, revealing it and elevating it to the status of a subject of
discourse. To be understood, however, discourse generally requires a
cultural meta-language that can have to do with a certain coherence within
the milieu in which it is deployed. This remains true for the following
sequence.

In this sequence, Atchori receives Moni-Sam's wife and mother-in-law.
It is to be noted that the office of the 'un-doer of sorcery' contains no cross,
and yet the man still invokes God's help. He then hands over to Jisset a
protective object that the latter is supposed to wear for seven days without
washing and subsequently throw it in the river. Once again, Daniel Kamwa
elucidates the contradictions that exist between two forms of the occult.
He almost always juxtaposes the evil sequences involving The Prince with
the beneficial ones of Atchori, who is fighting against the forces of evil. The
film also attributes Jisset's power and temerity to the fact that he is so
frequently in the company of Atchori, as is shown in the instance of the
missed, un-enacted 'mystical' gift and surrounding aggression.

In effect, Moni-Sam tries to marry Mlle Siffo. Jisset also is accompanied
by the same girl that Moni-Sam tries to use to bring harm to the journalist.
During an apparently chance meeting, noticing The Prince, Moni-Sam asks
Siffo to buy cigarettes and then give the change from the purchase to a
'beggar' who is sitting close by. As she is about to carry out the request,
Jisset appears. Since he is well acquainted with the practices of the invisible,
he quickly leads away his female friend, convinced she was about to be
'offered' to The Prince. It is at this point that the spectator remembers that
during a meeting at the cemetery, Moni-Sam suggests to The Prince that he
is about to marry a girl The Prince would not find displeasing.[13] What are
we to conclude?

As we have seen in the case of Moni-Sam, membership in a circle of the
invisible happens by choice; here, we see instead, in the case of the failed
'sacrifice' of Siffo, that one can also involuntarily become implicated in the
actions of the forces of darkness through manipulation. This 'sacrifice' is an
action brought about through some instrument/agent and introduces an

important symbolic dimension of the transactions of mystery. The victim is not always a relative; as we see here, she is introduced into the 'circle' against her wishes. The victim is generally naive and not 'armoured' the way Jisset is, thanks to Atchori's active protection, a protection that in a way recalls the herbalist in *Yaaba*.

During a reception, shown in slow motion, Jisset's hand shakes violently when he is about to drink a glass of beer that Mamy Nyanga has left. In the preceding shot, the woman is seen quickly sneaking an object into the journalist's glass and thus poisoning it. Jisset forbids Siffo to swallow it, proposing instead that she eat some fruit. A few minutes later he hurts himself and cleans his finger with a rag.[14] Jisset suspects nothing, but he has a nightmare in which he sees The Prince. During the 'battle' that takes place between Atchori and The Prince in the film's final scenes, The Prince, waving about the white, bloodstained rag, announces that Jisset has given his blood to him and must die. We thus understand that the story has proceeded through the ellipsis of a sequence and that an important transaction has been carried out. After failing in the attempted poisoning, Mami Nyanga and Moni-Sam regained possession of the piece of rag and took it to their master as a guarantee of their allegiance, a fact which justifies their aggression. The blood and the red represent an important symbol here with respect to pacts that are imposed through manipulation.[15] Atchori, who shows himself to be stronger in fights where the faces of the participants can hardly be seen in the poor light, orders The Prince to move away from Jisset. Realizing that he has been had by his faithful followers, The Prince turns around; filmed in a subjective camera, following a dissolve, we see Mami Nyanga and her group in the act of celebrating their deadly successes in stopping the 'harmful results of devaluation', because, as they say, 'under-development is not a curse'.

The scene that best illustrates the occult's capacity to do harm is without a doubt the one that portrays the death of Moni-Sam's son. While the child is dying in hospital, an alternating montage shows, in slow motion, a young boy being pursued in the bush by The Prince. This alternation occurs three times, right up to the moment when the mystic seizes the boy and smothers him in his arms. There is a close-up on the helpless doctor, then on the heart monitor that is displaying a horizontal line. The sick boy has just died and the next shot takes us to Moni-Sam's home where mourning has begun. What can we deduce about the relationships between representations of the invisible and the discourse of sorcery?

Although we cannot exactly situate the timelines in *Yaaba*, the director of *Wend Kuuni* indicates that his film takes place between the fifteenth and nineteenth centuries (Pfaff, 1996, 230), and it is clear from the images and the information conveyed by the 'madman' Elie's radio that *Delwende* takes place in contemporary Burkina Faso. Idrissa Ouedraogo makes it clear that his film is inspired by the universe of the fantastic tales he was once told. He then adds that 'village life is exactly as we show it in the film, there is no reconstitution, everything was shot in natural settings' (Pfaff, *ibid*). This supports the anthropological approach used by Pfaff in his article. The whole argument of Kamwa's film is built around the devaluation of the CFA franc in 1993: the narrative movement that results in the resolution of Moni-Sam's financial troubles, who then embarks on his particular itinerary, follows the devaluation of that currency. Linking this devaluation, a politico-economic phenomenon, to sorcery, is the kind of stretch that only fiction can carry off. Is this maybe a way of taking things to the extreme, to exaggerate a political event that so marked the destiny of colonized people? The fact remains that *Le Cercle des pouvoirs* also reveals a constant in postcolonial experiences, and elsewhere as well: political problems are often resolved through assassination. This reality will be aided and abetted by the forces of darkness.

The language of sorcery is consistently present at certain moments in the political life of every group, whether urban or rural, in spaces where the State is absent, hence making any national(ist) project almost irrelevant. These languages allow for the establishment of relations of domination. But as we pass from pre-colonial times to the present, from West Africa to Central Africa, practices of the occult diversify and change radically, although aggression, both 'real' (shown, staged) or supposed (imagined by the community) remains a permanent fixture. Given the trajectory of Moni-Sam, we can even advance the hypothesis that it would be more difficult for him, and by extension for anyone, to activate their evil power in a society not devoured by individual appetites and in which political power is not obsessed with perpetuating itself. The occult, as shown in the Cameroonian and Burkinabe films, is in essence a narration and discourse on socio-political disorder and panic. In joining an 'anti-sorcerer' like Atchori to The Prince, however, Kamwa gives social justice a bit of a chance. The films of Kaboré, Yaméogo and Ouedraogo are a cautionary tale against evolutionist theories; they point out the need to question group values. Kamwa's film, on the other hand, reveals the dark side of modernity and the invisible dynamics of the manner in which the postcolonial State functions when it's not in fact dysfunctional; for it is truly a sorcerer-state. Thus 'mystical' discourse, although it in fact elucidates sudden and puzzling social inequities and explains new vocations, ceases to be a perception solely 'from below' of (super)natural phenomena, as Geschiere says (1997, 24). This discourse is in fact what inspires and drives people in the higher echelons of the political system.

We can also note that the 'circle of those in power' is like a mafia, with its rules and godfathers. One can reject its rules only on pain of death, the language of which is, in that circle, permanent and unavoidable. In other words, the mystical is intimately linked to blood. In order to obtain fortune or political glory a person must always liquidate any debt that they have taken on through authorizing or suffering aggression; mystical organizations are always holders of debts in blood, while their members are always debtors. The link that Geschiere establishes between kinship and occult practices holds here only in the case of Moni-Sam, who sacrifices his own son. He has no relationship with Siffo, but he tries nonetheless to eliminate her, as he does Jisset. Practitioners of the occult can claim anyone's blood in order to fulfil their ambitions that have little to do with national(ist) projects.

There are without a doubt beneficial aspects of the occult, but in this case there is still a problem, albeit a different one. Recourse to these forces seems to be nothing but a reaction to aggression, a fact which at least in part elucidates the path travelled by the journalist Jisset. In Africa, we might ask, the question is whether any public life, any significant social or professional success, is possible without important mystical protections as most people, from all social scales, tend to adopt it. The question becomes even more relevant in the context of the proliferation of French mystical groups in public life and the place of the occult in popular narratives. Even though he is removed from political office at the end of the film, Moni-Sam achieves a certain success and resolves his financial problems. Jisset assiduously keeps the company of Atchori, without whom he would have lost his life given the number of acts of aggression of which he is victim. The occult is a permanent presence in the lives of those who must protect themselves and conquer new social and professional domains.

As we have seen, the social sciences are very cautious when dealing with the question of the 'reality' of the occult. Geschiere says several times that is not the object of his book. Kamwa's film has however come to the aid of researchers by showing them, through symbolic narration and interpretation, just how the forces of darkness function. This help, which comes about through an iconic articulation that can be resolved individually or collectively, gives the filmic image the advantage of being placed within society. This society in turn does not submit it to the same constraints of 'proof' that are required by so-called 'scientific' discourse. The syntactic ordering of *Le Cercle des pouvoirs* in fact *constructs* a causal relation between mystical practices and illness, political power and accumulation of wealth. We must wonder whether it is however enough merely to see a story involving the occult in order to conclude that it exists and, along with Gugler, one of the few researchers in the social sciences, admit that, 'The revelation of the occult confirms its existence, enhancing the credibility of beliefs in the occult … In their distorted fashions these stories reflect a reality' (Gugler, 2003, 178). Is not cinema an imaginary and even magical *construction*?

It must also be mentioned that these films speak of phenomena that are in essence invisible. To represent them is thus, in fact, to *interpret* them, and that, in a way, changes their essence. Therein lies the problem; for seeing, here, is not enough to believe. Despite the fact that the syntactic organization of Kamwa's film elucidates the practices of dark forces, we cannot help but note that Moni-Sam also traffics a lot in contraband goods, for the film shows him engaged in illicit practices. We are led to believe that this might in fact be the true source of his fortune, from a strictly empirical standpoint. By exploiting the poor and ruining the State, the new elite class takes away the State's resources, which it should be using to save others from death. They thus, as we see with Moni-Sam, ensure that they will die a deferred but ineluctable death. Certainly, his political success, as with many elements of his life, cannot coherently be explained; this in a sense validates an explanation that appeals to sorcery, a symbolic interpretation of facts. We must not forget that Moni-Sam becomes a practitioner in the realm of the forces of darkness, in politics and in contraband, only after a political event, namely the devaluation of the CFA franc. How then is one to approach new situations that cannot be controlled without recourse to the occult? But although this 'reality' remains a problem that we cannot accuse researchers of avoiding, it remains true that the occult offers a truth: it is the truth of a society in crisis, in the face of which subjects develop different responses to the questions asked of them.

This chapter has shown that filmic discourse offers cultural (symbolic) explanations for real (objective) phenomena that have little to do with nation building. It takes up but goes beyond anthropological thinking about the occult, which remains obscure. Maybe that is the secret of the interest in sorcery: the fact that it defies all un-nuanced elucidation. But it also accounts for the trajectory and significance of phenomena in the realms of darkness, at every stage of social evolution. The dysfunctional nature of postcolonial States as well as the proliferation of magico-religious practices in Africa and elsewhere indicates that the mystical and even the incoherent are present in questions of government. From Sana, the sorcerer created in the universe of *Yaaba*, to the services of Atchori, to the misdeeds of The Prince in *Le Cercle des pouvoirs*, African films deploy invisible forces that allow people to question and represent the torments of an era, as well as all that is at stake in society. Through the paths followed by Moni-Sam and Jisset, the forces of darkness are also clearly identified as impediments to the democracy whose failures they in fact help us understand. But at least we can *see* these forces at work, elucidating for us the dysfunctional nature of power. The inherent opacity of postcolonial power renders it even more mysterious, puzzling and difficult to understand; it also multiplies questions that neither anthropological discourse nor the medium of film can address. Of course this is only fitting, for, thus exposed, the occult would cease to be occult.

Notes

1　We must note that this problem does not arise only with the outbreak of the occult in politics. In the social sciences it is as if it were impossible to study Africa in a similar manner. For example, since the analyses of Jean-François Bayard on corruption, we tend to forget that 'la politique du ventre' is not an exclusively African phenomenon. One wonders also if the discourse of political scientists will change following the 'ethnic' conflicts of former East-Europe. When we include Africa in a 'modernity' to which we seek to compare it, it is only in order to emphasize its atavastic nature.

2　In *The Invention of Africa*, V. Y. Mudimbe (1988, 189–90) deconstructs the tradition-modernity dichotomy and then goes on to conclude that 'the discovery of primitiveness was an ambiguous invention of a history incapable of facing its own double' (190). In the same vein, Bernard Mouralis argues in *L'Europe, l'Afrique et la folie* that the reductionistic ideas that circulate in the Africanist Western discourse are due to an inability to think the Other, to think onself and, therefore, to think at all (1993, 13).

3　From the title of Bernard Hours's book, *L'Etat sorcier. Santé publique et société au Cameroun*. Paris, L'Harmattan, 1986.

4 We should note that in one of the films by Michel Ocelot, Kirikou must conquer a sorceress.

5 French original: '*Face à l'insécurité matérielle et symbolique, le sentiment des catégories dominées est que les conditions de possibilité d'attaque en "sorcellerie" sont multiples. Cette insécurité n'épargne point les dominants. Dans les moments de crise de gouvernabilité des sociétés, les hommes et les femmes se mettent en quête de stratégies thérapeutiques, de rituels et de prescriptions qui leur épargnent de mort'.*

6 The question seems inevitably to be linked to postcolonial power. In *Les Magiciens du repentir. Les Confessions de Frère Dominique* (1995), Pius Ngandu Nkashama outlines the frightening dimensions of this phenomenon as found in Congo-Kinshasa under Mobutu. In *Illusions identitaires* (1996), Jean-François Bayart demonstrates that African leaders, among them Sékou Touré, Mathieu Kérékou, Félix Houphouët-Boigny and even Thabo Mbeki, turn to the forces of darkness every day. In the same vein, Pierre Péan describes the case of Omar Bongo in *Affaires africaines* (1983). In Sembène Ousmane's *Guelwaar,* after the disappearance of Guelwaar's body, which has been mistakenly buried in a Muslim cemetery, a nurse tells the deceased's son dead bodies are used by politicians and businessmen for occult purposes in order to guarantee their success.

7 This common identity that is ascribed to power, to 'sorcery' and to cannibalism is also taken up in literary texts. In *Destins parallèles* (1995), Kitia Touré writes: '*Le pouvoir est comme un cercle de sorcières. Il faut être sorcière pour y entrer et quand on y entre, il faut être anthropophage comme les autres, et avec les autres, au risque de se faire manger comme un dissident /* Power is like a circle of witches. You have to be a witch to enter it, and when you do so, you have to be a cannibal like the others, and with the others, or else risk being eaten as a dissident' (167). Also, '*En politique, il ne faut pas faire de sentiment. C'est comme dans la sorcellerie. Il faut détruire avant d'être soi-même détruit /* In politics, you cannot be sentimental. It is like the world of sorcery. You have to destroy before being yourself destroyed' (297–298). This, in fact, always involves 'witches' and not male sorcerers.

8 *Mont Kupé* and *Famla* are places where, according to popular stories, all occult events take place. For a more detailed account, I direct the reader to the studies of Peter Geschiere. In their analyses of the situation in South Africa, the Camaroffs (1999) call these people, who have been enslaved into the invisible world, 'zombie workers'.

9 The reader should note the homophony between the character's name, 'Moni', and the English word 'money'.

10 Although it is situated at a time when slaves were being shipped to the Americas, Maryse Condé's novel, *Moi Tituba sorcière ... Noire de Salem* (1986) presents a discourse of the invisible that belongs to the discursive categories underlying this chapter. It again involves a woman, Tituba, who is tried along with other women who have been accused of 'plotting with Satan'. They are to be hanged following an unorthodox trial. However, this heroine deploys her powers in exact accordance with the perspectives noted by De Rosny. Beyond

many other examples found in the text, the following two illustrate her at work: she inflicts an awful illness on her mistress Susanna Endicott, who continually humiliates her, but she cures Elizabeth Parris at a moment when they are getting ready for her imminent burial. What is most important is the way in which the text characterizes the 'sorcerer', knowledge of the cosmos and the many instances in which Tituba communicates with the invisible. The narrator, Tituba, speaks of a 'gift' (26), of 'superior grace' (34) and of 'art', of 'knowledge' (59), and of 'science' (89, 109), etc. At several points in the book, we see sophisticated thinking about the nature of a complex phenomenon that always escapes any Cartesian or Christian rational reasoning. Finally, we must note that in Condé's novel, sorcery is also linked to power to the extent that it constitutes a mechanism of defence for the weak, because slaves use it with wondrous results.

11 The choice of adjective here is deliberate because in the other films, if an act of aggression has indeed taken place, people are unjustly accused of being responsible, whereas in this film, the story 'proves' culpability.

12 There is an agreement: Moni Sam must either die or look for a substitute who would die for him. In short, he needs a saviour.

13 It is worth noting that some of these representations may not be easily understandable if the viewer is not sufficiently familiar with Cameroon's narratives of the occult.

14 Again, a non-Cameroonian spectator may not fully understand this scene. Such a reaction is possible only when the subject is protected with 'armour,' in other words, is 'mystically' protected against death by poisoning. This is also called the 'casse-verres/glass-breaker': the poisoned glass shatters when a protected person tries to put it to his lips. An identical scene takes place in *Quartier Mozart* in which Mad Dog's glass shatters at the table (Mad Dog presides over a chaotic polygamous family). He reacts saying this to his wives, whom he suspects of making an attempt on his life: 'I armoured. You can do nothing to me'.

15 In some sorcery-based stories of the *Famla*, to drink a glass of red wine signifies to make a gift of your own blood or of the blood of a loved-one.

Conclusion

What is African cinema (today)?

'Is there anything in this cinema which is not African?
Fantasy, myth, we got.Walt Disney, we got.
Lion King, we got. Massacres, we got.
Comedians, music, we got. Paul Simon, we got.
Aristotle, catharsis, and kola nut, we got.
What don't we got?'

Jean-Pierre Bekolo (*Aristotle's Plot*, 1996)

The purpose of this book was to revisit the cultural, historical and political considerations that had almost systematically dominated African film scholarship over the past decades. I have examined some important aesthetic, generic and representational trends that have been precipitated by several contemporary cinematic productions. In these films, novel formal experimentations are admittedly determined by both local and global concerns. Conceptualizations of nationhood, identity, race, Africa and social contestations appear at times to be almost completely absent. One of the immediate consequences of this new reconfiguration of the cultural landscape is the deconstruction of the tenacious and yet avowedly reductionist category 'African cinema'. This 'cinema' was until now characterized by cultural, anthropological and ideological discourses that were substantially determined by a political institution, namely the FEPACI. As the previous chapters have shown, the cinematic field has unquestionably become so diverse that defining African cinemas today is more challenging than ever before.

When Paulin Soumanou Vieyra (1975, 7) emphatically argued for the need to use the singular ('cinema') to describe African films that could not, in his opinion, be varied or numerous enough to be considered part of a specific 'national cinema', it was certainly because of the then dominant Panafricanism, as well as its attendant political discourse. In contemporary postnational spaces, Africa has itself become a more complex entity; its cinemas (and I emphasize the plural) do not necessarily aim at portraying a specifically 'African' identity. Reacting to the increase in films on immigration in Europe, for example, Olivier Barlet asked a question that is crucially important in current transnational settings: 'Are the new films of Africa African?' (Olivier Barlet 2003, 43–49). In other words, is a cinematographic or cultural identity conceivable, and must one define it in relation to a specific national, continental or racial framework? Is it possible to unequivocally define, in a way that is coherent and acceptable, the fundamental constituents of an 'African cinema'? In addition to issues pertaining to identity, current scholarship does not seem to have sufficiently documented the criteria that can help rigorously determine the diverseness of African films. Should the assumed diversification of these cinemas, as Samuel Lelièvre suggests, be only assessed on the basis of various (generally external) sources of financing available to African filmmakers (2003, 10–13)? Would aesthetic, generic, representational or discursive evaluations not be better benchmarks?

The stakes of Lelièvre's and Barlet's enquiries, as this book has also endeavoured to assess, are greater than a mapping of the territoriality of African cinemas. More radically, they involve the very possibility of determining an 'African' identity or, more specifically, of defining the formal, discursive or representational features of African narratives in a context of large-scale cultural, political and economic circulations. As David Murphy once pointed out, there is a profound (in my opinion, insurmountable) difficulty in grasping the concept of the 'true African' because 'the reality of Africans filming has not produced a unified "authentic" African cinema. Rather, it has produced a series of complex and often contradictory visions of a continent' (Murphy, 2000, 240). Such multiple, contradictory and hybrid identities, these tensions and dialogues between possible film languages, were identified, although not sufficiently documented, by Manthia Diawara (1992, 164–165), when he convincingly suggested that unlike the 'return to the source' films (1992, 159–164), the other narratives in his typology, namely social realist and confrontation films (141–159), define their Africanness within *dominant cinematic forms*. Although he also cautioned that it would be 'simplistic to single out *Yeelen* or *Tilaï* as the new direction in African cinema and to judge other films by their relative affinities to this film' (165), Diawara rightly brought attention (quite early) to the necessarily mixed configuration of African cinematic language. If such aesthetic formation did not need to be necessarily regarded as mixed, how could one account for the fact that confrontation films, for example, which challenged political and cultural subjugation, use *dominant forms* to convey their proclaimed message? Such apparent contradiction clearly indicates that from their inception, African films were positioned within a global cultural circulation and distribution to which they could not possibly be immune. Such exposure has certainly had a lasting effect that appears to have intensified over the years. These effects are in turn actually more apparent in the post-1990 films, which have revealed a completely transformed and diverse landscape. In another essay, Diawara is very critical of the idea of an essentialist and immutable 'African cinema':

> I do not believe that there is such a thing as an authentic African
> film language, whether it is defined in terms of commonalities
> arising from liberation struggles against colonialism and
> imperialism, or identity politics or Afrocentricity. … there are
> variations, and even contradictions, among film languages and
> ideologies, which are attributable to the prevailing political
> cultures in each region, the differences in the modes of
> production and distribution, and the particularities of regional
> cultures. (Diawara, 2000, 81)

Such rejection of an imaginary homogeneity is endorsed in even stronger terms by filmmakers themselves, in different terms. In addition to Joseph Gaï Ramaka and Jean-Pierre Bekolo, whose opinions have been discussed throughout this book, several other directors firmly contest what they perceive as a reductive 'Africanness'. For example, Idrissa Ouedraogo (1995, 336) disapproves of the fact that African films appear to be permanently homologized by a dominant perception that African directors work neither on the same data, nor in keeping with the same aesthetic values, as Western directors. For Ouedraogo, in spite of its unique philosophy and distinctive originality, every film produced in Africa is lumped in advance in the box 'African cinema'. Gabonese director Imunga Ivanga equally rejects the uniform 'African box' into which all films by

African directors are relegated. For him, such simplification is unacceptable given the continuing expansion of a borderless, mobile and diversified world, where 'authenticity' has revealed itself to be a concept fraught with confusion and exclusion. Some of his questions are crucial:

> What can be said about films from the south which by far outpace their 'undocumented' (*'sans-papier'*) authors in portraying the national character of the north? As a matter of fact, initial definitions [relating to authenticity or Africanness] quickly become inoperative because these creators' desires and status cannot be yoked into an iron shackle. *The so-called filmmakers from the south define themselves according to the same terms as Truffaut, Godard, Rohmer, Chabrol, all authors of the New Wave.*
> (Ivanga, 2005, 176, my emphasis)[1]

In his interview with Nwachukwu Frank Ukadike, Jean-Pierre Bekolo is even more radical and, equally, almost dismissive of any generalized idea of 'African cinema'. After openly acknowledging what he calls his 'inclination for Hollywood' as well as the weight of Western influence and rationalities on his work, he emphatically states: 'I don't know about African cinema. I never studied it, and it's not my field' (2002, 220). He further adds, 'having clearly examined what cinema is, I feel there is no cinema. There are African films, but I do not know if there is cinema in it' (Ukadike, 2002, 223). In *Africa for the Future* (2009) a theoretical and philosophical book where he discusses his opinions regarding culture, he emphatically addresses the necessary interconnectedness of cinema productions on a global scale. In such a context, it is critical for Africans, in his opinion, to initiate what he calls '*Désobéissances Narratives*/Narrative Disobedience' (59), processes through which postcolonial subjects renounce liberationist narratives that have become nothing but *déjà vu* and *déjà su* (59). Bekolo equally advocates a '*république universelle*/universal republic', a new, possible rather than utopian, territory for shared cultural values (91). By (almost naively) denying any role to ideology in new cosmopolitan contexts (113), Bekolo is not far from Reda Bensmaïa's perception of writers' homeland which does not refer to a specific land, native soil, or culture any more; it rather refers to migrations among lands, languages and cultures, a circulation that makes identities necessarily hybrid and inter-correlated (2003, 126). It is clear, then, that for many postcolonial directors, the era of 'isolated' subjectivities is irreversibly over, and they are now in a fast moving terrain where identity and otherness are not so clearly separated.

From the work of Diawara, among others, we learn that in spite of the constitution of some specifically local/African features (the import of oral forms, African dance/languages as well as the strategic positioning of a target audience), African cinemas have in fact historically been diverse and heterogeneous. The focus of most scholarship on the work of Djibril Diop Mambéty as an early 'dissonant' aesthetician (Harrow, 2007 or Niang, 2002 among others) should not occlude the fact that 'Western' aesthetics have consistently impacted African filmmaking in various ways (cf. Sada Niang (2008) and myself (2008)). What is new, though, is that several post-1990 narratives have underscored the incorporation of 'dominant', 'global' and 'foreign' components in a more pronounced way; significantly, these components have, in turn, been substantially subverted. Some of these innovations are illustrated in the genres and representations I have outlined throughout this book. They include the construction of a comedic register where African films are positioned as a form of entertainment. Such entertainment combines local and global components to represent the decidedly non-nationalist anxieties of the lower social classes. New postcolonial subjects also define a different social, rather than political or military, heroism, which involves undertaking activities as ordinary as dancing in order to articulate specific personal projects. With these films where sex, laughter and alcoholism prevail, the postcolonial authority regresses from triumphant power to a marked decline in crime narratives that subvert the rules of this genre. The subjects portrayed in recent productions have equally undergone another major transformation: they are no longer ascetic freedom fighters or social critics; they are now ordinary characters who claim the right to enjoy sexual liberties that break with rigid moral or social codes. Although censorship prevails in the form of strategic directorial choices, sex has undeniably become a social commodity and a topic open to public discussion. Sex(uality) is thus viewed not only as an obstacle for a successful nation building project, but also as a perfect ingredient for tragedy and other political disruptions. The mythical linkage of sexual desire to the Fall and social disintegration in several postcolonial films illustrates that they belong to a postnationalist regime. This new perspective remains true even in contexts of epic constructions. As I have outlined, the post-resistance epics studied in this book revisit the past without necessarily glorifying it or invoking anxiety over a lost grandeur. This post-liberation mode also prevails in sorcery narratives that seek to offer symbolic explanations for objective phenomena in situations where the State is completely absent.

Given the above, I want to argue that Diawara's dated, albeit useful taxonomy (1992) needs to be updated because it does not sufficiently consider the new dynamics of production and aesthetic experimentations at work in films that involve Africa. In looking at the continent *as a category of representation*, one can start by examining a category of films in which Africa is perceived by 'the other'. Although this is a rather 'classic' investigation, my conception takes into account the fact that not all Western directors have constructed a colonial or exotic representation of Africans. Some of them like Chris Marker and Claude Vauthier can be convincingly positioned within the liberationist Third Cinema trend because of the revisionist discourse contained in their work. These must be positioned against what may be called the 'Griot Camera,' namely all the dominantly nationalist films that have been erroneously perceived as representing a monolithic 'African cinema'. A third category would mainly consist of the numerous post-1990 directors like Jean-Pierre Bekolo or Idrissa Ouedraogo who believe nationalist praxis is exhausted and that African cinemas need to be positioned within global cultural transactions. Those who argue that this is the case tend to emphasize the fact that African directors use the same categories as their Western counterparts, and their work should consequently be examined using similar frameworks and criteria.[2] Some of those include the genres and representations outlined in this book, all which put to rest, at least partially, the obsolete 'exceptionalism' which David Murphy and Patrick Williams (2007) criticized. A final group of films that deserves full investigation, and which also consists of separate multiple sub-categories and typologies, is made of the thousands of narratives produced by the video industries in West and Central Africa. Whether they constitute a (national) cinema is a huge theoretical issue that remains to be addressed; this exploration is all the more urgent given that they are the most watched and the most available in African households.

Another element that needs to be documented by further research is the undeniable nationalization and regionalization of African cinemas. Although the nature, depth and breadth of such growth are yet to be rigorously illustrated, one must admit, following Diawara (2000), that the decadence of the nation-state has stimulated the emergence of alternative film praxis and aesthetics in which nation formation is not a central preoccupation. In spite of notable and numerous similarities within specific geographic territories (for example, films from West Africa have features not easy to identify in those from Central Africa), new ways seem to be paved for specific national (or regional) cinemas that nevertheless continue to position themselves *within tumultuous trans-continental and cosmopolitan dynamics.* That is why, notwithstanding the singular in the title of her book *50 ans de cinéma maghrébin* (2009), Denise Brahimi goes on to use a plural determinant in the first sentence in order to describe films from the region she studies. Another compelling example is provided by Keyan G. Tomaselli (2006) who uses the plural in the subtitle of his work: *Encountering Modernity: Twentieth Century South African Cinemas.*

The third element I wish to emphasize relates to the obvious decline of (cultural) nationalism in films, an important component which scholarship has so far failed to sufficiently address. As I have argued, several directors like Mwenze Ngangura, Idrissa Ouedraogo and Jean-Pierre Bekolo have become very critical of nationalist filmmaking which has successfully transformed 'African cinema' into what Tahar Cheriaa called a 'monster' or a 'biological anomaly', that is, a head (the filmmakers and their films) without a body (a market and a public) (1978, 8–9). For Bekolo in particular (2009, 42), social agency amounts to a complete lack of understanding of *the medium cinema* on the part of both artists and 'intellectuals' who historically have failed to use cinema as a real 'tool for self empowerment'. According to him, nationalist and didactic narratives left the African landscape vacant and thus vulnerable to foreign images. Ironically, as indicated by Ngangura, this situation has resulted in African films alienating African spectators. Worse, thanks to a pertinent remark by Diawara, these committed directors were all using dominant narrative forms to question colonial subjection.

The need, therefore, to rethink African film scholarship, to go beyond nationalism, is essential. The 'Third Worldist [and nationalist] terms' (Haynes, 2005, 113) that have saturated the field of African cinemas must be reconsidered in order to determine the new articulations of an increasingly post-resistance era that has pushed nation formation to the margins. As paradoxical as it may be, 'writing' (Bill Ashcroft et al 2002) or 'shooting' (Melisa Thackway 2003) 'back' actually links colonial and postcolonial subjects in a rather perverse way: they appear to be two sides of the same coin. By this I mean that postcolonial directors (and critics) legitimize their praxis by reproducing and perpetuating (although by contesting) the imperial order they claim to challenge. Polemically, a possible implication could be that the existence of postcolonial cultures that limit themselves only to a resistance mode is bound to disappear when nationalist struggles meet their ultimate goals. In other words, liberationist aesthetics and productions would become useless or vanish with a total collapse of the imperial order because they position colonialism as a central (and unique) reference point. Nationalist and 'oppositional' African film scholarship is dependent on productions that echo resistance which, albeit dominant (and domineering), is not, in any way, the only form of postcolonial subjectivity. As Achille Mbembe rightly pointed out, 'to account for both the mind-set and the effectiveness of postcolonial relations of power, we need to go beyond the binary categories used in standard interpretation domination' (2001, 103). What is more, for him, 'it is only through a shift in perspective that we can understand that the postcolonial relationship is not primarily a relationship of resistance or of collaboration but can best be characterized as convivial, a relationship fraught by the fact of *commandement* and its "subjects"' (104).

Several directors considered in this book offer such balanced reconsiderations of postcolonial relations and subjectivities by establishing a 'third' or middle space between poles that for a long time were supposedly binary. Although a radical nationalist, Guelwaar in Sembène Ousmane's *Guelwaar* is also a fervent Catholic who accepts help from his prostitute daughter. Although he is viewed as the local hero, he is equally notorious for his lasciviousness. In *Madame Brouette,* Mati the unfortunate female protagonist is also a smuggler who uses questionable strategies to meet her personal social goals. In *Ndeysaan*, victim and criminal become interchangeable poles, and a whole community ends up being united in what is a permanent grief after a former murderer is almost forgiven. In *Keita,* Djeliba, the last protector of African memory in a transformed world, advocates a combination of Western and African education. Jean-Marie Teno's openly militant (and tragic) *Afrique, je te plumerai* ends with a meta-fictional comic performance. *Bal Poussière* and *Les Couilles de l'éléphant* combine a discourse on sex and unparalleled comic components. Most important, and central to the argument of this book, all these 'intermediary' spaces are located within post-resistance, postnationalist frameworks where the nation, its fragments and components have become peripheral, if not absent.

In view of the above, it becomes evident that African cinemas today are far from a set of monotonous didactic narratives of the 1960s. They are certainly not the same 'shit' that Bekolo's character deplores in *Aristotle's Plot*. They now consist of transformed genres and forms which aim at entertaining and making culture popular, since pioneer films, by all accounts, hardly connected with a significant audience. By starting to focus on the quotidian, adopting categories like comedy, tragedy, musicals, dance, epic, sexuality or witchcraft that generally target/involve middle to low class heroes, renouncing social agency and aggressive ideological considerations, there is no doubt that contemporary African directors have opened up new directions that will substantially shape the cultural field for years to come. There are increased and active efforts to identify new markets (both local and international), to cross existing boundaries and position productions within global economic or cultural rationalities that involve both identity and otherness. Already, as mentioned earlier, technological advancement and state negligence have resulted in the growth of private video productions that generally focus on categories like crime, violence, comedy, sex and witchcraft. Although the Nigerian *Nollywood* is the most documented (Barrot, 2008), it must be noted, to give two rapid examples, that Boubakar Diallo has experienced an immense success with his low-budget films in Burkina Faso; similarly, the television series *Ma Famille* as well as the videos of *Les Guignols*, all shot and produced in Côte d'Ivoire, are widely available and discussed in francophone circles in Africa and abroad. The reason for mentioning these cheap, rudimentary quality 'films' is compelling: they use or expand on all the categories studied in this book, and it is certain that future research will focus more thoroughly on this new spectacular cultural phenomenon. These image producers and directors have succeeded where most postcolonial filmmakers have almost collectively failed, that is, in generating narrative forms that would make African cinemas truly *popular*. Several filmmakers, including those I have examined, have in various ways made a decisive step towards that goal by redefining African cinemas in the new terms proposed by Bekolo's character Essomba Tourneur: *What don't we got?*

Notes

1 French original: '*Que dire des films du sud arborant plus facilement que leurs auteurs 'sans papiers' la nationalité du nord? En réalité, les définitions initiales sont vite dépassées par les envies des créateurs, leurs statuts ne peuvent être enserrés dans un carcan. Les cinéastes dits du Sud sont des auteurs qui se définissent selon les mêmes termes que l'on fait Truffaut, Godard, Rohmer, Chabrol, tous les acteurs de la Nouvelle Vague. Ils ne récusent pas cette chaleur qui court le long de leurs films*' (Ivanga, 2005, 176).

2 I provide an extensive analysis of these categories in an earlier work. For more, see Alexie Tcheuyap (2006).

Bibliography and filmography

Bibliography

Achebe, Chinua (1958). *Things Fall Apart*. (London, Heinemann Educational Books).

Adesokan, Akin (2008). 'The Challenges of Aesthetic Populism: An Interview with Jean-Pierre Bekolo', *Postcolonial Text*, 4 (1), pp. 1–11.

Adetunji Osinubi, Taiwo (2009). 'Cognition Warp: African Speculations on Near-Future Risks', *African Identities*, 7 (2), pp. 257–276.

Akudinobi, Jude (1995). 'Tradition/Modernity and the Discourse of African Cinema', *Iris*, 18, pp. 25–37.

——— (2001). 'Nationalism, African Cinema, and the Frames of Scrutiny', *Research in African Literatures*, 32 (3), pp. 123–142.

——— (2006). 'Durable Dreams: Dissent, Critique, and Creativity in *Faat Kiné* and *Moolaadé*', *Meridians: Feminism, Race, Transnationalism*, 6 (2), pp. 177–194.

Altman, Rick (1999). *Film/Genre*. (London: BFI Publishing).

Ambrosio, Nora (2006). *Learning About Dance: Dance as an Art Form and Entertainment*, 4th edition. (Dubuque, Iowa: Kendall/Hunt Publishing Company).

Anderson, Benedict (2006). *Imagined Communities*. (London: Verso).

Andrew, Dudley (2010). 'Time Zones and Jetlag: The Flows and Phases of World Cinema', in Nataša Durovicová and Kathleen Newman (eds.), *World Cinemas, Transnational Perspectives*. (New York and Oxon: Routledge), pp. 59–89.

Angounou, Ebale (undated). Blood: Biya's Power Lotion. Electronic web publication.

Appadurai, Arjun (2005). *Modernity at Large: Cultural Dimensions of Globalization*. (Minneapolis: University of Minnesota Press).

Appiah, Kwame Anthony (1992). *In my Father's House: Africa in the Philosophy of Culture*. (New York: Oxford University Press).

Apter, Andrew (2005). *The Pan-African Nation: Oil and the Spectacle of Culture in Nigeria*. (Chicago: University of Chicago Press).

Aristotle (1990). *Poétique* trans. Michel Magnien. (Paris: Editions LGF).

Armes, Roy (1987). *Third World Filmmaking and the West*. (Berkeley: University of California Press).

—— (2006). *African Filmmaking North and South of the Sahara*. (Edinburgh: Edinburgh University Press).

Ashcroft, Bill et al. (1995). *The Post-Colonial Studies Reader*. (New York: Routledge, 1995).

—— (2002) *The Empire Writes Back*. (London: Routledge).

Azodo, Ada Uzoamaka and Ngozi Eeke, Maureen (2007) (eds.). *Gender and Sexuality in African Literature and Film*. (Trenton: Africa World Press).

Bakari, Imruh and Mbye, Cham (1996) (eds.). *African Experiences of Cinema*. (London: British Film Institute).

Bakhtin, Mikhail (1981). *The Dialogic Imagination: Four Essays*. Ed. M. Holquist, trans. C. Emersib and M. Holquist. (Austin: University of Texas Press).

—— (1984). *Rabélais and His World* trans. H. Iswolsky. (Bloomington: Indiana University Press).

Bakupa-Kanyinda, Balufu (1996). 'De l'exception historique.' *L'Afrique et le centenaire du cinéma*. (Paris: Présence Africaine), pp. 24–33.

Barlet, Olivier (2000). *African Cinemas: Decolonizing the Gaze* trans. Chris Turner. (New York: Zed Books).

—— (2003) 'Les Nouveaux Films d'Afrique sont-ils africains?' *CinémAction*, 106, pp. 43–49.

—— (2010) 'The New Paradoxes of Black Africa's Cinemas', in Nataša Durovicová and Kathleen Newman (eds.), *World Cinemas, Transnational Perspectives*. (New York and Oxon: Routledge), pp. 217–225.

Barrot, Pierre (2008). *Nollywood. The Video Phenomenon in Nigeria*. (Oxford: James Currey).

Barthes, Roland (1981). *Camera Lucida: Reflexions on Photography* trans. Richard Howard. (New York: Hill & Wang).

Bassori, Timite and Rahaga, Jean-Claude (1974). 'Le Problème d'un langage cinématographique original', *Présence Africaine*, 90, pp. 142–159.

Bayart, Jean-François (1996). *L'Illusion identitaire*. (Paris: Fayard).

Bekolo Obama, Jean-Pierre (2009). *Africa for the Future: Sortir un Nouveau Monde du Cinéma*. (Paris: Dagan).

Benali, Abdelkader (1998). *Le Cinéma colonial au Maghreb: L'Imaginaire en trompe l'œil*. (Paris: Cerf).

Benjamin, Walter (2000). *Œuvres: Tome II* trans. Maurice de Gandillac. (Paris: Gallimard).

Bensmaïa, Reda (2003). *Experimental Nations, or The Invention of the Maghreb*. (Princeton: Princeton University Press).

Benveniste, Emile (1971). *Problems in General Linguistics* trans. Mary Elizabeth Meek. (Coral Gables, Fla: University of Miami Press).

Bergson, Henri (1910). *Le Rire: Essai sur la signification du comique*. (Paris: Alcan).

Bickford-Smith, Vivian and Mendelsohn, Richard (eds.) (2006) *Black and White in Color: African History on Screen*. (Oxford: James Currey/Athens: Ohio University Press/Cape Town: Double Storey).

Bidima, Jean-Godefroy (1995). *La Philosophie africaine*. (Paris: PUF).

Bordwell, David (1989). *Making Meaning*. (Cambridge, MA: Harvard University Press).

Borges, Jorge Luis (1988). *Ultimes dialogues avec Osvaldo Ferrari*. (Paris: Editions Zoé/Editions de l'Aube).

Boughédir, Férid (1974). 'Comment le cinéma peut œuvrer à l'indépendance et l'autorité culturelle africaine.' *Présence Africaine*, 90, pp. 123–139.

—— (1976). *Cinéma africain et décolonisation: Étude des conditions culturelles et économiques de l'émergence de cinémas nationaux indépendants en Afrique dans la période postcoloniale*. (PhD Dissertation, Paris: University of Sorbonne.)

—— (1987). Le *Cinéma africain* de *A à Z*. (Bruxelles : OCIC)

—— (1992). *African Cinema from A to Z*. (Brussels: OCIC).

—— (2000). 'African Cinema and Ideology: Tendencies and Evolution' in June Givani (ed.) *Symbolic Narratives/African Cinema: Audiences, Theory and the Moving Image*. (London: BFI Publishing), pp. 109–121.

Boulanger, Pierre (1975). *Le Cinéma colonial: De L'Atlantide à Lawrence d'Arabie*. (Paris: Seghers).

Bourdieu, Pierre (1977). *Outline of a Theory of Practice* trans. Richard Nice. (Cambridge: Cambridge University Press).

Brahimi, Denise (2009). *50 Ans de cinéma maghrébin*. (Paris: Minerve).

Brennan, Timothy (2008). 'Postcolonial Studies and Globalization Theory', in Revathi Krishnaswarmy and John C. Hawley (eds.) *The Postcolonial and the Global*. (Minneapolis, MN: University of Minnesota Press), pp. 37–53.

Brunovska Karnick, Kristine and Jenkins, Henry (eds.) (1995). 'Funny Stories.' *Classical Hollywood Comedy*. (New York: Routledge), pp. 63–86.

Camaroff, Jean and Camaroff, John (eds.) (1997) *Modernity and its Malcontents: Rituals and Power in Post-Colonial Power*. (Chicago: University of Chicago Press).

—— (1999). 'Occult Economies and the Violence of Abstraction: Notes from the South African Postcolony.' *American Ethnologist*, 26 (2), pp. 279–303.

Carroll, Noël (1991). 'Notes on the Sight Gag', in Andrew Horton (ed.), *Comedy/Cinema/Theory*. (Berkeley: University of Clifornia Press), pp. 25–42.

Castaldi, Francesca (2006). *Choreographies of African Identities*. (Chicago: University of Illinois Press).

Cavell, Stanley (1982). *Pursuits of Happiness: The Hollywood Comedy of Remarriage*. (Cambridge, MA: Harvard University Press).

Césaire, Aimé (1969). *The Tragedy of King Christophe* trans. Ralph Manheim. (New York: Grove Press).

CESCA (1986). *Cemra Nigra: Le discours du film africain*. (Paris: OCIC L'Harmattan).

Chabal, J.P. and J-P. Daloz (1999). *L'Afrique est partie: Du désordre comme instrument politique*. (Paris: Economica).

Cham, Mbye Boubacar (1982). 'Sembene Ousmane and the Aesthetic of African Oral Tradition', *Africana Journal*, 13, pp. 24–38.

—— (2004). 'Film and History in Africa: A Critical Survey of Current Trends and Tendencies', in Françoise Pfaff (ed.) *Focus on African Films*. (Indianapolis: Indiana University Press), pp. 48–68.

Chatterjee, Partha (1993). *The Nation and its Fragments: Colonial and Postcolonial Histories*. (Princeton: Princeton University Press).

Cheriaa, Tahar (1978). 'Le Cinema africain et les "réducteurs de têtes"', *L'Afrique Littéraire et Artistique*, 49, pp. 8–9.

Chinweizu et al (1980). *Towards a Decolonization of African Literature: African Fiction and Poetry and their Critics*. (Enugu: Fourth Dimension Publishing).

Christian, Ed (ed.) (2000). *The Post-Colonial Detective*. (New York: Palgrave).

Ciekawy, Diane and Geschiere, Peter (1998). 'Containing Witchcraft: Conflicting Scenarios in Postcolonial Africa.' *African Studies Review*, 41 (3), pp. 1–14.

Clavreuil, Gérard (1987). *Erotisme et Littératures*. (Paris: Acropole).

Condé, Maryse (1986). *Moi Tituba sorcière... Noire de Salem*. (Paris: Mercure de France).

Conteh-Morgan, John and Olaniya, Tejumola (2004). *African Drama and Performance*. (Indianapolis: Indiana University Press).

Cornell, Drucilla (ed.) (2000). *Feminism & Pornography*. (New York: Oxford University Press).

Cowen, Tyler (2002). *Creative Destruction: How Globalization Is Changing the World's Cultures*. (Princeton: Princeton University Press).

Cowie, Elizabeth (1997). *Representing Women: Cinema and Psychoanalysis*. (Minneapolis: University of Minnesota Press).

Crawford, J. R. (1967) *Witchcraft and Sorcery in Rhodesia*. (London: Oxford University Press).

Dagan, Esther (ed.) *The Spirit's Dance in Africa: Evolution, Transformation, and Continuity in Sub-Sahara*. (Westmount, QC: Galerie Amrat African Art Publications).

Defays, Jean-Marc (1996). *Le Comique*. (Paris: Seuil).

Dérive, Jean (ed.) (2002a). *L'épopée, unité et diversité d'un genre*. (Paris: Karthala).

—— (2002b). 'Y a-t-il un style épique?' in *L'épopée, unité et diversité d'un genre*. (Paris: Karthala).

—— (2002c). 'Le Cas de l'épopée africaine', in *L'épopée, unité et diversité d'un genre*. (Paris: Karthala).

Derrida, J. (1981). *Positions* trans. Alan Bass. (Chicago: University of Chicago Press).

—— (1982) *Margins of Philosophy* trans. Alan Bass. (Chigago: University of Chicago Press).

Diawara, Manthia (1987). 'Oral Literature and African Film: Narratology in *Wend Kuuni*', in Jim Pines and Paul Willemen, *Questions of Third Cinema*. (London: British Film Institute), pp. 198–221.

—— (1992). *African Cinema· Politics and Culture*. (Indianapolis: Indiana University Press).

—— (1996). 'Popular Culture and Oral Traditions in African Films.' *African Experiences of Cinema*. (London: British Film Institute), pp. 209–219.

—— (1998). 'Toward a Regional Imaginary in Africa', in Frederic Jameson and Masao Miyoshi (eds.) *The Cultures of Globalization*. (Durham: Duke University Press), pp. 103–124.

—— (2000) 'The Iconography of West African Cinema', in June Givani (ed.) *Symbolic Narratives/African Cinema: Audiences, Theory and the Moving Image*. (London: BFI Publishing), pp. 81–89.

—— (2005) 'L'autoreprésentation dans le cinema africain', in Simon Njami (ed.) *Africa Remix. L'art contemporain d'un continent. Catalogue de l'exposition*. (Paris: Editions du Centre Pompidou), pp. 285–291.

Dixon, Wheeler Winston (ed.) (2000). *Film Genre 2000: New Critical Essays*. (Albany: State University of New York Press).

Dovey, Lindiwe (2009). *African Film and Literature: Adapting Violence to the Screen*. (New York: Columbia University Press).

Durovicová, Nataša and Newman, Kathleen (eds.) (2010). *World Cinemas, Transnational Perspectives*. (New York and Oxon: Routledge).

Duval, Maurice (1985). *Un Totalitarisme sans état: Essai d'anthropologie politique à partir d'un village burkinabé*. (Paris: L'Harmattan).

Dworkin, Andrea (2000). 'Against the Male Flood: Censorship, Pornography and Equality', in Drucilla Cornell (ed.) *Feminism & Pornography*. (New York: Oxford University Press), pp. 19–38.

Eagleton, Terry (2003). *Sweet Violence: The Idea of the Tragic*. (London: Blackwell Publishing).

Ebanda de B'beri, Boulou (2000) (ed.) 'Ecritures dans les cinémas d'Afrique noire'. *CiNéMAS*, 11 (1).

—— (2006). *Mapping Alternative Expressions of Blackness in Cinema: A Horizontal Labyrinth of Transgeographical Practices of Identity*. (Bayreuth: Bayreuth African Studies).

Eidsvik, Charles (1991). 'Mock Realism: The Comedy of Futility in Eastern Europe', in Andrew Horton (ed.) *Comedy/cinema/theory*. (Berkeley: University of California Press), pp. 91–105.

Elley, Derek (1984). *The Epic Film: Myth and History*. (Boston: Routledge & Kegan Paul).

Esonwanne, Uzoma (2007). 'The "Crisis of the Soul": Psychoanalysis and African Literature'. *Research in African Literatures*, 38 (2), pp. 140–142.

Evans-Pritchard, E. E. (1937) *Witchcraft, Oracles and Magic Among the Azende*. (Oxford: Calderon Press).

Fanon, Frantz (1967). *Black Skin, White Masks* trans. Charles Lam Markmann. (New York: Grove Press).

—— (1968). *The Wretched of the Earth* trans. Constance Farrington. (New York: Grove Press).

Feinberg, Leonard (1967). *Introduction to Satire*. (Iowa: Iowa University Press).

FEPACI (1995). *L'Afrique et le centenaire du cinéma*. (Paris: Présence Africaine).

Ferro, Marc (1993). *Cinéma et histoire*. (Paris: Gallimard).

Fila, David-Pierre (2003). 'Cinéma noir, public blanc', in Elisabeth Lequeret, *Le cinéma africain. Un continent à la recherche de son propre regard*. (Paris: Les Cahiers du cinema), pp. 78–79.

Finnegan, Ruth (1970). *Oral Literature in Africa*. (Oxford: Oxford University Press).

Fisiy, Cyprian F. and Geschiere, Peter (1990). 'Judges and Witches, or How Is the State to Deal with Witchcraft? Examples from Southern Eastern Cameroon', *Cahiers d'Etudes Africaines*, 118, pp. 135–156.

—— (1993). 'Sorcellerie et accumulation. Variations sous-régionales', in Peter Geschiere and Piet Konings (eds.) *Itinéraires d'accumulation au Cameroun: Pathways to Accumulation in Cameroon*. (Paris: ASC-Karthala), pp. 99–129.

Foucault, Michel (1970). *The Order of Things: An Archaeology of the Human Sciences*, (London: Tavistock Publications).

—— (1972). *The Archaeology of Knowledge and the Discourse on Language* trans. Alan Sheridan. (New York: Pantheon).

—— (1977). *Discipline and Punish. The Birth of the Prison* trans. Alan Sheridan. (New York: Pantheon Books).

—— (1978). *The History of Sexuality* trans. Robert Hurley. (New York: Pantheon Books).

—— (1997). *Il faut défendre la société. Cours au Collège de France, 1975–1976*. (Paris: Seuil).

Fougeyrollas, Pierre (1987). *La Nation: Essor et déclin des sociétés modernes*. (Paris: Fayard).

Frindéthié, K. Martial (2009). *Francophone African Cinema: History, Culture, Politics and Theory*. (Jefferson, NC and London: McFarland & Company, Inc.).

Gabara, Rachel (2006). *From Split to Screened Selves: French and Francophone Autobiography in the Third Person*. (Stanford: Stanford University Press).

Gabriel, Teshome H. (1982) *Third Cinema in the Third World. The Aesthetics of Liberation*. (Ann Arbor: UMI Research Press).

—— (1995). 'Towards a Critical Theory of Third World Films', in Michael Martin (ed.) *Cinemas of the Black Diaspora*. (Detroit: Wayne State University Press).

Gardies, André (1989). *Cinéma d'Afrique noire francophone: L'Espace miroir*. (Paris: L'Harmattan).

Gauthier, Alain (1992). *Trajectoire de la Modernité: Représentations et images*. (Paris: Presses Universitaires de France).

Genette, Gérard (1982). *Palimpsestes: La Littérature au Second Degré*. (Paris: Seuil).

Geschiere, Peter (1988). 'Sorcery and the State in Cameroon.' *Critique of Anthropology*, 8 (1), pp. 35–63.

—— (1995). *Sorcellerie et politique en Afrique: La viande des autres*. (Paris: Karthala).

—— (1997). *The Modernity of Witchcraft: Politics and the Occult in Post-Colonial Africa* trans. Peter Geschiere and Janet Roitman. (Charlottesville: University Press of Virginia).

—— (2000) 'Sorcellerie et modernité. Retour sur une étrange complicité', *Politique Africaine* 79, pp. 17-32.

—— (2003). 'On Witch-doctors and Spin Doctors: The Role of "Experts" in African and American Politics', in Birgit Meyer and Peter Pels (eds.) *Magic and Modernity, Interfaces of Revelation and Concealment*. (Stanford: Stanford University Press), pp. 159–183.

Geschiere, Peter and Konings, Piet (eds.) (1993). *Itinéraires d'accumulation au Cameroun. Pathways to Accumulation in Cameroon*. (Paris: ASC-Karthala).

Geschiere, Peter and Nyamnjoh, Francis (1998). 'Witchcraft as an Issue in the "Politics of Belonging": Democratization and Urban Migrants' Involvement with the Home Village.' *African Studies Review*, 41 (3), pp. 69–91.

Gilroy, Paul (1993). *The Black Atlantic: Modernity and the Double Consciousness*. (Cambridge, MA: Harvard University Press).

Girard, René (1977). *Violence and the Sacred* trans. Patrick Gregory. (Baltimore: John Hopkins University Press).

Givani, June (ed.) (2000). *Symbolic Narratives / African Cinema: Audiences, Theory and the Moving Image*. (London: BFI Publishing).

Glissant, Edouard (1996). *Introduction à la poétique du divers*. (Paris: Gallimard).

Gobineau, Arthur (1967). *The Inequality of Human Races* trans. Adrian Collins. (New York: Howard Fertig Inc.).

Gomel, Elana (1995). 'Mystery, Apocalypse and Utopia: The Case of the Ontological Detective Story.' *Science-Fiction Studies*, 22, pp. 343–356.

Grant, Barry Keith (2003). *Film Genre Reader III*. (Austin: University of Texas Press).

—— (2007). *Film Genre: From Iconography to Ideology*. (New York: Wallflower).

Gugler, Josef (2003). *African Film: Re-Imagining a Continent*. (Bloomington: James Currey/Indiana University Press).

Gunning, Tom (1995). 'Crazy Machine in the Garden of Forking Paths: Mischief Gags and the Origins of American Comedy', in Kristine Brunovska Karnick and Henry Jenkins (eds.) *Classical Hollywood Comedy*. (New York: Routledge), pp. 69–86.

Habermas, Jurgen (2001). *The Postnational Constellation. Political Essays* trans., ed. and with an introduction by Max Pensky. (Cambridge, MA: MIT Press).

Haffner, Pierre (1978). *Essai sur les fondements théoriques du cinéma Africain*. (Dakar: Nouvelles Editions Africaines).

Hall, Stuart (1989). 'Cultural Identity and Cinematic Representation', *Framework*, 36, pp. 68–81.

—— (1996). 'The Local and the Global: Globalization and Ethnicity', in Anthony King (ed.) *Culture, Globalization and the World System*. (Minneapolis: University of Minnesota Press), pp. 19–39.

Hall, Stuart et al (eds.) (1980). *Culture, Media, Language*. (London: Routledge).

Harrow, Kenneth (ed.) (1995) *Research in African Literatures, Special Issue: African Cinema*, 26 (3).

—— (ed.) (1999). *African Cinema. Post-Colonial and Feminist Readings*. (Trenton: Africa World Press).

—— (2002). *Less Than One and Double: A Feminist Reading of African Women's Writing*. (New York: Heinemann).

—— (ed.) (2001). *Research in African Literatures, Special Issue: African Nationalism*, 32 (3).

—— (2007) *Postcolonial African Cinema. From Political Engagement to Postmodernism.* (Bloomington and Indianapolis: Indiana University Press).

—— (2010). 'What's an Old Man Like You Doing with a Saignante Like Me?' in Toyin Falola and Fallou Ngom (eds.) *Facts, Fiction, and African Creative Imagination.* (New York and London: Routledge), pp. 190–206.

Hartman, Geoffrey H. (1981). *Saving the Text: Literature, Derrida, Philosophy.* (Baltimore: John Hopkins University Press).

Hayari, Farida (1996). 'Images of Women', in Mbye Cham and Imruh Bakari (eds.) *African Experiences of Cinema.* (London: British Film Institute), pp. 181–184.

Haynes, Jonathan (2005). 'African Filmmaking and the Postcolonial Predicament: *Quartier Mozart* and *Aristotle's Plot*', in *Cinema and Social Discourse in Cameroon.* (Bayreuth: Bayreuth African Studies), pp. 111–136.

Hegel, George (1956). *The Philosophy of History.* (New York: Dover).

Higbee, Will and Lim, Song Hwee (2010). 'Concepts of Transnational Cinema: Towards a Critical Transnationalism in Film', *Transnational Cinemas*, 1 (1), pp. 7–21.

Higginson, Pim (2005). 'Mayhem at the Crossroads: Francophone African Fiction and the Rise of the Crime Novel', *Yale French Studies*, 108, pp. 160–176.

—— (2007). 'A Descent into Crime: Explaining Mongo Beti's Last Two Novels', *International Journal of Francophone Studies*, 10 (3), pp. 377–391.

Hjort, Miette (2010). 'On the Plurality of Cinematic Transnationalism', in Nataša Durovicová and Kathleen Newman (eds.), *World Cinemas, Transnational Perspectives.* (New York and Oxon: Routledge), pp. 12–33.

Hoefert de Turégano, Teresa (2004). *African Cinema and Europe. Close-up on Burkina Faso.* (Florence: European Press Academic Publishing).

Horton, Andrew (ed.) (1991). *Comedy / cinema / theory.* (Berkeley: University of California Press).

—— (1991). 'Introduction', in Andrew Horton (ed.) *Comedy / cinema / theory.* (Berkeley: University of California Press), 1–21.

Hours, Bernard (1986). *L'Etat Sorcier. Santé publique et société au Cameroun.* (Paris: L'Harmattan).

Hutchinson, John and Smith, Anthony D. (eds.) (1994). *Nationalism.* (New York: Oxford University Press).

Ivanga, Imungu (2005). 'Au Sud, des cinémas', in Catherine Ruelle (ed.) *Afrique 50: Singularités d'un cinéma pluriel.* (Paris: L'Harmattan), pp. 175–176.

Jansen, Jan (2001). *Epopée, histoire, société, le cas de Soundjata.* (Paris: Karthala).

Johnson, John William; Hale, Thomas A and Belcher, Stephen, (eds) (1997). *Oral Epics from Africa: Vibrant Voices from a Vast Continent.* (Bloomington: Indiana University Press)

Jost, François (1982). 'Où en est la narratologie cinématographique?' *CinémAction*, 20, pp. 37–46.

—— (1987). *L'Oeil-Caméra. Entre film et roman.* (Lille: Presses Universitaires de Lille).

Jouvenel, Bertrand de (1972). *Du pouvoir.* (Paris: Hachette).

Julien, Eileen (1992). *African Novels and the Question of Orality.* (Indianapolis: Indiana University Press).

Kane, Mohamadou (1974), 'Sur les formes traditionnelles du roman africain', *Revue de Littérature Comparée,* Vol III (4), pp. 536-568.

Kane, Momar Désiré (2004). *Marginalité et errance dans la littérature et le cinéma africains francophones.* (Paris: L'Harmattan).

Kemedjio, Cilas (1999). *De la négritude à la Créolité. Edouard Glissant, Maryse Condé et la malédiction de la théorie.* (Frankfurt: Main).

Kesteloot, Lilyan and Dieng, Bassirou (1997). *Les Epopées d'Afrique noire.* (Paris: Karthala).

Ki-Zerbo, Joseph (1975). 'Ethique. Cinéma et développement en Afrique', *Afrique Littéraire et Artistique,* 49, pp. 159–164.

Knepper, Wendy (2006). 'Confession, Autopsy and the Postcolonial Postmortems of Michael Ondaatje's *Anil's Ghost*', in Christine Matzke and Susanne Mühleisen (eds.) *Postcolonial Postmortems: Crime Fiction from a Transcultural Perspective.* (New York: Rodopi), pp. 35–58.

Koffi, Michel (2003). 'La Tradition Ivoirienne de la comédie', in Samuel Lelièvre (ed.) *Cinémas d'Afrique noire: Une oasis dans le désert? CinémAction,* 106, pp. 146–147.

Kom, Ambroise (1999). 'Littérature africaine. L'avènement du polar.' *Notre Librairie,* 136 (January–April), pp. 16–25.

―――― (2002). 'Violences postcoloniales et polar d'Afrique', *Notre Librairie,* 148, pp. 36–43.

Kuoh-Moukoury, Thérèse (1977). *Les Couples dominos.* (Paris: Julliard).

Krishnaswamy, Revathi and Hawley, John C. (eds.) (2008). *The Postcolonial and the Global.* (Minneapolis: University of Minnesota Press).

Lacan, Jacques (1988) *The Seminar of Jacques Lacan Book I.* ed. Jacques–Alain Miller. trans. John Forrester. (Cambridge: Cambridge University Press).

Larkin, Brian (2004). 'Degraded Images, Distorted Sounds: Nigerian Video and the Infrastructure of Piracy', *Public Culture,* 16 (2), pp. 289–314.

Lazarus, Neil (1999). *Nationalism and Cultural Practice in the Postcolonial World.* (Cambridge: Cambridge University Press).

Leitch, Thomas M. (2002). *Crime Films.* (Cambridge: Cambridge University Press).

Lelièvre, Samuel (ed.) (2003) *Cinémas d'Afrique noire: Une oasis dans le désert? CinémAction,* 106.

―――― (2003). 'Du cinéma africain ... aux cinémas africains'. *CinémAction,* 106, pp. 10–13.

Lequeret, Elisabeth (2003). *Le Cinéma Africain. Un continent à la recherche de son propre regard.* (Paris: Les Cahiers du cinema).

Loftus, Maria (2009). *Le Cinéma documentaire en Afrique noire. Du documentaire colonial au documentaire Africain (1899–1985).* (PhD thesis. University of Strasbourg).

Mabrouki, Azzedine (1993). 'L'Algérie et la question du cinéma: Une question bouleversée', *Cinéma et Libertés. Présence Africaine,* pp. 37–42.

Malkmus, Lizbeth and Armes, Roy (2000). *Arab and African Filmmaking*. (London: Zed Books).

Mamani, Abdoulaye. (1980), *Sarraounia*. (Paris: L'Harmattan)

Martin, Michael T. (2008). 'I am not a Filmmaker *Engagé*, I am an Ordinary Citizen *Engagé*: A *Black Camera* Interview with Joseph Gai Ramaka.' *Black Camera*, 22 (2) and 23 (1), pp. 24–34.

Matzke, Christine and Mühleisen, Susanne (eds.) (2006). *Postcolonial Postmortems. Crime Fiction from a Transcultural Perspective*. (New York: Rodopi).

Mazrui, Ali (1995). 'Pan-Africanism: From Poetry to Power.' *Issue: A Journal of Opinion*, pp. 35–38.

Mbembe, Achille (1986). 'Pouvoir des morts et langage des vivants: Les errances de la mémoire nationaliste au Cameroun', *Politique Africaine*, 22, pp. 37–72.

—— (1988). *Afriques indociles: Christianisme, pouvoir et état en société postcoloniale*. (Paris: Karthala).

—— (2001). *On the Postcolony*. (Berkeley: University of California Press).

—— -(2002a). 'African Modes of Self Writings' trans. Steven Rendall. *Public Culture*, 14 (1), pp. 239–273.

—— (2002b). 'On the Power of the False' trans. Judith Inggs. *Public Culture*, 14 (3), pp. 629–641.

—— (2003). 'Necropolitics', *Public Culture*, 15 (1), pp. 11–40.

McCluster, Audrey Thomas (2009). *The Devil You Dance With. Film Culture in the New South Africa*. (Urbana and Chicago: University of Illinois Press).

Meyer, Birgit (1999). 'Popular Ghanaian Cinema and "African Heritage"', *Africa Today*, 42 (2), pp. 93–114.

Meyer, Birgit and Pels, Peter (eds.) (2003). *Magic and Modernity, Interfaces of Revelation and Concealment*. (Stanford: Stanford University Press).

Meyer, Brigit (2003). 'Ghanaian Popular Cinema and the Magic in and of Film', in Birgit Meyer and Peter Pels (eds.), *Magic and Modernity: Interfaces of Revelation and Concealment*. (Stanford: Stanford University Press), pp. 200–222.

Meyer, Michel (2003). *Le Comique et le tragique: Penser le théâtre et son histoire*. (Paris: Presses Universitaires de France).

Metz, Christian (1982). *The Imaginary Signifier: Psychoanalysis and the Cinema* trans. Celia Britton. (Indianapolis: Indiana University Press).

—— (1990). *L'Enonciation Impersonnelle ou le site du film*. (Paris: Méridiens Klincksieck).

Monga, Célestin (2009). *Nihilisme et négritude: Les arts de vivre en Afrique*. (Paris: Presses Universitaires de France).

Moore, Henrietta L. and Sanders, Todd (eds.) (2001). *Magical Interpretations, Material Realities: Modernity, Witchcraft and the Occult in Postcolonial Africa*. (New York: Routledge).

Moorman, Marissa (2001). 'Of Westerns, Women, and War: Re-Situating Angolan Cinema and the Nation', in Kenneth Harrow (ed.) *Research in African Literature, Special Issue on Nationalism*, 32 (3), pp. 103–122.

Morreall, John (1983). *Taking Laughter Seriously*. (Albany: SUNY Press).

Mouralis, Bernard (1993). *L'Europe, l'Afrique et la folie*. (Paris: Présence Africaine).

Mudimbe, V. Y. (1988) *The Invention of Africa: Gnosis, Philosophy and the Order of Knowledge*. (Indianapolis: Indiana University Press).

Mukendi, Ntite (1974). 'Comment le cinéma peut œuvrer à l'indépendance et l'autorité culturelle africaine', *Présence Africaine*, 90, pp. 99–122.

Murphy, David (2000). 'Africans Filming Africa: Questioning Theories of an Authentic African Cinema', *Journal of African Cultural Studies*, 13 (2), pp. 239–49.

Murphy, David and Williams, Patrick (2007). *Postcolonial African Cinema: Ten Directors*. (Manchester: Manchester University Press).

Ndebele, Njabulo (1994). *South African Literature and Culture: Rediscovery of the Ordinary*. (New York: Manchester University Press).

Neale, Steve (2000). *Genre and Hollywood*. (London: Routledge).

Nébié, Bali (2004). *Le Crépuscule des ténèbres*. (Ouagadougou: Sidwaya).

—— (2004). 'Interview', *L'Evènement*, 54, 25 October.

Nelson, T. G. A. (1990). *Comedy: An Introduction to Comedy in Literature, Drama and Cinema*. (Oxford: Oxford University Press).

Newman, Kathleen (2010). 'Notes on Transnational Film Theory: Decentered Subjectivity, Decentered Capitalism', in Nataša Durovicová and Kathleen Newman (eds.) *World Cinemas, Transnational Perspectives*. (New York and Oxon: Routledge), pp. 3–11.

Ngandu Nkashama, Pius (1977). *La Délivrance d'Ilounga*. (Paris: P.J. Oswald).

—— (1989). *Ecritures et discours littéraires: Etudes sur le roman africain*. (Paris: L'Harmattan).

—— (1993). *Théâtres et scènes de spectacle: Etudes sur les dramaturgies et les arts gestuels*. (Paris: L'Harmattan).

—— (1995). *Les Magiciens du repentir: Les confessions de Frère Dominique (Sakombi Inongo)*. (Paris: L'Harmattan).

Ngangura, Mweze (1996). 'African Cinema: Militancy or Entertainment?' in Imruh Bakari and Mbye Cham, *African Experiences of Cinema*. (London: BFI), pp. 60–64.

Niang, Sada (1996) (ed.). *Littérature et cinéma en Afrique francophone: Ousmane Sembène et Assia Djebar*. (Paris: L'Harmattan).

—— (2002). *Djibril Diop Mambéty: Un cinéaste à contre courant*. (Paris: L'Harmattan).

—— (2008). 'Du Néoréalisme en Afrique: Une relecture de *Borom Sarret*', *Présence Francophone*, 71, pp. 76–90.

Niang, Sada and Gadjigo, Samba (2008). 'Ousmane Sembène, cinéaste', *Présence Francophone*, 71.

Nkonlak, Romuald (2007). 'Jean-Pierre Bekolo Obama: Censurer *Les Saignantes* aurait été un ratage', *Mutations*, 4 April.

Nyamnjoh, Francis (2001). 'Delusions of Development and the Enrichment of Witchcraft Discourses in Cameroon', in Henrietta L. Moore and Todd Sanders (eds.) *Magical Interpretations, Material Realities: Modernity, Witchcraft and the occult in Postcolonial Africa*. (New York: Routledge), pp. 28–49.

Okpewho, Isidore (1983). *Myth in Africa.* (Cambridge: Cambridge University Press).
—— (1992). *African Oral Literature. Background, Character, and Continuity.* (Bloomington: Indiana University Press).
—— (1979). *The Epic in Africa. Towards a Poetics of Oral Performance.* (New York: Columbia University Press).
O'Regan, Tom (1996). *Australian National Cinema.* (New York: Routledge).
Ortigues, Marie-Cecile and Ortigues, Edmond (1966). *Oedipe africain.* (Paris: Plon).
Oscherwitz, Dayna L. (2008). 'Of Cowboys and Elephants: Africa, Globalization and the Nouveau Western in Djibril Diop Mambety's *Hyenas*', *Research in African Literatures*, 39 (1), pp. 223–238.
Ottenberg, Simon (1997). 'Introduction: Some Issues and Questions on African Dance', in Esther Dagan (ed.) *The Spirit's Dance in Africa: Evolution, Transformation, and Continuity in Sub-Sahara.* (Westmount, QC: Galerie Amrat African Art Publications).
Ouedraogo, Idrissa (1995). 'Le cinéma et nous', *L'Afrique et le centenaire du cinéma.* (Paris: Présence Africaine), pp. 336–341.
Oyono, Ferdinand (1966). *Houseboy.* Trans John Reed. (Oxford; Portsmouth, N.H.: Heinemann).
Paré, Joseph (2000). '*Keita! L'héritage du griot:* L'esthétique de la parole au service de l'image.' *CiNéMAS*, 11 (1), pp. 45–60.
Paré, Joseph and Curtius, Anny Dominique (1996). '*Le Mandat* de Sembène Ousmane ou la dialectique d'une double herméneutique', in Sada Niang (ed.) *Littérature et Cinéma en Afrique francophone.* (Paris, L'Harmattan), pp 139–148.
Péan, Pierre (1983). *Affaires africaines.* (Paris: Fayard).
Pearson, Roberta E. and Simpson, Philip (eds.) (2000). *Critical Dictionary of Film and Television Theory.* (New York: Routledge).
Petty, Sheila J. (ed.) (1996). *A Call to Action: The Films of Ousmane Sembene.* (Westport, CT: Praeger).
—— (2008). *Contact Zones: Memory, Origin and Discourses in Black Diasporic Cinema.* (Detroit: Wayne State University Press).
—— (2009). 'The Rise of the African Musical: Postcolonial Disjunction in *Karmen Geï* and *Madame Brouette*', *Journal of African Cinemas*, 1 (1), pp. 95–112.
Pfaff, Françoise (1984). *The Cinema of Ousmane Sembène: A Pioneer of African Film.* (Westport, CT: Greenwood Press).
—— (1996). 'Eroticism in Sub-Saharan African Films,' in Imruh Bakari and Mbye Cham (eds.) *African Experiences of Cinema.* (London: BFI).
—— (1996). 'Africa from Within: The Films of Gaston Kaboré and Idrissa Ouedraogo as Anthropological Sources', in Imruh Bakari and Mbye Cham (eds.) *African Experiences of Cinema.* (London: BFI).
—— (ed.) (2004). *Focus on African Films.* (Indianapolis: Indiana University Press).
Pines, Jim and Willemen, Paul (1989). *Questions of Third Cinema.* (London: British Film Institute).

Présence Africaine (1974). 'Le Rôle du cinéaste africain dans l'éveil d'une conscience de civilisation noire', 90.

Présence Africaine (1993). 'Cinéma et libertés'. Contribution au thème du FESPACO '93.

Primus, Pearl (1996). 'African Dance', in Kariamu Welsh Asante (ed.) *African Dance: An Artistic, Historical and Philosophical Inquiry*. (Trenton, NJ: Africa World Press, Inc.).

Pyrhönen, Heta (1994). *Murder from the Academic Angel: An Introduction to the Study of the Detective Narrative*. (Columbia: Camden House).

Quayson, Ato (2000) *Postcolonialism: Theory, Practice or Process?* (Oxford: Polity Press).

—— (2003). *Calibrations: Reading for the Social*. (Minneapolis: University of Minnesota Press).

Rafter, Nicole (2006). *Shots in the Mirror: Crime Films and Society*. (Oxford: Oxford University Press).

Robert, Marthe (1980). *Origins of the Novel* trans. Sacha Rabinovitch (Bloomington: Indiana University Press).

Rosny, Eric de (1981). *Les Yeux de ma chèvre: Sur les pas des maîtres de la nuit en pays Douala*. (Paris: Plon).

—— (1992). *L'Afrique des guérisons*. (Paris: Karthala).

Rowe, Kathleen (1995). 'Comedy, Melodrama and Gender: Theorizing the Genres of Laughter', in Kristine Brunovska Karnick and Henry Jenkins (eds.) *Classical Hollywood Comedy*. (New York: Routledge), pp. 39–62.

Ruelle, Catherine (2005) (ed.). *Afrique 50: Singularités d'un cinéma pluriel*. (Paris, L'Harmattan).

Rushdie, Salman (1991). *Imaginary Homelands: Essays and Criticism 1981–1991*. (London: Penguin).

Russell, James (2007). *The Historical Epic and Contemporary Hollywood: From 'Dances with Wolves' to 'Gladiator'*. (New York. Continuum).

Rutherford, Blair (1999). 'To Find an African Witch: Anthropology, Modernity and Witch-Finding in North-West Zimbabwe.' *Critique of Anthropology*, 19 (1), pp. 89–109.

Santas, Constantine (2008). *The Epic Film: From Myth to Blockbuster*. (Toronto: Rowman & Littlefield Publishers Inc.).

Sassen, Saskia (2008). 'The Many Scales of the Global: Implications for Theory and for Politics', in Revathi Krishnaswamy and John C. Hawley (eds.) *The Postcolonial and the Global*. (Minneapolis: University of Minnesota Press), pp. 82–93.

Semujanga, Josias (1999). *Dynamique des genres dans le roman africain : éléments de poétique transculturelle*. (Paris, L'Harmattan).

Senghor, Léopold Sédar (1964). *Liberté I*. (Paris: Seuil).

Shaka, Femi Okiremuete (2004). *Modernity and the African Cinema*. (Trenton: Africa World Press).

Shelby, Tommie (2005). *We Who Are Dark: The Philosophical Foundations of Black Solidarity*. (Cambridge: Harvard University Press).

Shohat, Ella and Stam, Robert (1994). *Unthinking Eurocentrism: Multiculturalism and the Media.* (New York: Routledge).

Simon, Jean-Paul (1979). *Le Filmique et le comique.* (Paris: Méridien Klinsieck).

Sinaté, Ibrahima (1994). *Med Hondo: Un cinéaste rebelle.* (Paris: Présence Africaine).

Snipe, Tracy D. (1996) 'African Dance: Bridges to Humanity', in Kariamu Welsh Asante (ed.) *African Dance: An Artistic, Historical, and Philosophical Inquiry.* (Trenton: Africa World Press, Inc.).

Soro, Gabriel (2002). 'Le Héros épique et son entourage dans La Chanson de Roland et dans Soundjata ou l'épopée mandingue', in Jean Dérive (ed.) *L'épopée, unité et diversité d'un genre.* (Paris: Karthala), pp. 147–168.

Sotinel, Thomas (2008). 'Grandeur et misère du cinéma africain.' Interview. *Le Monde,* 7 February.

Souriau, Etienne (1970). *Les Deux cent mille situations dramatiques.* (Paris: Flammarion).

Sow, Alfâ Îbrahîm (1980). *Anthropological Structures of Madness in Black Africa* trans. Joyce Diamanti. (New York: International Universities Press)

—— (1977) *Psychiatrie dynamique africaine.* (Paris: Payot)

Soyinka, Wole (1976). *Myth, Literature and the African World.* (Cambridge: Cambridge University Press).

Spencer, Paul (1985) (ed.). *Society and the Dance: The Social Anthropology of Process and Performance.* (New York: Cambridge University Press).

Spillers, Hortense J. (1996). '"All the Things You Could Be by Now If Sigmund Freud's Wife Was Your Mother": Psychoanalysis and Race Author(s)'. Critical Inquiry, Vol. 22 (4), pp. 710–734.

Stam, Robert and Spence, Louise (1983). 'Colonialism, Racism and Representation.' *Screen,* 24 (2), pp. 2–20.

Steiner, George (1980). *The Death of Tragedy.* (New York: Oxford University Press). First published by Alfred A. Knopf (1961).

Stoneman, Rod (1996). 'South/South Axis: For a Cinema Built by, with and for Africans', in Imruh Bakari and Cham Mbye (eds.) *African Experiences of Cinema,* (London: BFI), pp. 175–180.

Stott, Andrew (2005). *Comedy.* (New York: Routledge).

Tcheuyap, Alexie. (2008). 'De la fiction criminelle en Afrique. Relecture des films de Sembène Ousmane.' *Présence Francophone* 71, pp 56-75.

—— (2006) 'Esquisse d'une typologie des cinémas en Afrique noire' *International Journal of Francophone Studies,* Vol 9 (2), pp. 203-221.

—— (2005). *De l'écrit a l'écran: Les réécritures filmiques du roman africain francophone.* (Ottawa: University of Ottawa Press).

—— (ed.) (2005). *Cinema and Social Discourse in Cameroon.* (Bayreuth: Bayreuth African Studies).

Teno, Jean-Marie (1995). 'La Liberté de dire non', in FEPACI (ed.) *L'Afrique et le centenaire du cinéma.* (Paris: Présence Africaine), pp: 375–377.

Thackway, Melissa (2003). *Africa Shoots Back: Alternative Perspectives in Sub-Saharan Francophone African film.* (Bloomington: Indiana University Press).

Thomas McCluskey, Audrey (2009). *The Devil You Dance With. Film Culture in the New South Africa*. (Urbana and Chicago: University of Illinois Press).

Thompson, Jon (1993). *Fiction, Crime and Empire: Clues to Modernity and Postmodernism*. (Chicago: University of Illinois Press).

Thompson, Kirsten Moana (2007). *Crime Films. Investigating the Scene*. (London and New York: Wallflower).

Tiérou, Alphonse (1983). *La Danse africaine c'est la vie*. (Paris: Maisonneuve et Larose).

—— (1989) *Dooplé, Loi éternelle de la danse africaine*. (Paris: Maisonneuve et Larose).

—— (2001). *Si sa danse bouge, l'Afrique bougera*. (Paris: Maisonneuve et Larose).

Tomaselli, Keyan G. (2006). *Encountering Modernity: Twentieth Century South African Cinemas*. (Amsterdam: UNISA Press).

Tomaselli, Keyan G., Shepperson, Arnold and Eke, Maureen (1995). 'Towards a Theory of Orality in African Cinema.' *Research in African Literatures*, 3 (Fall), pp. 18–35.

Touré, Kitia (1995). *Destins parallèles*. (Abidjan: NEI).

Ukadike, Nwachukwu Frank (1994). *Black African Cinema*. (Berkeley: University of California Press).

—— (ed.) (1995). 'New Discourses of African Cinema/Nouveaux Discours du cinema africain'. *IRIS*, 18 (Spring).

—— (2002). *Questioning African Cinema: Conversations with African Filmmakers*. (Minneapolis: University of Minnesota Press).

Vail, Leroy and White, Landeg (1991). *Power and the Praise Poem: Southern African Voices in History*. (Charlottesville: University Press of Virginia).

Vanoncini, André (2002). *Le Roman policier*. (Paris: Presses Universitaires de France).

Vieyra, Paulin Soumanou (1961) 'Le Cinéma et la révolution africaine', *Présence Africaine*, 34–35, pp. 92–103.

—— (1975). *Le Cinéma africain de ses origines à 1973*. (Paris: Présence Africaine).

Vokouma, François (1995). 'Produire nos propres images… Malgré l'état de l'Afrique', in FEPACI (ed.) *L'Afrique et le centenaire du cinéma*. (Paris: Présence Africaine) pp. 269–275.

Welsh Asante, Kariamu (ed.) (1996). *African Dance: An Artistic, Historical and Philosophical Inquiry*. (Trenton NJ: Africa World Press, Inc.).

Wetmore, Kevin, J., Jr. (2002) *The Athenian Sun in an African Sky: Modern African Adaptations of Classical Greek Tragedy*. (Jefferson: McFarland & Company, Inc.).

Williams, Adams (ed.) (2002). *Film and Nationalism*. (New Brunswick, NJ: Rutgers University Press).

Williams, Drid (1991). *Anthropology and the Dance: Ten Lectures*. (Chicago: University of Illinois Press). 2nd edition 2004.

Wittgenstein, Ludwig (1968). *Philosophical Investigations*. (Oxford: Blackwell).

Yewah, Emmanuel (1990). 'Traditions, Politics and African Detective Fiction', *Ufahamu: Journal of African Activist Association*, 18 (3), pp. 66–76.

Zacks, Stephen A. (1995). 'The Theoretical Construction of African Cinema', *Research in African Literatures*, 3 (Autumn), pp. 6–17.

Zemon Davis, Nathalie (2000). *Slaves on Screen: Film and Historical Vision*. (Toronto: Vintage).

Zimmer, Christian (1970). *Cinéma et politique*. (Paris: Seghers).

Žižek, Slavoj (1989). 'Looking Awry', *October*, 50, pp. 31–35.

Zumthor, Paul (1990). *Oral Poetry: An Introduction*. (Minneapolis: University of Minnesota Press).

Filmography

Adanggaman (2000). Directed by Roger Gnoan M'Bala, France/Switzerland/Côte d'Ivoire/Burkina Faso/Italy, Abyssa Film, 90 min, DVD.

Africa Paradis (2007). Directed by Sylvestre Amoussou, Benin/France, Tchoko Tchoko 7ème Art, 86 min, DVD.

Afrique, je te plumerai (1992). Directed by Jean-Marie Teno, Cameroon/France/Germany Les Films du Raphia, 88 min, DVD.

Afrique sur Seine (1955). Directed by Paulin Soumanou Vieyra, Senegal, 21 min.

Bal Poussière (1988). Directed by Henri Duparc, Côte d'Ivoire, Focale 13, 90 min, DVD.

Bamako (2006). Directed by Abderrahmane Sissako, Mali/USA/France, Archipel 33, 115 min, DVD.

Bana in Oakville (2009). Directed by Meni Tchoko, Canada, Noutchal Productions, 89 min, DVD.

Bronx Barbès (2000). Directed by Eliane de Latour, France, Les Films d'Ici, 110 min, 35mm.

Caramel (2004). Directed by Henri Duparc, Côte d'Ivoire, Focale 13. 88 min, 35mm.

Clando (1996). Directed by Jean-Marie Teno, Cameroon/France/Germany, Les Films du Raphia, 98 min, VHS.

Code Phoenix (2007). Directed by Boubakar Diallo, Burkina Faso, Les Films du Dromadaire, 90 min.

Dakan (1997). Directed by Mohamed Camara, Guinea/France, Films du 20ème, 87 min, VHS.

Daratt (2006). Directed by Mahamat Saleh-Haroun, Chad/France/Belgium/Austria, Chinguitty Films, 96 min, DVD.

Delwende (2005). Directed by Pierre Yaméogo. Burkina Faso/France/Switzerland, Les Films du Safran, 89 min, DVD.

Djeli, conte d'aujourd'hui (1981). Directed by Kramo Lanciné-Fadika, Cote d'Ivoire, 90 min.

Dossier brulant (2005), Directed by Boubakar Diallo, Burkina Faso, Les Films du Dromadaire, HDTV, 90 min.

Faat Kiné (2000). Directed by Ousmane Sembène, Senegal, Films Doomireev, 120 min, 35 mm & DVD.

Finye (1982). Directed by Souleymane Cissé, Mali, Cissé Films, 100 min, DVD.

Finzan (1989). Directed by Cheikh Oumar Sissoko, Mali, Kora Films, 107 min, VHS.

Gito l'ingrat (1992). Directed by Leonce Ngabo, France/Burundi, 90 min, DVD.

Guelwaar (1992). Directed by Ousmane Sembène, Senegal/Channel IV/Films Doomireev/France 3 Cinéma/Galatée Films/New Yorker Films/ Westdeutscher Runnfund (WDR), 115 min, DVD & 35mm.

Hyènes (1992). Directed by Djibril Diop Mambéty, Senegal/ADR Productions/ Thelma Film AG, 110 min, DVD & 35 mm.

Inspecteur Sory, le Mamba (2005). Directed by Mamadi Sidibé, Gabon/Guinea, Adelaïde Productions, 94 min.

Karmen Geï (2001). Directed by Joseph Gaï Ramaka, Senegal/Canal + Horizons, 86 min, DVD.

Keita The Heritage of the Griot. (1995). VHS. Directed by Dani Kouyaté, France/ Burkina Faso, 94 min, VHS & DVD.

Kirikou et la sorcière (1998). Directed by Michel Ocelot, France/Belgium/ Luxembourg, Gébéka Films, 74 min, DVD.

Kirikou et les bêtes sauvages (2005). Directed by Michel Ocelot, France, Facets, 75 min, DVD.

Le Ballon d'or (1994). Directed by Cheik Doukouré, France/Guinea, 90 min, DVD.

La Belle, la brute et le berger (2006) Directed by Boubakar Diallo, Burkina Faso, Les Films du Dromadaire, HDTV, 100 min.

La Colère des Dieux (2003). Directed by Idrissa Ouedraogo, France/Burkina Faso, Nabil Nouss. Prod/Les Films de la Plaine / NDK Productions, 90 min, 35 mm.

La Genèse (1999). Directed by Cheick Oumar Sissoko, France/Mali, 102 min, DVD & 35 mm.

Le Malentendu colonial (2004). Directed by Jean-Marie Teno, Cameroon/France/ Germany, Les Films du Raphia, 78 min, DVD.

La Noire de.... (1966) Directed by Ousmane Sembène, Senegal, Films Doomireev, 65 min, 16 mm & DVD.

La Vie est belle (1987). Directed by Mweze Ngangura, Belgium/France/Zaïre, 87 min, DVD.

Le Cercle des pouvoirs (1998). Directed by Daniel Kamwa, Cameroon/France, DK7 Communications, 115 min, DVD.

Le Complot d'Aristote (1996). Directed by Jean-Pierre Bekolo, France/Zimbabwe, JBA Productions, 70 min, 35 min.

Le Grand Blanc de Lambaréné (1995). Directed by Bassek Ba Kobhio, Gabon/ Cameroon/France, LN Productions, 94 min DVD.

L'Enfant noir (1995). Directed by Laurent Chevalier. France/Guinea: Les Films du Paradoxe, 92 min, VHS.

Les Couilles de l'éléphant (2002). Directed by Henri-Joseph Koumba Bididi. Gabon/France, Adélaïde Productions/Ce.Na.Ci/Terre Africaine, 98 min, 35mm.

Les Maîtres fous (1955). Directed by Jean Rouch, France, Documentary Educational Ressources, 36 min, 16mm.

L'Or des Younga (2006), Directed by Boubakar Diallo, Burkina Faso, Les Films du Dromadaire, HDTV, 100 min.

Les Saignantes (2005). Directed by Jean-Pierre Bekolo, France/Cameroon, Quartier Mozart Films/E4 Television Production, 92 min, Digital betacom.

Le Truc de Konaté (1998). Directed by Fanta Régina Nacro, Burkina Faso, Les Films du Défi, 33 min, VHS.

Madame Brouette (2002). Directed by Moussa Sène Absa, Canada/France/Senegal, Les Productions La fête Inc, 104 min, DVD.

Mossane (1996). Directed by Safi Faye, France/Senegal, 106 min.

Ndeysaan The Price of Forgiveness (2001). Directed by Mansour Sora Wade, Ban Film, 90 min, DVD.

Open Water (2005), Directed by Boubakar Diallo, Burkina Faso, Les Films du Dromadaire, 90 min.

Pièces d'identité (1998). Directed by Mweze Ngangura, Congo/Belgium, 93 min, VHS, DVD and 35 mm.

Quartier Mozart (1992). Directed by Jean-Pierre Bekolo, Cameroon. Kola Case, Cameroon Radio Television, 80 min, 16 mm, blown up to 35 mm & DVD.

Sam le Caid (2008). Directed by Boubakar Diallo, Burkina Faso, Les Films du Dromadaire, HD Cam, 100 min.

Samba Traoré (1992). Directed by Idrissa Ouedraogo, Burkina Faso/France/Switzerland, Films A2, 85 min, VHS.

Sambizanga (1972). 16mm. Directed by Sarah Maldoror, Angola, Isabelle Films, 102 min.

Sango Malo (1991). Directed by Bassek Ba Kobhio, Cameroon/Diproci/Fodic/Les Films Terre Africaine, 94 min, VHS & DVD.

Sarraounia (1986). Directed by Med Hondo, Burkina Faso/Mauritania/France, Spiamedia Productions, 120 min.

Série noire à Koumbi (2006), Directed by Boubakar Diallo, Burkina Faso, Les Films du Dromadaire, TV Series.

Sofia (2004), Directed by Boubakar Diallo, Burkina Faso, Les Films du Dromadaire, Dvcam 105 min.

Tilaï (1990). Directed by Idrissa Ouedraogo, Switzerland/UK/France/Burkina Faso/Germany, 81 min, DVD.

Totor (1994). Directed by Daniel Kamwa. Cameroon/France, DK7 Communications, 115 min, DVD.

Touki Bouki (1973). Directed by Djibril Diop Mambéty, Senegal, Cinegrit, Studio Kankourama, 85 min, 35 mm & DVD.

Traque à Ouaga (2004), Directed by Boubakar Diallo, Burkina Faso, Les Films du Dromadaire, Dvcam, 40 min.

Visages de femmes (1985). Directed by Désiré Ecaré, Côte d'Ivoire, Films de la Langune, 105 min, VHS.

Wend Kuuni (1982). Directed by Gaston Kaboré, Haute Volta, Dirction du Cinéma de Haute Volta, 85 min, VHS.

Xala (1974). Directed by Ousmane Sembène, Senegal, Société Nationale de Cinématographie/Films Doomireew, 123 min, DVD.

Yaaba (1989). Directed by Idrissa Ouedraogo, Burkina Faso, Les Films de l'Avenir/Thema Films AG, 90 min, DVD & VHS.

Yeelen (1987). Directed by Souleymane Cissé, Mali, Atriascop Paris/Burkina Faso Ministry of Cooperation/Centre National de la Cinématographie (CNC)/ French Ministry of Cooperation/French Ministry of Foreign Affairs/Les Films Cissé/Les Films du Carosse/Mali Government/Midas/French Ministry of culture/UTA/Westdeutscher Rundfunk (WDR), 105 min, DVD.

Yellow Fever Taximan (1985). Directed by Jean-Marie Teno, Cameroon, 30 min, VHS.

Index

Note: 'n' after a page number indicates the number of a note on that page